Property of the
CPE
people teaching people
Center for Participant Education

Queen Silver

Queen Silver

THE
GODLESS
GIRL

Wendy McElroy

 **Prometheus Books**

59 John Glenn Drive
Amherst, New York 14228-2197

Photographs courtesy of the Queen Silver Estate.

Published 2000 by Prometheus Books

Inquiries should be addressed to
Prometheus Books, 59 John Glenn Drive, Amherst, New York 14228–2197.
VOICE: 716–691–0133, ext. 207.
FAX: 716–564–2711.
WWW.PROMETHEUSBOOKS.COM

04 03 02 01 00   5 4 3 2 1

Library of Congress Cataloging-in-Publication Data

McElroy, Wendy.
    Queen Silver : the godless girl / Wendy McElroy.
       p.   cm.
    Includes bibliographical references and index.
    ISBN 1–57392–755–4 (alk. paper)
    1. Silver, Queen, d. 1998. 2. Socialists—United States—Biography.
3. Radicals—United States—Biography. 4. Women and socialism—United
States. I. Title.
HX84.S527M345   1999
335'.0092—dc21
[B]   99–045067
                                     CIP

Printed in the United States of America on acid-free paper

To Don Latimer,
the man at Queen's side.
In the many years they were together,
I never heard a harsh exchange—
nothing but affectionate concern for the other's welfare.

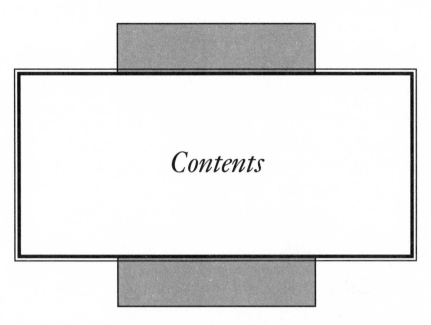

Contents

Part 1: Biography

Part 2: Selected Writings

Acknowledgments

I WISH TO thank the following people. First and foremost, Don Latimer. Don not only assigned Queen's papers to me from the estate and, so, enabled this book to exist, he also provided me with emotional and moral support that continues to this day. I literally cannot thank Don enough.

The Valle family constituted a second home for Queen. Sylvia Valle, in particular, devoted many hours to organizing a portion of Queen's posthumous papers for my use. Robert Seeman was a constant presence at the hospital and convalescent home and, then, provided welcome companionship as I sorted through books and papers at Queen's home.

A list of the people who visited Queen during the last months would certainly leave out many people deserving of thanks. Many of them offered me anecdotes and insights about Queen. To avoid offending individuals, let me collectively thank the entire membership of two organizations—Atheists United and the Humanist Association of Los Angeles—who could not have been kinder or more supportive.

Two people in particular have generously reviewed the book for accuracy. Don Latimer's careful eye and his knowledge of Queen's life (which he shared) kept the book on track. The prominent freethinker Annie Laurie Gaylor provided invaluable feedback on points of atheist history. I also thank librarian Arthur Pond for his feedback and his involvement in the special memorial held for Queen by librarians.

Special thanks are due to my editors at Prometheus Books, Steven L. Mitchell and Mary A. Read, for the care with which they handled this project. Chris Kramer went an extra yard to make sure the book was on schedule.

To my perfect husband, I offer what is a constant refrain, "Thanks for putting up with me." Not to mention proofreading, offering comments, repairing computer crashes, scanning photos...

Introduction

ON JANUARY 7, 1998, Queen Silver died at the age of eighty-seven. The Los Angeles and New York *Times* did not run her obituary, although she had frequently appeared on the front pages of prominent newspapers decades before.

As a child and a young adult, Queen had been one of the most prominent figures in the freethought movement, a movement loosely comprised of atheists, skeptics, and those espousing rationalism. She was an ardent feminist and an early voice for socialism, active in the Industrial Workers of the World.[1] By the age of eight, she was heralded as a "child wonder," "a girl scientist," and a bright hope for twentieth-century radicalism in America. It is no wonder that the director Cecil B. DeMille used Queen as a role model in his movie *The Godless Girl*. With the Palmer Raids (circa World War I) that were aimed at quashing radicalism, and with the McCarthy hearings of the 1950s, she joined a legion of voices that were forced to retreat from politics. Although the name Queen Silver evokes no recognition today, hers was among the most prominent voices silenced. Her reemergence into political life in the 1970s—predominantly into freethought and feminism—did not cast a spotlight on her former and amazing career in radicalism. Instead, she chose to remain largely behind the scenes rather than to seek notoriety.

Queen Silver was probably the closest woman friend I will ever know. Because I ran away from home at sixteen, Queen became my substitute family and she, in turn, referred to me as "the daughter I never had." We met at a lecture sponsored by Atheists United, and she immediately invited me out to lunch. I declined, making a lame excuse. The real reason: she was two generations older than me and I have always been uncomfortable around "older" people. But, as I continued to attend lectures, a realization dawned. Queen was always the most interesting person in the room. We started "doing lunch." Queen became the person to whom I looked for advice on everything from men to the institutional analysis of society. On the latter subject, we disagreed significantly. I am an individualist-anarchist who favors free-market solutions to social problems. Queen was an old-fashioned socialist with a deep suspicion (to say the least) of the marketplace's ability to deliver social justice.

Because the two of us profoundly differed in our visions of society, this book steps back from my own views. Instead, it uses Queen's own words to provide the political perspective. Her equally remarkable mother, Grace Verne Silver, is also represented in her own words in order to give a better sense of their personalities as well as their politics. Grace had carried her ten-day-old daughter onto a socialist stage where she was to deliver a lecture and she remained the dominant ideological force in Queen's life thereafter.

This book is primarily an intellectual history of Queen's life. As such, it stresses her intellectual development, the content of her articles and lectures, and the political impact of her life. But since she lived her principles, it is not possible to separate her personal life from politics.

As a feminist, she stood up in court to defend her mother against criminal charges at the age of fourteen—and won. As a socialist, she watched as men from the American Legion repeatedly burned the stock of her mother's socialist bookstore. As a freethinker, her pamphlet on evolution—written at eleven years old—circulated to acclaim at the Scopes Monkey Trial (1925). In short, although my emphasis is intellectual, I have attempted to blend the political with the personal.

My research material came from Queen Silver's estate, the papers of which I inherited.[2] The papers include correspondence, an almost complete archive of *Queen Silver's Magazine*, manuscripts, lectures on tape and video, boxes of press clippings, boxes of photographs, a genealogy, legal documents, and business records. Whenever possible, I have completely cited all sources, but this was not always possible. For example, Grace maintained Queen's press clippings and she did not always indicate the page number of the newspaper on which Queen had appeared. Thus some footnotes are incomplete.

Part 2 of the book consists of reprints from Queen's lectures and articles. With one exception, the earlier reprints are from *Queen Silver's Magazine* and have not been edited. The reprints from Queen's later life have been edited extensively. Because she spoke from note cards inscribed only with key words, Queen tended to deliver the same basic lecture over and over, with the presentation varying. With each of these later lectures, I took several versions and edited them together, preserving what seemed to be the best wording. The lecture identified as the source is the one containing the material I employed most.

Finally, I do not mean for this book to be a definitive treatment of either Queen or Grace Verne Silver. Indeed, I hope it serves as a springboard for future research into these fascinating women.

Notes

1. For more on the definition of freethought, see page 243 of this work.

2. After my research on Queen and her mother is completed, I intend to donate the papers and xeroxes thereof to various foundations to make them available to other scholars.

Part One
Biography

1

A Radical Is Born and Molded

(1910–1918)

QUEEN SILVER WAS born at 3:30 P.M. on December 13, 1910, in Portland, Oregon. Her mother, Grace Verne Silver (1889–1972), had paused her multistate lecture tour on socialism and labor reform for the Socialist Party in order to give birth. A feminist, socialist, and freethinker, Grace insisted that the blank on the birth certificate list her "usual occupation" as "Socialist Lecturer." The tour might well have had to be suspended in any case, however. Shortly before Grace had arrived in Portland, her voice had given out from the strain of continuously exhorting audiences, so that she was unable to speak. Accordingly, the Portland socialists took the diminutive young agitator under their wing, and made certain she had a place to live and an allowance to cover her expenses.[1]

The turn of the century was a heyday for socialist agitation in the United States. For example, it ushered in the Industrial Workers of the World (the IWW, also known as the Wobblies)—an organization that aimed at industrial unionism through direct action, such as strikes. Organized in 1905, by the time of Queen's birth it had already participated in an impressive number of successful strikes. For example, in 1906, restaurant and hotel strikers in Goldfield, Nevada, were successful in their bid for an eight-hour day. In Portland, three thousand sawmill workers had gone on strike for a nine-hour day and higher wages, and won some improvements in working conditions. When the economic panic of 1907 caused some industries to shut down, unemployed workers became even more militant and willing to join labor unions.

The Pacific Northwest with its sawmills and shipping became especially fertile ground for Grace's brand of soapbox radicalism. And the IWW with its clear goal of organizing labor into one huge union, regardless of the worker's sex, would have appealed deeply to her feminist passions. In the truest sense of the words, Queen Silver was literally born into the radicalism that would define her life in a dramatic ebb and flow until her death at eighty-seven: feminism, freethought, and socialism.

One factor was absent from her birth, however. Queen's father was not present and she never met him subsequently. On the birth certificate, his name is listed as Parker Vaughn, with this description: "a forty-seven-year-old white mechanic." Vaughn was Grace's second cousin, descended from the same branch of the Silver family as she was, the branch that had settled in Massachusetts in 1630. Thirty-three years after Queen's birth, on August 18, 1943, Grace would sign a notarized statement to aver that the birth certificate was mistaken due to a clerical error on the part of the hospital. Although she did not retract the claim to have been married at the time of Queen's birth, Parker Vaughn remains a mysterious figure who does not appear in other family records.

On the birth certificate, the yet unnamed Queen was referred to simply as "Baby Vaughn Silver." In later life Queen intimated to me that her mother might have lied to the hospital either about being married or about the father's name. Unfortunately, this was the sort of information about which Queen was always vague. If anyone dared to ask after specifics, she would smile and offer the standard response of, "That's classified information."

The Drama of Queen's Birth

No similar vagueness surrounds the physical circumstances of Queen's birth thanks to a later magazine article written by Grace entitled "Motherhood without Fear."[2] There, Grace graphically described the event. Except for a hoarse throat, the twenty-one-year-old Grace had been in perfect health and she was determined to save money by going through the birth process naturally and alone. After the labor pains had lasted six hours, Grace changed her mind and attempted to check into a hospital. Although she had cash in hand, no hospital would take her without a referral from a family doctor. She tried to explain that, from the moment of her own birth, she had never seen a physician. To no avail. Now, alone and three thousand miles away from her family in New England, the half-dozen doctors she attempted to visit all said they were too busy to attend her.

Finally Grace appealed to fellow socialists in Portland who advised her, "Wait as long as possible, pick out a hospital, and go there alone and demand admission." If she were refused, the organization's attorneys assured her they would sue for damages because hospitals were legally required to admit maternity cases.

After eighteen hours of labor, Grace found herself taking a streetcar and walking three blocks to Multnomah Hospital, where she offered to pay in advance to be admitted. Then, she outright begged for admission. At last, the hospital acquiesced and she was taken to the general ward and "told to go to bed." Only after the other women on the ward staged what Grace described as a "virtual riot" did she receive medical attention—after a fashion. Grace recounted the grueling experience:

> I was taken to the bathroom, left alone to bathe; a less strong woman would have fainted, probably, and drowned in the tub. When I was walked to the operating room and told to climb on the shining table I was too terrified to speak. The doctor got out a knife; I thought they were about to cut me open, but I did not care. They could have saved me from that fear by assuring me that the "operation" I dreaded was merely shaving.... The doctor had one arm about a nurse's waist; with

his rubber-gloved hand he ruffled the hair of another while the girls giggled. With the same hand, when it was over... he sewed six stitches where I'd been torn. I heard him say, "That's the largest and hardest-headed baby ever born in this hospital." In the ten days I remained I never saw him or any other doctor again.[3]

Grace pleaded to see the newborn, but hospital rules intervened once more and Grace was left untended. Grace recalled:

I was left alone; not even a student nurse appeared. I'd been drenched with cold water, containing disinfectant, before they left me. The bed was wet with blood and water from my shoulders to my feet. A sheet was pulled over me, and the wind blew cold from the Pacific Ocean through the large open window. My teeth chattered so I could not sleep; it was the middle of December.[4]

For fourteen months thereafter, Grace was plagued by an agonizing cough, but a sound New England constitution allowed her to survive without further damage. Such neglect-induced illness was not the greatest peril Grace faced in the hospital, however. Queen was finally brought to her the next morning, but the matron demanded Grace give her daughter up for adoption. The stern woman was fended off only when Grace summoned an attorney, who discovered that the woman received five dollars for each baby she procured from new mothers too weak or too frightened to withstand her pressure.

Unlike those more vulnerable women, Grace Silver walked out of the hospital with a daughter firmly clutched in her arms. The baby was a fourth cousin of President Rutherford B. Hayes, and a lineal descendant of both Henry Knox, first secretary of war, and Samuel Spencer, a leader of the Boston Tea Party. Later in life, Queen would always refer to herself as a "twelfth- or fourteenth-generation American revolutionist" but, perhaps with revolutionary discretion, she never mentioned the presidential connection. Grace left the hospital with her august daughter and, in Queen's own words, "I made my first public appearance on a platform with my mother the night she had her 'coming out' party at which she was the guest speaker.... [S]he came out of the hospital, and then she went back onto the road to lecture. I was about ten days old."[5] Queen sometimes added in private that she may well have received her evening meal at the meeting as well.

Grace left Portland with more than a baby. She took away a bitter lesson that she would teach Queen: fear hospitals. Grace later wrote, "A general hospital, no matter how good, is no place for a woman to have a baby.... [A] mother is better off at home, in the care of a woman friend or relative, and a doctor. Her physician will at least have more personal interest in her recovery."[6] For her entire life, Queen would be deeply suspicious of hospitals and doctors, always preferring home remedies and frequenting health-food stores far before it was fashionable.

And so began the most unique childhood I have encountered in person or print. Virtually from her first breath, Queen was imbued by her mother and other radical associates with a hostility toward authority and institutions, with a commitment to socialist causes, and the passion to be an independent woman.

The Lecture Trail Leads Grace Back Home

As she rode the trains to lecture in different cities, Grace developed the habit of reading newspapers, lecture notes, and books aloud to herself. Often she continued to read aloud late into the night while in her hotel room. It was a habit she maintained after Queen's birth. Moreover, without a babysitter or relatives on hand, Grace toted her baby daughter to every meeting and lecture she attended. She described Queen's response:

> Beginning at the age of four months, she attended every lecture I gave, lying on a pillow, or sitting on a chair later on, eyes fixed on me throughout the evening, watching every look and every motion. Every night, back at the hotel, I read aloud. On the train I read aloud. She listened just as some babies listen to their mothers' lullabies or nursery rhymes.[7]

Although Grace later chronicled Queen's intellectual development during those first years, most of the other circumstances surrounding her infancy remain a mystery. Most details come from conversations Queen had much later with friends or from comments scattered through Grace's articles. For example, in an article entitled "Making Your Child a Genius," Grace described her daughter's physical constitution:

Queen, delicate from birth, required constant care and careful han-
dling. Yet, beginning with a fourteen-hundred-mile railway journey at
the age of two weeks, she and I traveled fifty-five thousand miles
before she reached the ripe age of six, in all weathers and altitudes, in
dust and fog, snow and rain.[8]

At some point before Queen was six years old, Grace returned with
what must have been great reluctance to the family home in Brockton,
Massachusetts. The proximate cause of her return was a poverty so extreme that Grace became unable to feed herself and Queen. The poverty
had already caused one tragedy: the death of Queen's younger brother.
Although Queen was characteristically sketchy about the details of this
misfortune, she once briefly explained to me that her brother had died
because Grace could not afford the proper nutrition or medical care that
both of her children badly needed at the time.[9] Queen had been injured in
an accident just as her brother fell severely ill. Grace was forced to choose
between the two children. As it was clear that Queen would recover with
medical care, Grace made her decision. She watched her son die.

The birth of this second child, whose name I never heard and the
name of whose father was never mentioned, had been described by
Grace in her article "Motherhood without Fear."

> Three years later [after Queen's birth] I had enough fear to demand,
> and get, proper attention.... I was still traveling, lecturing as usual. A
> few days before the time I hunted up a physician who had been highly
> recommended.[10]

Although that particular physician did not work out, he did refer
her to another doctor who ably assisted Grace in giving birth to "a nine-
pound boy, born without pain, without ever losing consciousness,
without a mark of forceps on the child or a tear of my flesh, with no
after-nausea."[11]

The son was delivered in a hotel room, with none of the staff or
other guests suspecting the event, until it was over. Queen would have
been almost four years old at that time. And, since she and her mother
moved to Los Angeles when she was six (and the two of them lived tem-
porarily in Brockton beforehand), her brother must have died of starvation and the lack of medical care in his first or second year.

From Queen's later descriptions of her harsh and puritanical maternal grandfather, Samuel N. Silver (1846–1927), nothing short of such a traumatic event would have prompted Grace to return home.[12] During the question and answer period of a lecture she delivered on November 5, 1995, at the Humanist Association of Los Angeles, Queen described Samuel N. Silver.

> My late and unlamented grandfather was a brilliant person in many ways, very intelligent, and he developed a number of inventions, including the water-powered printing press which published the *Lewiston Maine Journal* for many years, and which was so complicated that no one else could fix it except for my grandfather. During his younger years, he had actually been an associate of people like Victoria Woodhull and Colonel Blood.[13]

A sense of the younger Samuel can be gleaned from musings he had written which were included in a file of genealogical information in Queen's personal papers. On January 1 "in early dawn," 1870, the twenty-four-year-old Samuel wrote,

> What is life but thought? The more you are able to think, the more you will be able to live. The more you train your thought, the better can you mold your life. The higher you grade your thought, the higher will be the tone of your life.
>
> Water can rise no higher than its source. Man can rise no higher than his ideas. All things are made as from a pattern. Ideals are the patterns—the germ-kernels of your life. Ideals are the source of all habits—the directors of all energy. Habits are but the ripened fruits of your thoughts—the crystallization of your ideas. O man what shall the harvest be!? What shall the harvest be!?
>
> Shall we know better than we build, or
> Shall we build better than we know?
>
> S. N. Silver,
Bloomfield, Vermont

This was not the grandfather Queen knew or of whom she heard stories from Grace, however. In the aforementioned lecture, she continued to describe the grandfather to whom Grace had introduced her both in person and through personal accounts:

> But at some point—probably in his thirties—he got religion and he got it in a particularly vicious form. He went through several denom-

inations and later on went through several more, until he took up with what were called the Russellites, which were the forerunners of the present Jehovah's Witnesses. But he went through a number of different religions and he actually ended up with the reorganized Church of Jesus Christ of the Latter Day Saints.

At the same time he got religion, he also got the idea that the Lord did not want him to waste his time going out and earning a living. The Lord wanted him to stay home and read the Bible, which he did. He started in at the first chapter of Genesis and went through to the last chapter of Revelations, and then started back over again. His family lived on cornmeal mush and beans and whole-wheat bread from one year's end to the next in order that he wouldn't be wasting the Lord's time in going out and trying to earn more money. He would work enough to bring in a minimum.

... Sometime after her mother died when she [Grace] was five, she told my grandfather that if he was going to go to heaven she did not wish to go. I don't think she ever had any religion. As she said later on, he carefully explained to her what was wrong with all the other religions and she could see clearly what was wrong with his own without any explanation....

I don't know whether he beat my mother when my grandmother was alive, but she was beaten up consistently afterward.

In an article written by Grace entitled "The Bunk of Symbolism" she describes a dream that had haunted her pleasantly since childhood: it was of flying. The dream came from a childhood game she had played with her mother. Grace related:

Till I was about ten I could summon the dream at will, even when awake. It was pleasant with no sense of fear, no abrupt ending as in the falling dreams. By accident, at the age of ten ... we [Grace and her father] had returned to the house in which I had been born. My first act was to stare in amazement at a flight of stairs.

"That," I told my father, "is the same stairway I always dream of flying down." Over and over I had, in imagination, floated down those stairs; I tried to do it then and fell the whole length. A few months later an uncle came to visit us.

"I'll bet you can't remember how I used to stand at the head of those stairs and throw you down to your mother every morning," was one of the first things he said to me. For nearly a year, before I was two years old, it had been their regular stunt.... I would have never known the origin of that flying dream if he had not accidentally returned to visit us.

It is unlikely that Grace was beaten while her mother lived. Although little is known of Azuba Glidden Silver, the scant facts indicate that she had a strong personality and would have been able to stand up to her husband. Azuba had gone to work in the cotton mills in Maine when she was eight years old, where she worked sixteen to eighteen hours a day, from half past five in the morning until after ten at night. Apparently all her sisters had done the same. She died when Grace was five years old, as a result of consumption that she contracted in the mills. Another thing Azuba contracted there was a hatred of child labor practices, against which she spoke out. Thus, Queen would proudly announce that she was the third generation of a family of women who didn't know their place.

A sense of the marital relationship between Azuba and Samuel was rendered in an article written by Grace entitled "That 'Sterile' Period":

> My father belonged to a small religious sect which taught that all intercourse was sinful unless solely for the purpose of procreation. He claimed that, in accordance with these principles, he never at any time approached my mother except during the night following the end of her menstruation. They were married eight years before I was born. My mother did not share his views and, knowing that the birth of one child only was desired, and that said birth would be followed by immediate and virtuous separation, steeped an herb which grows wild in Maine and drank the concoction every month as a "regulator."[14]

After her mother's death, Grace was thrashed every day of her life at home. The beating was saved up until bedtime, presumably so it could be anticipated throughout the day. Samuel punished her on the grounds that if he didn't know anything she'd done to deserve it, then she must have done something he hadn't yet found out about.

Fortunately, Samuel had acquired a good-sized and well-rounded library in his younger days, including all of the lectures of Robert G. Ingersoll, the foremost freethought lecturer in America of that day. As Queen explained,

> They were up in the attic. Whenever my grandfather was away, she would get one of the books and go into the woods, read it, and bring it back. She also received help from one of the neighbors across the street who happened to subscribe to *The Appeal to Reason*, which was the big socialist paper of that period. He gave her his copies of *The Appeal to Reason*, as well as other things, which she gave back. By the

time she was seventeen, she had read her way through the public library, which included three volumes of Marx's *Capital*. She had become a convinced socialist.

On the day before she was eighteen, my grandfather beat her unmercifully because she had looked up a word in the dictionary after he had told her the definition. He said he was enough dictionary for any daughter of his. On the following day, he presented her with a gold watch for her birthday and told her she was now free to leave home, or she was welcome to stay. But if she stayed she would be under his submission, living the same way she had been. It probably took her about thirty seconds to make the decision and another five minutes to pack what clothing she had and she was gone.

She had $5 she had won in some sort of an essay contest.[15] With that she put as much distance between her and him as $5 could. In those days, it took her all the way into Boston where she had two aunts, both of whom hated her father intensely and who were happy to help her get established.

In turn, she made connections with the Socialist Party in Boston. They took to her. She was one of the very few native[-born] American women in the movement at that time—most of them were immigrants, especially Russian. Mother was one of the very few socialists whose ancestors just missed the *Mayflower* in terms of moving to America. She was young, eighteen, and she had a good education, so the socialists trained her to be a soapbox speaker. They did so by having her talk across a canyon to them, with pebbles in her mouth. Then, that summer, with a burly man standing protectively on either side of her, Grace stood up and delivered her first speech in Boston Common. Because she was a slim and attractive young woman, the organizers would start the meeting by putting her up there, with the instructions "stay for as long as you have something to say." When the words ran out, she relinquished the box to someone else. Throughout the summer Grace spoke out on Boston Common.

Then, in the fall, they sent her to the state organizer in Maine, which took her back home. An odd little sidelight is that, although she and my grandfather were not speaking to each [other] and he felt her activities had disgraced him completely, nevertheless he felt that if she was going to disgrace the family she should do it in style. He rented the town hall in Auburn for her to speak, so she could make a proper appearance. She probably delivered the first socialist speech in Auburn, Maine.

It was to this situation that Grace returned with her infant daughter, again presumably to save them both from starvation. It is difficult to imagine Grace making the choice to return in the presence of any less severe an alternative. And, yet, from a faded photograph, the family home appears to be a spacious, comfortable, and carefully tended farmhouse, sitting amid picturesque surroundings. Under gentler circumstances, such a home would have served as a sanctuary for a young mother whose life was crowded with controversy and, now, tragedy. But any circumstances that included Grace's father could not be described as gentle.

Even now I stare at a stiff-backed browned photograph of Samuel N. Silver, and I wonder at the unknown aspects of the family story. What led him to discover such a cruel God that he was prompted to beat his own motherless child? Samuel stares back at me from middle age, with a full beard and moustache—a handsome man—with piercing grayish eyes that do not tolerate or forgive. On the back of the photograph Grace has penciled in a message to Queen, "Samuel N. Silver. Born Bloomfield, Vermont, 1852, died Brockton, Massachusetts, about 1928, I think.[16] This is the one you saw when back east and was my father. His grandfather was Arad Silver."

Queen remembered very little of her experience "back east," though she developed a lifelong antipathy to snow as the result of a terrifying fall through a snowbank. She remembered eating corn mush every morning for breakfast and often for the other meals as well. She remembered having to be quiet all the time. The details Queen provided were sketchy.

Several things seem clear through deduction, however. Samuel, who left almost all of his estate to the Church of Latter Day Saints, could not have been pleased with his daughter who openly rejected the Bible and religion as damaging to women. Nor could he have related well to Queen who, even at the age of four, showed a precocious interest in all matters scientific. As a father and grandfather in the New England Puritan tradition, he took them in and fed them. He did his duty.

For her part, after growing up in the anarchistic atmosphere of the socialist and freethought movements, Queen could not have been pleased with the stern rules and silence of her grandfather's house. Another thing is certain: Queen would have recalled being beaten by Samuel, which indicates that Grace stood as a barrier between her father and her child. And, as soon as she could manage it, Grace took Queen as far away from the family home as she could. She traveled across the continent to Los Angeles, never to return.

Unfortunately, such a family schism makes for bad history. No family photographs record Queen's successive birthdays, no diary entries from aunts or uncles provide the family gossip. There are not even the oral histories from elderly relatives that most people rely upon to remember their earliest years. Instead, virtually the only accounts that exist of Queen's first seven years are those related by Grace in subsequent magazine articles.

The injury previously alluded to was one of the watersheds of Queen's young life. At the age of three, she was blinded in her left eye by a cigarette that was flung from a passing car and fell into her carriage. Although full sight very slowly returned and there was no lasting deformity, the injury caused Queen agony for years and was so debilitating that she could not venture outside during daylight hours for many months. The expense of treating this injury and Grace's need to conform her own schedule to Queen's—thus, precluding the travel and lecturing from which she made a living—probably caused the poverty that had driven Grace briefly home.

Years later, Grace gave an account of the accident's continuing impact upon her daughter:

> For eight years, Queen has been handicapped by blindness in one eye, while for months at a time, both of her eyes have pained her unbearably. For three years, she was unable to read because she could use neither eye for more than a few minutes at a time, and for eight months was confined in a dark room. Had it not been for the accident which caused this loss of eyesight and consequent suffering, she would now be much further advanced than she is.[17]

"Making Your Child a Genius"

The second pivotal event in young Queen's life also occurred at the age of three: she pronounced her first word, and she did so in a remarkable manner. Grace explained,

> That first word ever pronounced developed into a speech, delivered when some friends lifted her to the platform, while I stood out of sight in the wings, and someone told her to "make a speech" like Mother. She talked over five minutes, repeating verbatim the peroration of a speech I had been giving at one-night stands all winter.[18]

At that instant Grace probably decided to mold her daughter into a lecturer and writer along her own style by using an innovative technique of home schooling. On November 1, 1916, when Grace and the almost six-year-old Queen arrived in Los Angeles, one of the first places they visited was the Los Angeles Central Public Library from which Queen obtained a borrower's card. She proudly wrote, rather than printed, her own name on it. Queen's lifelong affair with books had begun. The public library became an integral aspect of Grace's ambitious plan to raise a girl wonder—although she always insisted, a bit disingenuously, that Queen was merely an average child who had been given "proper" instruction. The "proper" education of other children, however, hardly included speaking on soapboxes at outdoor meetings of atheists and other radicals.

Until the late twenties, the city of Los Angeles had a "free speech zone" that extended between 1st and 2nd Avenues on Los Angeles Street. Along this stretch, speakers were permitted to set up soapboxes and audiences were allowed to gather in an atmosphere relatively free from interference by police.[19] It was a favorite outdoor auditorium for evangelists and radicals of all causes.

Much later in life, Queen gave a sense on how the free speech zone in Los Angeles had evolved:

A woman named Dorothy Johns in 1908…along with three other women…was arrested for using the streets of L.A. to speak on freethought since preachers were allowed to freely speak on religion. Thirty-five men were also arrested. The prisoners were all acquitted.

Queen quoted a commentator who observed:

The Socialists and Freethinkers of Los Angeles have won a notable victory for free speech—that is, the right to speak unmolested on the street—and religious ranters no longer enjoy a monopoly given them by pinheaded officials afflicted with the idea that only believers in the Christian superstition have any rights under a secular government.[20]

Queen also reminisced about her own experience of the free speech zone,

By the time Mother and I arrived in Los Angeles, the free speech zone was well established. With the exception of people throwing rocks occasionally and of a truck that purposefully drove into a meeting one night killing two people and injuring several—Mother jumped off the soapbox just in time to avoid injury—there were no incidents. That is, as far as the law was involved, we had no problems, except that my mother did get arrested once during a speech. She read a clipping out of the newspaper which said that the army camp near Riverside had issued a command that people should not kiss each other publicly on the streets of Riverside. The army people explained that they needed to protect the morals of the soldiers who were stationed at the camp. So my mother said that if these soldiers hadn't all had good Christian upbringings, they wouldn't need someone to pass a law to protect their morals. For that she got taken off on the charge of disturbing the peace.[21]

Several photographs exist of Queen as a child lecturer, standing on a tabletop in the open air of Los Angeles Street. In one, Queen—who was always diminutive—is a tiny seven-year-old, poised on a soapbox with arms spread wide open in front of a fascinated crowd of men. In another, her back is to the camera, her hands rest demurely by her side, and there is no podium to hold any notes because she is speaking extemporaneously. To one side of Queen and slightly closer to the camera, with her face inclined downward, Grace is seated and seems to be following Queen's speech from a sheath of papers in her lap. Again, a few dozen men have gathered and seem to be listening intently. How large the audience actually is in either case cannot be ascertained as the photograph captures only a segment of the scene.

Queen had become her mother in miniature.

Decades later, Grace would still be grooming Queen to take her rightful place on the lecture circuit. On June 8, 1934, Grace wrote to her twenty-three-year-old daughter,

> Now that I am traveling again I recall several rules for traveling speakers which you might also find useful: 1. The first thing when you get into a new town, before you leave the station, find out and write down what time the train (etc.) leaves for your next stop, and how much it will cost to get there.
>
> 2. Get mail at P.O. first thing when you arrive and last thing before you leave. There might be something important. When you leave forwarding order, have mail forwarded to where you expect to be a week later. The P.O. is too slow to catch up with you sooner than that.

3. Look for a room somewhere within three or four blocks of the main library. It is likely to be fairly reasonable, in the business district—or near—and semirespectable at least. Besides, you can use the library.

4. Get some kind of city map and study it so you know where you are. Can get them free on hotel folders.

5. Pack suitcases, if you have two, so that literature for first meeting, and clothes for that night, will both be in same case and the other and heaviest case can be checked from one town to another and left twenty-four hours without charge at the station.

6. Sleep on trains or boats or buses with all your clothes on except dress and shoes. Better yet, if you must take off a dress, use another dress, not a nightgown, to sleep in. Then if anything happens you are at least dressed. No nightgown or kimonos when traveling. Use a loose dress instead.

7. Take your own collection if possible and watch that helpers in meetings don't go away with half your literature money.[22]

But Los Angeles County would not merely be a stop on a lecture tour: it became home for both Grace and Queen who would stay there virtually without an absence for the rest of their lives.[23]

Inevitably, the spectacle of a girl wonder delivering radical speeches in the streets of L.A. stirred curiosity.

Grace's home-schooling philosophy was given credit and her methodology was later chronicled in an article that appeared in *National Brain Power Monthly* entitled "Making Your Child a Genius."[24] It was written by Henry H. Roser, whom Grace married in 1921 making him Queen's stepfather. The article was subtitled, "Grace Verne Silver Tells the Secret of the Home Teaching Methods that Have Made Queen Silver the Marvel of the School World."[25]

Roser described Grace as a "noted author, lecturer, and mother and educator of a so-called child prodigy." Like Grace, he claimed Queen was an ordinary little girl who had fulfilled the intellectual promise available to any other child who was appropriately educated.

Grace is quoted within the article as criticizing the public school system for inculcating compromise and mediocrity into its students. She contended:

The educators of our schools worship a holy trinity of their own, namely, *Average, Authority,* and *Standardized Methods....* We are fast becoming a nation of *average* people. Instead of statesmen, we have politicians of average ability; we aim at an average weight and height for every child and adult, at an average wage rate, based upon an average standard of life.... Average is the great god of modern life....

A sausage machine is a fine thing—with which to make sausages. School administrators have generally considered it a good method of making brains for children.[26]

Among the "fundamental principles of education" that Grace believed were universally ignored by the current education system were: developing constructive thought until it became a reflex action; directing the child's energy into constructive pursuits, rather than destructive ones that wasted time; allowing a child's mind to develop according to its own natural tendencies, just as the body grew naturally; realizing that the child inherits its "chief bias" from its mother; and, understanding that a successful education leaves the child with ultimately more knowledge than the adult from whom it learns.

Grace explained the process by which she tutored Queen, which included *no* lullabies or nursery rhymes. "A woman once repeated a nursery rhyme to her," Grace recounted. " 'Stop, stop,' she [Queen] cried, 'that sound hurts my ears.' Another told her a fairy tale. 'Is that true?' she asked me. Upon being informed that it was not, Queen remarked, 'That woman must think that I am as ignorant as she is!' She was four years old at that time."[27]

In the early years of Queen's development, Grace claimed that she had subordinated her own career:

> I gave up traveling and remained in Los Angeles in order to make use of the unusually good library facilities in that city. In one year, between [the ages of] six and seven, I took her through the first six grades of grammar school work in reading, arithmetic, grammar, history, and much besides....
>
> At seven and a half she was reading Darwin's *Coral Reefs*, and *Expression of the Emotions in Man and Animals*. Soon after, she began to read Haeckel's *Natural History of Creation*.

Roser went on to add that Queen had also been taught self-reliance and, from the age of seven, had been earning her own money by writing, speaking, and working in motion pictures.[28]

Details on how Grace and Queen actually supported themselves during this period are vague. Despite Roser's claims of Queen earning money, she later spoke of how desperately poor she and her mother had been. Certainly, they picked up money working as extras in the movie industry that had sprouted in Los Angeles.

In the manuscript of a later article, Grace commented on the process of finding work as an extra. It involved nothing so much as constant driving. "There was no Central Casting Agency in those days, and all us extras used to make the rounds from one studio to another, morning and night, when we were not working. Universal City, Culver City, Hollywood, back and forth. One might easily drive fifty to seventy-five miles a day, looking for work and not getting it."[29]

Several photos of Grace "in costume" exist. In one photograph, a saronged Grace with her skin browned to a Polynesian hue embraces a distressed monkey. In another, she poses in the all-concealing Puritan garb of eighteenth-century New England. Meanwhile, because Roser sported a beard and owned a six gun (that probably didn't shoot), he generally received extra pay for work in cowboy movies. For her part, Queen used to speak delightedly of one movie set on which she had to climb up a rope to board a ship that was made to rock as though in a gale. In a letter dated July 23, 1982, written by a seventy-one-year-old Queen, however, she seemed to minimize her film experience, stating, "While I did do some movie work it was much earlier (1917–1928) and was only extra work."[30]

At some point, probably in the early 1920s, the family moved to what Queen always referred to as "the half-acre" in Inglewood, California. There they raised chickens for eggs and lived largely off vegetables from their substantial garden.

The Radical Backdrop of Childhood

Part of Queen's self-reliance that was not covered in Roser's article, "Making Your Child a Genius," was later related to me by Queen herself: it was political street sense. And she acquired it while most other children were having *Peter Rabbit* read to them. Upon arriving in Los Angeles, Grace and Queen may have first visited the public library, but making connections in the freethought and socialist communities had not been far behind. In 1916, the main freethought organization in the city was the Los Angeles Liberal Club, of which the well-known libertarian radical Charles T. Sprading was president.

Sprading became something of a point of contention between Queen and me. As a staunch libertarian, I often and openly favored individual and free-market solutions to the social problems for which Queen often and openly favored collective and legal solutions. On many occasions she and I found ourselves at ideological loggerheads, with our conflicting political assumptions allowing no chance of resolution. At some point in such conversations, Queen would exercise seniority and call a halt by saying, "As always, we must agree to disagree." The exaggerated patience of her tone left little doubt that she hoped libertarianism was a political phase I would outgrow.

Immediately after we experienced such a dispute, Queen would often recount a childhood encounter with Sprading, whom she knew I admired.[31] The libertarian guru had attended a freethought meeting in someone's home, at which Grace and Queen were also present. He spoke with what must have been great enthusiasm or outrage on some subject or, perhaps, he was merely given to gesturing. The diminutive Queen stood beside him, listening. As Sprading drove home an argument, an impulsive sweep of his hand lightly hit her head, which must have come up to about his waist level.

She looked up at Sprading and stated, "Don't do that again." The meeting went on, passions flowed anew until, lo and behold, he did it again. Whereupon, Queen kicked him in the shins so hard that Sprading was still limping hours later when the meeting concluded and he left the house. Queen told me the story several times. She always smiled when she did so.

As well as connecting with the freethought movement, Grace and Queen quickly sought out socialist organizations in Los Angeles, especially the IWW. Unfortunately, by late 1916, this organization was careening toward the brink of disaster. On April 6, 1917, Congress declared war on Germany and the first of a long series of alien enemy regulations were issued, regulations that would be used against labor radicals.

Queen once observed to me that every period had its official smear words. When her mother had been on the farm, the smear word had been "anarchist." When she went on the lecture trail, the word had been "socialist." During World War I, it was "Bolshevik" or, in California, "Wobblie."

The American government—preparing to enter World War I and panicked to its core by the Bolshevik Revolution that swept Communists into power in Russia—began to crack down on labor radicals, who were often antiwar as well as socialistic. To make matters worse, the membership of the IWW consisted largely of immigrants, especially from Russia and Germany: this made them "suspicious foreign nationals" in the eyes of the authorities and of American patriots. Moreover, the IWW tactic of declaring strikes ran directly counter to the government's need to maintain high levels of wartime production.

The mass arrests began. One of the first occurred on August 27, 1917, in Tripp, South Dakota, when thirty German nationals were arrested for violating the Espionage Act because they signed a petition against the draft. The list of such incidents would fill many pages. The victims were not always "alien enemy" nationals and the attackers were not always the authorities. As World War I progressed, the attacks became more violent and they were directed more indiscriminately to include native-born pacifists and anyone who refused to buy war bonds. Often, the violence was committed by groups of enraged citizens.

In September 1917, after simultaneously raiding forty-eight IWW meeting halls across the country, government agents arrested 165 leaders of that organization. Eventually, over a hundred of them went on trial for violating the Espionage Act: that is, they encouraged desertion from the American military, promoted strikes, and spoke out against the draft. After a five-month trial, every defendant was found guilty, though the sentences meted out varied widely. "Big Bill Haywood," the Wobblies' flamboyant leader, received a twenty-year prison sentence. He fled to the Soviet Union, where he died ten years later.

In slightly more than a decade of existence, the IWW had flourished, with its membership swelling to over 100,000 members in 1917. The Wobblies would now decline, with only a brief resurgence. This was the point at which Queen and Grace intersected with the IWW and other socialist groups in Los Angeles.

Grace's reaction was interesting. Well aware of the mayhem sweeping radical ranks, Grace ran in 1918 as the "Candidate of the Socialist Party for Representative in the Ninth Congressional District."[32] In "All Work and No Play," a semiautobiographical short story, as many of her stories seemed to be, Grace wrote years later,

Martha [the main character] couldn't see herself spending her life putting patches on the pants of the body politic; what society needed was a new suit of clothes.

Political work had followed, and she was one of the first women who ran for Congress. It had been in Los Angeles, in 1918, when that city had but two districts. She'd been candidate in one of them on the Socialist ticket, had got close to nine thousand votes—and been overwhelmingly elected—to stay at home, away from Congress forever. Nowadays, in less populated districts, men, and women too, have been elected with fewer supporters. Anyway, as Martha said, it really didn't matter.[33]

During the war years, Grace was somewhat protected from the widespread arrests of radicals and raids that were known as the Palmer Raids, so named after President Wilson's attorney general, A. Mitchell Palmer. The raids were primarily aimed at immigrant radicals who, as noncitizens, had little legal protection against harassment or deportation. Grace was not only native born, but also from a family whose roots were centuries deep in American soil and whose name sounded decidedly respectable. Moreover, because she was educated and politically aware, the authorities had to maintain at least a bare semblance of proper procedure in dealing with her.

But the authorities had an extremely good "informer" system within the more important radical organizations and they maintained thorough files on the memberships. With such resources at their command, the police and those groups aligned with the police used harassment as their preferred strategy against native-born radicals. Queen described one such incident of harassment which Grace experienced:

The Merchants and Manufacturers Association in Los Angeles at that time was the group maintaining the files. It was not done primarily by the police department, but by private organizations. When radicals were arrested, they were usually not taken—at least, my mother was not taken—to the police department. They were taken to the Merchants and Manufacturers Association. On one occasion, they showed my mother her file and read things to her from it. They had everything from the time she had left the farm, to her speaking on Boston Common and every organization she'd every spoken for and, I suppose, every man she'd been friendly with.

One particular thing showed how thorough they were.... There was a man by the name of Ed M. who became a rather famous prison-reform speaker. My mother was in Salt Lake City at the time that Ed

M. was going through so she interviewed him for the *International Socialist Review* for which she was writing at the time. She wrote all night to get the article ready to send into the review, then took it downstairs to proofread it over breakfast, but made the mistake of leaving behind in her room the pictures intended to go with the article. When she got back after breakfast she found her room had been ransacked and the pictures taken. The Merchants and Manufacturers Association file had notes on the interview and on the theft of the pictures. So they were very thorough.[34]

Although it is likely Queen attended the meeting at which her mother was swept up, it is unlikely that she, too, ended up at the Merchants and Manufacturers Association. Queen recounted many times how her mother, before taking her to a socialist or labor meeting, would press carfare into her hand. If trouble broke out at the assembly, Queen was to head directly out the door, away from the crowds, and go to a "safe" prearranged address. Queen was to stay there until someone she trusted came to get her.

Queen gave another example of a meeting that had been disrupted:

My mother, and then stepfather [Henry H. Roser] and I had gone to hear the speaker Anna Marie Strong at the Blanchard Hall, which isn't there anymore. And when the person got up to make a collection speech, that was a signal to all the American Legion people in the audience to arrest the one or two people who were beside them, as they had been deputized to do. Mother was one of the people arrested. They were all turned loose later on. It was harassment, which the American Legion was fond of doing.[35]

The American Legion was also responsible for the closing of the first socialist bookstore in Los Angeles, which had been established by Grace. In a talk delivered before the Humanist Association of Los Angeles, Queen recalled,

My mother had a bookstore which was raided three times by the Legion.... A truckload of books were taken out and burned, not only socialist literature but also scientific things by Darwin and Haeckel, fiction by Jack London and Mark Twain, and everything was burned. This happened three times. Afterward she didn't try to open up again because the money simply ran out.[36]

As well as learning from books, Queen was clearly receiving an education in political reality. Over and over, she recounted vivid memories to me...of seeing a man beaten up in daytime on the streets of Los Angeles for no other reason than that he had put on a red tie that morning.[37]...Of an IWW meeting into which members of the American Legion burst: one of them grabbed a young child and dipped his legs into a cauldron of scalding coffee. At a meeting in San Pedro, she said a child had been killed.

It must be remembered that Queen was a child herself when she witnessed other children being brutalized for their political associations. And Grace, as a mother witnessing the same events, continued to bring her daughter to meetings and to encourage her to speak out. Queen did so but, in the process, she acquired a healthy respect for and fear of "strangers."

Notes

1. Their generosity can be partially explained by the prominent role Grace was already playing in the socialist movement. She was a delegate to the Socialist convention of 1910 and she reported on the one in 1912 for the *International Socialist Review*. There, she met most of the communist and socialist leaders of the day, including Emma Goldman. Transcribed from an informal lecture delivered by Queen in Los Angeles, April 16, 1981.

2. The article was published in *Your Body* (November–December 1936). My quotations come from the original manuscripts in my possession, which may have been slightly edited in published form.

3. "Motherhood without Fear," manuscript, p. 8.

4. Ibid., p. 9.

5. From the transcription of the question and answer period from an informal lecture delivered in a living room in Los Angeles, April 16, 1981.

6. "Motherhood without Fear," p. 9.

7. As quoted in an article entitled "Making Your Child a Genius" by Henry R. Roser, Grace's husband, published in *National Brain Power*, September 1922, p. 54.

8. Ibid.

9. To my knowledge, Queen related this family story to only one other person, Don Latimer, a much-loved friend and companion of her last decades, but she provided no more detail to him than she did to me.

10. "Motherhood without Fear," p. 10.

11. Ibid.

12. Although Grace refers elsewhere to her father's death as occurring circa 1929, the executor's (Myron C. Fisher's) first and final account of the estate (No. 36,835, Commonwealth of Massachusetts, Plymouth) covered the period "beginning with the twenty-eighth day of November, A.D. 1927, and ending with the fourteenth day of December, A.D. 1928." No copy of the actual death certificate was available.

13. Some parts of the description come from the informal lecture delivered in Los Angeles, April 16, 1981. Queen always referred to Samuel Silver as "my late and unlamented grandfather." Victoria Woodhull was notorious for advocating free love and for being the first woman to run for president of the United States. Colonel Blood was her partner, both in intellectual and intimate terms.

14. As quoted from the manuscript of "That 'Sterile' Period," p. 5. It has the notation, "Published in *Sexology*, April 1935." The article also states, "... my father married again, treated his second wife the same way, and she bore a child ten months later. They got virtuous, too; she left him...." The second wife was named Annie Soper, and she bore a son named Norman. It is my impression, however, that the marriage took place after Grace left home, when Samuel would have needed a new housekeeper.

15. Queen may have remembered the amount of money incorrectly. Grace maintained detailed files of her published writing which she passed onto Queen and, from Queen, to me. One article entitled "Courtship" has a publication date of March 1908, and is marked in Grace's hand as "my first article" and "$8.00 prize won early in 1908." Ironically, the article calls for family members to make friends with each other. The "byline" is Auburn, Maine.

16. It is significant that Grace did not know the date and, in fact, misstated it. She meticulously recorded other dates of importance in Queen's life, which means she must have severed all contact with her father after leaving home for the second time.

17. *Queen Silver's Magazine* 1, no. 2 (First Quarter 1924): 2. In a sense, the psychological impact of the injury continued all of Queen's life. On insurance forms and other applications, when asked about injuries, Queen would mention that the accident required her to wear eyeglasses, then carefully point out that there had been no lasting disfigurement.

18. Elsewhere, the story differed slightly. In *Queen Silver's Magazine* 1, no. 2, Grace explained, "... from the time she learned to talk she was educated and trained for public speaking. She began at the age of four to give ten-minute talks, gradually lengthening the time, and learning how to handle an audience and answer their questions" (p. 2).

19. Thereafter, the "free speech zone" was moved to the Los Angeles Plaza. Queen later explained, "The Plaza wasn't too terribly satisfactory. You were supposed to be seventy-five feet from any other platform and it was difficult. They [the city] finally created an area on a street east of the Hollywood freeway near the exchange, called Boston Street, and it ran for about a block. You went into it from Sunset Boulevard, I think. It went into a little park, which

was actually a mass of concrete and I doubt whether they have kept even that up over the years. The officials who set it up seemed somewhat aggrieved that no one went down there after they went to all this trouble. But no one wanted to go down on a hot day with smog coming in from two or three freeways and no shade, and the concrete." (From an informal talk given April 16, 1981, in Los Angeles.)

20. From "Heroines of Freethought" speech delivered at the Humanist Association of Los Angeles (HALA).

21. From an informal talk given April 16, 1981, in Los Angeles. Grace received a week in jail and a $50 fine for disturbing the peace.

22. This was one in a long series of letters Grace wrote to Queen in mid-1934 from Ketchikan, Alaska. Another letter from Grace, undated, enclosed a diagram for converting a canvas chair into a soapbox. Using cleats, a board was put across the canvas top, with ropes stretched between the legs to be tight when opened. Grace explained, "First time I used it, it was hard to stand still, but one gets used to it, use a light board for top. Your own weight helps to make it more solid. It is light and easy to carry." Later, she referred to a soapbox she had either patented or intended to patent. I presume this was the box in question.

23. Queen lived in San Francisco for a brief time when she was eighteen.

24. *National Brain Power Monthly* was a McFadden publication in the vein of a self-help magazine. The magazine had run a contest for stories about those who had overcome handicaps. After Roser submitted a sketch of Queen's triumph over her eye problem, the magazine requested a feature article.

25. According to George B. Wright writing in *Queen Silver's Magazine* 2, no. 3, "Prior to her [Queen's] eighth birthday her education was conducted exclusively by her mother.... Since that time Henry H. Roser, teacher, and retired attorney, has, under her mother's direction, assisted in her tutoring, especially in languages" (p. 13). Later in life, on various forms she filled in applying for advance in the civil service, Queen indicated that Roser had a teaching certificate from the Wisconsin Normal School and that he ceased to tutor her in 1928.

26. Grace Verne Silver as quoted by Henry H. Roser in "Making Your Child a Genius," p. 29. The home-schooling aspect of Queen's genius seemed particularly appealing to many admirers. The famed botanist Luther Burbank wrote to Queen in a letter dated July 24, 1923, "How happy you should be in not having an education. You know I am called quite a botanist and plant improver, well I never studied botany in school and am glad of it. We learn very little at school anyway except to clutter up our minds with things that we never have occasion to use. Most of the men and women who have led the world have had very little or no education in the schools but an abundance of education which nature gives us freely."

27. Ibid., p. 54.

28. George B. Wright in *Queen Silver's Magazine* 2, no. 3, writes, "She was compelled to wait upon herself, buy her own clothing, after the age of seven, regulate her expenditures according to a weekly allowance, earn her own

money, and allowed absolute control of the spending of all she earned" (p. 13). In a letter dated September 3, 1923, W. S. Bryan wrote to twelve-year-old Queen, "I notice that you get your own meals in your room, and this makes me feel of kin to you." In a letter to Ethan Allen Gates, dated January 15, 1923, Queen speaks of making a choice between buying an *Encyclopaedia Britannica* or lumber to expand her room in Inglewood. She chose the lumber, but with regret because "Los Angeles is so far away I can get to it but once a week." Like many well-wishers, Gates donated books to the child wonder.

29. As quoted from the manuscript, "I Was a Co-Respondent."

30. Grace's experience may have been more extensive. In a letter Grace wrote to Queen dated June 23, 1934, from Ketchikan, Alaska, she shed some insight on their movie experiences. She wrote, "John Barrymore and Dolores Costello and the two kids are up here on his…private yacht *Infanta*.…Met all four on the street the other day and he tipped his hat and bowed to us. I was looking at her and thinking I knew her somewhere and did not realize just who they were till a couple days later.…She was in the *Sea Beast* when I was in *Java Village*. He probably thought he'd seen us some place, too. I had the brown monkey and he sent for me to bring the monkey over to his car one day.…"

31. Indeed, Queen generously presented me with several books by Sprading from her own library, including *Liberty and the Great Libertarians* (Los Angeles: Golden Press, 1913), *The Science of Materialism* (New York: The Truth Seeker Co., 1942), and *Science Versus Dogma* (Los Angeles: The Libertarian Publishing Co., 1924), inscribed on the inside cover "Dec. 13, 1925 [Queen's fourteenth birthday]. To Queen Silver from Henry H. Roser."

32. I have two identical photographs—obviously used for political promotion—under which this caption runs. One identifies the "candidate" as Grace Verne Silver. The other lists her as Grace Silver Henry. I have no explanation for the difference. If "Henry" was one of Grace's married names, that fact has not survived the generations. Indeed, Grace and Queen were so private about such matters that no one—not even I, whom Queen called "her confidante"—knew she had been married once, let alone twice. The most likely explanation, however, is that Grace was using a pseudonym.

33. Queen's papers included a great many articles, short stories, and one-act plays written by her mother, which were often published in popular magazines as a source of income. Most of them have handwritten notations on when, where, and for what fee they were published. "All Work and No Play" was without annotation.

34. From the transcript of an informal talk delivered April 16, 1981, in a Los Angeles living room.

35. Ibid.

36. Transcribed from a cassette recording of HALA lecture November 5, 1995. In the prologue to an award—the "HALA-NEGRI Award" (December 20, 1993)—presented to Queen by HALA in recognition of a lifetime of dedication to freethought, Maxine Negri stated, "At age fifteen…she [Queen] was

working in a book shop that sold the much-treasured Haldeman-Julius 'Little Blue Book' series." As this was a series issued by a freethought press, I presume the bookstore belonged to her mother, and this sets a time frame. The *Daily Worker* of November 20, 1925, stated, "A few years ago her stock of radical literature—1,500 dollars worth—was destroyed by the authorities." This places the bookstore circa 1922 in time.

37. Indeed, in the over twenty years of seeing Queen almost weekly, I cannot recall seeing her wear red as anything other than an accent, like jewelry, to an outfit.

2

The "Girl Wonder" Becomes a Lecturer

(1918–1923)

*H*ENRY H. ROSER'S article in *Brain Power Monthly*, "Making Your Child a Genius," featured several photographs of Queen. One of them would be widely reproduced by other periodicals: an eight-year-old Queen, with a huge soft bow gathering her hair loosely back, is raptly studying a book reported to be Haeckel's scientific treatise *Natural History of Creation.* The photograph is clearly posed, but very effective nevertheless. Queen's doll-like face, with apparently rouged lips, inclines slightly downward toward an opened book that seems too large for her hands. Light spills through a window, backlighting her in an almost ethereal manner. Indeed, from the soft focus, the picture may well have been shot through gauze. It is no wonder that this was the photograph Queen chose to have printed on a promotional card, even when she was approaching her teenage years.

Marketing the Girl Scientist

One aspect of the photo that was probably not staged was the choice of reading matter. The area of human study that drew the young Queen's most rapt attention was science. She expressed a special fondness for Haeckel, Darwin, and Huxley. As a result of her precocious reading and her soapbox lectures on evolution, the London Society of Social Science asked the eight-and-a-half-year-old to deliver six lectures at a large hall in Los Angeles.[1] The hour-and-a-half lectures were to be delivered on successive Sunday evenings. The announced titles were:

> Darwin's Theory of Evolution,
> From Star Dust to Man,
> Human Nature in the Animal World,
> Human Nature in the Plant World,
> The Conquest of Mexico by Cortez
> The Incas of Old Peru.[2]

The *Los Angeles Record* of December 24, 1919—the day before Christmas—had enthused:

> Eight-Year-Old Girl to Lecture on Darwinism. Queen is a little actress as well as lecturer and is going into pictures in emotional character work, she says. She has had considerable encouragement from D. W. Griffith and the Goldwyn studios.[3]
>
> A good share of Sunday night's address will be extemporaneously delivered. She has already traveled 50,000 miles in work on the stage and lecture platform.
>
> For pleasure she reads Roman and Greek history and geology. Algebra and geometry, she says, are "easy" subjects.

I can only imagine the expectant hush that fell over the crowded hall as the three-and-one-half-foot-tall little girl was introduced and walked to the center of the sprawling stage. Too small to use a lectern, Queen would have stood in full sight, probably with her hands loosely by her side as shown in several photographs. If she were clothed as in the photos, she would have worn a plain dress that came halfway down her calves, with sensible shoes and a hat that framed her face. Or perhaps she wore a large soft bow that pulled back her curled hair, as in the famous Haeckel photograph. A stunned silence must have settled over the attentive audience as Queen opened her first scheduled lecture on the evolutionary theories of Darwin. The impact would have deepened as she continued to elucidate for over an hour, without using notes.

The lecture series changed Queen's life. Newspapers rushed to exclaim over the girl wonder. The publicity did not die with the passage of months. The enduring attention Queen garnered can be partially explained by what could be called "good marketing." For example, at the age of ten, when the publicity from the original lecture series might well have been dying down, Queen made a strategic choice. Whether it was meant to be strategic or not, and how much it was guided by Grace, is not known. Queen offered an interpretation of the not-yet-published, but greatly anticipated theory of relativity by Albert Einstein. Einstein's revolutionary theory was the talk of the day, in and outside of the scientific world. And many scientists were at a loss to know how to evaluate it.

By offering a child's-eye view of relativity, Queen shared in the scientific limelight being shone upon Albert Einstein.[4] The famed botanist Luther Burbank expressed enthusiasm over her interpretation. The veteran and venerated freethought author William Smith Bryan proclaimed, "I never understood what Einstein meant by Relativity until I read her lecture on that subject. Possibly Einstein understood what he meant himself, but if he had employed Queen Silver to put his ideas into words, the world would have understood him better."[5] Thus Queen stole an iota of credit away from the august physicist who had just won the 1921 Nobel Prize for physics for discovering the photoelectric effect.

The *Los Angeles Record* of July 6, 1921, announced in page-two headlines: "Girl, 10, Explains Einstein. She Elucidates Relativity." The headline was followed immediately by an Editor's Note.

> Queen Silver, 10-year-old Hollywood girl, whose only school has been the Los Angeles public library, has written an article on Einstein's theory of relativity for *Record* readers. "Einstein's own book is not yet ready," she says, "and my article is, therefore, not so good as it

would be if I could have had his own work to study. If what I have written is not his theory, it is at least my theory of 'relativity' according to Einstein."

The *Los Angeles Record* published Queen's interpretation, which is reprinted here almost in its entirety:

The theory of Relativity in time and space, which Prof. Einstein is trying to demonstrate, is apparently "things are not what they seem." It is not a new theory; he is merely trying to demonstrate it mathematically. He is trying to calculate scientifically the amount of relativity involved in order to find out how greatly scientists are being deceived by appearances.

For examples of relativity, consider first things close at hand. Throw a ball; it comes finely to perfect rest—so you say. Einstein says the ball is still moving at the same rate of speed at which it is thrown, and that if it were not moving it would return to you. The Australian bushman put relativity to useful purpose when he made and threw the first boomerang.

Your watch goes faster if you are on a moving train than if you are standing still. Remember how the man in Jules Verne's *Around the World in Eighty Days* gained a day? And he never knew that relativity had anything to do with it!...

If you drive [a] car at the rate [of] sixty miles an hour alongside a moving train going in the same direction at the same rate of speed, then the automobile and the train are stationary in relation to each other. Helen Holmes [an actress] utilizes relativity when she jumps from one moving object to another. If both go at the same speed she jumps as safely from one to the other as if both were stationary, with only air velocity to overcome; and the relative speed of each may be so regulated as to discount even that. If, at some future time, an airplane should be constructed with such tremendous speed as to be able to go around the earth in twenty-four hours, a person on that plane would always be over the same spot on the earth's surface, and would continue to encircle the earth like a moon, unless arrested in his career by the force of gravitation. He would be stationary to the earth. We have never seen the opposite side of the moon for a similar reason—that the day on the moon is on the same length as the time required by the moon to encircle the earth.

People sitting in two trains passing in opposite directions at the rate of 60 miles an hour, on a double track, pass each other's faces at the rate of 120 miles an hour, though each really travels at only half that speed.

The sun's rays are dark and become light on coming in contact with atmosphere. We get no heat from the sun. Heat is made on earth by friction of the sun's rays on the earth's atmosphere. A relatively short distance above the earth, in space, it is dark and cold. These light rays come to us on a curve, never straight. We know this because we see the sun for 20 minutes before it has "risen" and for 20 minutes after it has "set" each day. At such a time we can look at the sun, or rather at the spot where the sun seems to be, without hurting our eyes. This is due to refraction of light—one of Prof. Einstein's points in the theory of Relativity.

The probability is that "fixed" stars appear stationary to us only because they are traveling in the same direction we are, carrying along our whole solar system at the same rate of speed as they themselves are going.

If the principle of Relativity be admitted, and Einstein's method of calculating the amount of relativity prove correct, it will be necessary to calculate the distance of all the heavenly bodies over again. Previous calculations of astronomical distances were made on the theory that light traveled in a straight line at the rate of a trifle over 186,000 miles per second. If light travels on a curve, then the real distance would be a little shorter than that previously calculated.

Prof. Einstein says that a straight stick is always crooked. This seems as unreasonable at first sight as the attempt to "square the circle" made by geometricians. Perhaps he can prove it. The fact that we cannot at all understand Prof. Einstein's higher mathematics, any more than we understand the "fourth dimension" or how to navigate a ship, need not be proof that his theory is wrong. Much of it seems very reasonable.

One vital point in the Einstein theory is this:

Everything ever seen, heard, or done, is registered in space somewhere. The application of the principle is this:

The nearest fixed star is so far away that it takes three and one-half years for light to come from it to our earth. If we had a telescope powerful enough to discern objects on that star, or people, if there were any, we should look through that telescope and see the very things that were happening there, not now, but three and one-half years ago.

People living on that body, if they have instruments of sufficient power to see this earth, are now looking at the panorama of the world war. Those still farther away, if they could look at us would be witnessing the Civil War, or the wars of Napoleon. Our fixed star is so far away from us that it requires 2,000 years for light to travel from it to our earth. Creatures on that body, if able to discern objects on our earth, are now looking at the rise of the Roman Empire. If we were able to wirelessly communicate with these various bodies, and if they have intelligent beings on them who could see and communicate with us, then our operators could telegraph to one star and find out what happened here ten years ago; to another and find out from people looking at our earth as we look at a motion picture, what Columbus did when he came to our side of the world; and we could ask another star why Napoleon lost the Battle of Waterloo; another to describe to us the death of Caesar; and still another, far away, to describe to us the building of the pyramids. This is what Prof. Einstein means when he says there is no time. Somewhere in the universe some distant star is looking on the solid earth of ours as a nebulous mass right now.

In the same way no motion is lost, but transformed. No matter is destroyed, but remade. Prof. Einstein did not discover relativity; he stated the problem in a new way, and is showing us curious things that may sometimes be brought about by the application of the Theory of Relativity.

Today, schoolchildren routinely watch television beamed from satellites that circle the earth, they work in science classes with models of the DNA structure, and take the principles of thermodynamics for granted. But, in the early 1920s, the Milky Way had just revealed its structure to astronomers, the chromosome theory had just been offered as a hypothesis to explain heredity, and the technique for "talking" motion pictures was in its infancy. It was almost unheard of for a child of ten (let alone a girl) to expound difficult scientific theories, especially ones by Nobel Prize winners which were sparking a revolution and mass debate within the scientific world.

In such a flamboyant and printworthy manner did Queen maintain her status as a child sensation, so that even foreign-language publications, from Yiddish to Esperanto, reprinted excerpts of her lectures along with glowing commentary.[6] Queen also continued to land on the front page of L.A. newspapers, such as the Sunday edition of the *Los Angeles Examiner*, October 15, 1922, whose headline declared, "Girl, Age 12, Expounds Wisdom of Centuries as Savants Marvel."

Over a period of three years (1922–1925), Queen repeatedly delivered the six lectures to large and eager audiences, adding several new topics to her repertoire. For example, she developed lectures entitled "The Pioneers of Freethought," "Evolution of Brain Power," and "Voltaire and the Fall of the Bastille." It was not unusual for hundreds of people to throng into halls for her lectures, with hundreds more being turned away at the door. On November 21, 1923, the editorial page of the *Bakersfield Morning Echo* boasted the headline: "A Wonderful Child." The editor declared, "When it is advertised that she [Queen] is to speak in a schoolhouse or other public building it is almost impossible to find standing room."

But the attention had an ominous side as well. The radical beliefs of Grace and Queen had not escaped the notice of authorities and "respectable" members of society. Many people were eager to silence the mother-and-daughter team. Indeed, Queen later told me that the only reason Grace married Roser was to prevent the real possibility that the authorities would consider her an unfit mother because she was single and take Queen away.

Some critics were willing to use violence. In the question and answer period of a lecture delivered in 1978, Queen spoke of receiving a tip over five decades earlier that the Ku Klux Klan intended to pay a night visit to Grace and her daughter. Grace told the well-wisher to return this message to the KKK, "We live out in the unincorporated territory of the county. There is no police protection within four miles, which is where the sheriff's office is and there is no fire protection except for what we provide for ourselves. But we have several axes behind the door and in the event anyone comes calling, we will not hesitate to defend ourselves in any way that becomes necessary." Queen concluded with the statement, "We never received a visit." To other friends, however—e.g., the librarian Arthur Pond—Queen spoke of running off a band of "visiting" KKK.

Most of Queen's critics were more subtle, however, and used the authorities—rather than naked violence—as a threat. In a letter dated July 6, 1923, fellow freethinker Robert F. Hester wrote to Queen, "I am very sorry that you are being interfered with by that petty organization [not identified] in Los Angeles. I am not at all surprised, however, considering that religionists have persecuted people of brains from time immemorial. ...I am glad they didn't succeed in arresting you and sending you to the detention home. I am sure your friends would never allow that, anyway."

Marriage to Roser not only gave Grace the most respectable of all commodities—a husband—it also provided her with a husband who was a lawyer. Grace managed to keep her daughter, but she did not escape public abuse.

In a letter dated July 20, 1922, with no addressee specified, the eleven-year-old Queen wrote, "The Los Angeles police have stopped all of us from speaking in the city of the 'Times' [presumably the *Los Angeles Times*], and forbidden us to sell any books. Mother has especially aroused the anger of the Christians, for she has talked here for six years, nearly, and they all know her. Of course we know they have no *right* to do this, but they seem to have the *power*. I wish we had a little power, too."

Queen went on to describe how the censors were attacking the movie industry "so hard that no company can make a good picture anymore, and some are afraid to spend money making any, for fear the picture will be either suppressed outright, or that enough will be cut out by the censors so that no one will want to see it." Since working as movie extras was a major source of income for both Grace and Queen, money became scarce. "[T]hat is another way the good people make life miserable for us," Queen wryly observed. "Mother says we will have to all depend on our writing for a living now. And that if our paper and postage stamps hold out, we will come out all right."[7]

The movie industry was being shaken to its roots not only by censorship, but by the introduction of "talkies." In the manuscript of an article entitled "I Was Once a Co-Respondent," Grace also commented on the impact of the latter.[8] "Talkies were a wonderful invention; but many a movie extra starved, even committed suicide in those days, when Hollywood imported stage actresses from New York, and threw us old-timers of the silent films overboard."

Despite economic setbacks, or perhaps because of them, Queen pressed on with her lecturing. The family must have been helped along financially by the literature Grace would spread out (police permitting) and sell as her daughter lectured. By this point (1922), Queen was twelve years old and already a veteran with over four years of public lecturing under her belt.

As could be expected, Grace played an energetic role in molding her daughter's continuing career as a girl wonder. Often, she assumed the role of promoter, making sure sufficiently large halls were available so Queen could fill them. In a letter to one of her benefactors, Ethan Allen Gates, Queen wrote,

> I expect to give my second lecture in Los Angeles, about the first of March—I may give two—repeat the last one, and give a new one. I also expect to repeat the last one in Huntington Park, in February.

Long Beach Rationalists thought they could not afford to hire a big enough hall, and have done nothing, so far toward getting up a meeting. Mother says we will wait till the weather is more settled, and then rent a theatre in Long Beach, and in San Pedro, and manage the meetings ourselves.[9]

But Grace did not remain as a power behind the scenes. She often took to the lecture stage and addressed the same audiences as Queen did, audiences who had presumably come to hear the daughter. The mother spoke first. For example, the *Los Angeles Record* of July 7, 1923, announced, "In commemoration of the signing of the Declaration of Independence and the destruction of the Bastille, a meeting will be held at Odd Fellow Hall at 2 P.M." Grace Verne Silver spoke on "The Evolution of Tyranny"; then Queen took the stage to lecture on "Voltaire and the Fall of the Bastille." Similarly, on July 14, the *Los Angeles Record* announced that "Queen Silver, famous 12-year-old orator would be lecturing upon 'The Rights of Children' on Sunday, July 15 at 2 P.M." On the same bill, Grace was slated to speak on "Selfishness, the Mainspring of Human Progress." After such meetings concluded, the mother and daughter team would often retire to a soapbox outside on the street where they would continue to answer questions.

In the photographs that Grace preserved of various L.A. street speeches, she and Queen are the only female faces in the crowd. The spectacle of a mother and daughter taking the stage and soapbox— Grace, thin with a determined face and haunted eyes; Queen, petite with hair flowing loosely along her shoulders—must have drawn the purely curious as well as those interested in their radical ideas.

Grace was more than merely a promoter and co-lecturer. She also acted as a press agent for Queen, whose clippings and pamphlets she mailed to editors across the country in the hope that they would review them in print. For example, she managed to have an article by Queen entitled "The War to End War" partially reprinted in a column entitled "Zoe Beckley's Corner" of the *N.Y. Evening Mail and Telegraph*, April 16, 1924 (page 13). Grace also maintained thick files of the clippings and any responses they drew for posterity. Under Grace's management, Queen continued to receive much the same headlines at twelve years old as she did at eight.

On April 6, 1923, the *Lyons Republican* ran the following story, offering the reviews of other publications, under a photo of the twelve-year-old lecturer. The *Republican* proclaimed,

> Miss Silver has attracted national and international attention for her genius....
>
> The *Los Angeles Sunday Examiner* speaking of her among other things says: Her remarkable genius establishes her as the greatest of child prodigies.
>
> The *National Brain Power Monthly* says: Queen Silver, still a sweet little girl, though knowing enough to be a college president.
>
> The *Los Angeles Evening Record* says: She has acquired enough education in four years to write and deliver a series of scientific lectures and write articles for the papers, explaining what this fellow Einstein is driving at.

On November 6, 1923, the *Inglewood News* ran a front-page story,

> Hawthorne boasts a girl scientist and lecturer, "Queen Silver" by name, whose lectures find thousands of persons fighting for a chance to hear her. The knowledge of things scientific of this girl of twelve might well be the envy of the president of any university.
>
> Professor Edgar L. Larkin [astronomer and mathematician] said of her, after listening to her lecture of the "Evolution of Brain Power," "I have heard from this child the greatest lecture on biology which I ever heard from any speaker."
>
> Another lecture...brought forth the statement that it would be considered a great lecture had it been delivered by any other person. But when it is considered that it was the effort of a child of but twelve years old, it is the more marvelous.

Writing again to her benefactor Gates, Queen commented on "Evolution of Brain Power," the lecture attended by Larkin. She observed mischievously,

> I lectured in Glendale last Friday....Prof. Larkin was there (the one who has charge of Mt. Lowe observatory), and he said...that Jesus Christ must have inspired it. That is the first time I ever heard that J. C. knew anything about evolution—or anything else. I had to work hard to keep from laughing till I got my pay![10]

Given Queen's talents, her irreverent attitude, and her marketing ability—which was arguably all Grace's ability—it is no wonder that

William Smith Bryan wrote into the main freethought periodical of the day, the *Truth Seeker*, to urge,

> Freethinkers ought to adopt little Queen Silver as their special lecturer and back her until she can make her own way. She has an intellect of a quality that has not before appeared in a child of her age, and there is no vanity or silliness connected with it. She has a style that any writer might envy, and her shafts go to the point with unfailing accuracy.[11]

Then, in another lecture undoubtedly calculated to provoke controversy and attention, Queen surpassed the stir that had been created by her interpretation of Einstein. The lecture was entitled "From Monkey to Bryan."[12] It was an arrow aimed directly at the populist politician William Jennings Bryan.[13] A noted orator, whom many believe would have won his 1896 Democratic bid for the presidency were it not for voting fraud, Bryan had become a leading crusader against the Darwinian theory of evolution and, especially, against teaching it in the public schools.

"Evolution from Monkey to Bryan"

Queen had been writing and lecturing on William Jennings Bryan since the age of eleven, and not politely so. In the *Truth Seeker* of April 15, 1922, Queen had published a commentary under the heading "The Laughter of a Child":

> Poor old William Jennings Bryan! He has always had the title of Champion Troglodyte of the World, and he was afraid some Christian idiot might take it away from him. He looked around to see what he could do next to make himself look foolish and sound silly, and so concluded to go after Darwin and evolution. He would have done so sooner, only he was so busy being a Presbyterian elder that he was very old before his education progressed far enough so that even he heard of evolution. When he did hear of it he came so near to having a real idea that it shocked him almost to death. He decided that a law ought to be passed right away to protect people from ideas, so no one would ever again run such a risk. The Kentucky legislature almost thought so too; only there proved to be one more descendant of Monkey than there was of MUD, and he had some sense and killed the proposed law.

Queen was responding to a challenge Bryan had issued in the *New York Times*, inviting advocates of evolution to come out of the trees and meet the issue fairly. In essence, he had issued a challenge to debate. Queen took him up on the offer.

> I'd be pleased to debate the question of evolution with him any time, provided he will hire the largest hall in the city and give me half as much for telling people the truth as he gets for telling them lies. I am eleven years old, and I suppose he would feel that I, with my superior intelligence, might take an unfair advantage of him, thereby making a monkey of him in public. We must apologize to the monkey for that last remark.[14]

In the same issue of the *Truth Seeker*, under the headline "The Laughter of a Child," the editor commented delightedly,

> The laugh in this case is on Mr. William Jennings Bryan, and the laugher is Queen Silver, a girl of 11 years who lives in Inglewood, California, and has educated herself by reading science and history books in the Los Angeles Public Library....Queen's handwriting is girlish, but her composition is accurate and needs no revision.[15]

Almost a full year after her article was published in the *Truth Seeker*, on March 11, 1923, Queen delivered the lecture "Evolution from Monkey to Bryan." As soon as C. H. Betts, editor of the *Lyons Republican* of Lyons, New York, heard of the lecture, he wrote to the twelve-year-old evolutionist, requesting permission to publish the text in his newspaper. It appeared in five installments, and afterward a thousand pamphlets were published. It received widespread acclaim, with Luther Burbank declaring it to be the best thing printed to date on the subject.[16]

Unfolding events on the American political scene were to make the pamphlet famous on a national and an international level. In the sweltering summer of 1925, a controversy called the Scopes Monkey Trial thrust the sleepy Bible-town of Dayton, Tennessee, into the center of national attention. The Butler Law of 1925 prohibited the teaching of evolution in Tennessee classrooms and the American Civil Liberties Union (ACLU) was determined to test the constitutionality of that law. The ACLU did so through providing for the defense of twenty-four-year-old John Thomas Scopes, a high-school biology teacher who was arrested for speaking out about evolution to his class in Rhea County High School.[17]

The defense attorney was the brilliant champion of the underdog, Clarence Darrow. The tent-revivalist, former secretary of state, and three-time candidate for president William Jennings Bryan volunteered to head up the prosecution. In the acclaimed 1960 movie by Stanley Kramer, *Inherit the Wind*, Spencer Tracy played Darrow to Frederic March's Bryan. Substantial passages of the script depicting the court trial came directly from the court dialogue, including the following exchange. Frustrated by having his expert witnesses barred from rendering testimony, Darrow finally put Bryan on the stand as an expert witness and asked him when the Great Flood occurred:

> Bryan: I never made a calculation.
> Darrow: What do you think?
> Bryan: I do not think about things I don't think about.
> Darrow: Do you think about the things you do think about?
> Bryan: Well sometimes.[18]

One can only imagine the unrestrained glee with which hardened reporters who covered the trial listened to such exchanges. The reporters included the rollickingly cynical H. L. Mencken who called Bryan the only man who could strut while sitting down. The reporters were delighted by another item as well. Arthur St. Claire, a friend of Queen's and a member of the Los Angeles branch of the American Association for the Advancement of Atheism, Inc. (the "4As"), attended the trial and wrote back from the scene. In a letter to Queen dated July 19, 1925, and signed, "Yours for Evolution," St. Claire enthused:

> Almost all of the newspaper reporters here are freethinkers at heart, though some have not the courage of their convictions. Many of them have read your pamphlet "Evolution from Monkey to Bryan," which is being surreptitiously circulated here. The local bookstore will not sell it; they are probably afraid of being raided. They sell Bryan's works openly. The cartoons have caused much merriment at Bryan's expense. Some are very curious about you, and can not believe it is your work. But I tell them about how many years you have been lecturing, and the numerous lectures and debates on scientific subjects you have given, and show them some of the clippings from the *Los Angeles Examiner, Record, News,* and other papers and magazines. It is curious to watch their reaction to the pamphlet and to the story of your career.[19]

Indeed, the pamphlet had been so well and widely received that efforts were made to raise money to send Queen to the Dayton trial in person. On June 29, 1925, the Inglewood, California, newspaper, the *Daily News*, splashed the headline across page 1: "Inglewood Girl Wonder May Go to Chattanooga, Aid Evolutionists."

> Inglewood's famous girl philosopher…may take part in the famous Dayton trial of Dr. Scopes who is alleged to have preached the theory of evolution in a public school. Queen Silver is an ardent evolutionist and in 1924 she challenged William Jennings Bryan to debate with her on the subject of evolution. The offer was not accepted.
>
> The *Chattanooga Daily Times*, a pro-evolutionary paper, is raising a subscription fund which has now reached $125, to pay the cost of sending Queen Silver to the scene of the trial to address a mass meeting on evolution. One thousand pamphlets of her essay "Evolution from Monkey to Bryan" will be distributed at Dayton preceding the trial, by a committee of radical evolutionists from Chattanooga, 35 miles from Dayton. If the Inglewood girl wonder makes the eastern trip she will address a mass meeting at Chattanooga on "Evolution." Judge J. H. Ryckman of Los Angeles will attend the trial to report for evolutionists of that city, and will act as guardian for Queen Silver if she decides to make the trip.

Alas, the trip never occurred, presumably due to lack of funds.[20] But the lecture "From Monkey to Bryan"—and, to a lesser degree, Queen's interpretation of Einstein's Theory of Relativity—had already borne impressive fruit in the form of *Queen Silver's Magazine*. It had been publishing for almost two years at the time of the Scopes monkey trial.

Notes

1. Identified in some newspaper reports as the London School of Social Science.

2. Elsewhere, some of the six lectures were identified by somewhat different titles. For example, in *Queen Silver's Magazine* 1, no. 2 (First Quarter 1924), they were identified as: From Monkey to Man; From Star Dust to Man; Human Nature Among the Animals; When Is a Plant an Animal?; Cortez and the Conquest of Mexico; and, The Incas of Old Peru (p. 2).

3. Again, it is not clear how much encouragement Queen actually received from movie luminaries such as D. W. Griffith. I suspect Grace or Queen sometimes exaggerated the truth for effect. For example, the front page

of the *Los Angeles Examiner* of October 15, 1922, declared, "She [Queen] has just completed her book, *The Ladder of Evolution.*" To my knowledge, no such book ever appeared. In fairness, this may be an example of the ubiquitous errors to which newspapers are prone.

4. The article, or a similar article based upon a lecture, seems to have been later reprinted in the first issue of *Queen Silver's Magazine.* I have been unable to locate a copy of that particular issue. The second issue of the magazine declared, "Regarding the Einstein article, published in the *Magazine.* It was written and first published two and one-half years ago" (1, no. 2 [First Quarter 1924]: 10). From the time frame provided, the referenced article is very likely to have been the one produced within this book.

5. As quoted from a letter to the editor in the *Truth Seeker,* September 29, 1923.

6. In a letter dated January 15, 1923, to Ethan Allen Gates, Queen commented on one such reprint, "I want to take advantage of my reputation, and have some meetings in other cities. The *Jewish Sunday Journal,* of New York, which is printed in Yiddish, had a picture and an article about my lecture in the issue of Nov. 12. We could get but one copy, and we can't read that."

7. Part of their coming out "all right" derived from Grace's habit of cultivating a garden upon which the family relied for food. Queen's letter to Gates continued, "We have a nice garden. Squash, cucumbers, string beans, carrots, beets, and strawberries are coming along all the time, and lot of other things will be ripe soon." Later in life, Queen rebelled against the quasi vegetarianism imposed upon her childhood by insisting upon meat with almost every meal. As she put it, "I do not graze."

8. The manuscript has the notation "Published Sept *Personal Adventures.* Accepted 9th time out."

9. The letter was dated January 15, 1923. Like many well-wishers, Gates donated money and/or books to Queen as he could afford to do so. Grace's hand could be seen in this process as well. In an undated letter circa 1923, Queen assured him, "I have plenty of room to store all the books I can get to store, and use. Mother says when we run out of wall space for wall bookcases we will build some revolving cases for the center of the room. I have room for several hundred more in my own room, and Mother says that if you send any of your books down for me to keep that I may have as many of the sectional bookcases with the glass fronts, as I need to put them in, or else she will get me some others with doors of glass."

On another occasion, he provided her with a violin bow as hers had broken strings, as she pointedly wrote to explain.

10. The letter is dated November 22, 1922, while the newspaper article is dated almost a year later. Perhaps the paper pulled a useful quote from its files.

11. As quoted from a letter to the editor in the *Truth Seeker* of September 29, 1923.

12. The lecture made into a pamphlet became a best-seller. For example,

in a letter dated July 6, 1923, Robert F. Hester wrote, "Mr. H. P. Burbage, Atty., wanted to know if you could have 1,000 copies of your lecture printed.... He wants to distribute them among his friends, also among his foes, the clergy. I loaned the copy you sent me to him, and he said it would come out in the *Libertarian* later. I think I can get it printed in 'The leading newspaper of South Carolina' the *Greenville News*, if you do not object."

In a letter dated July 18, 1923, the twelve-year-old noncapitalist replied, "Your friend Mr. Burbage can get my booklets for $7.50 per hundred, prepaid. Ten times that for a thousand prepaid. He can get about three hundred of the present edition, right away, if he sends for them—cash with order."

13. Queen's concurrent friendship with freethinker William Smith Bryan caused some confusion and the latter once urged her not to jokingly name a pet chimp "Bryan" lest people suspect she was referring to him.

14. "The Laughter of a Child," *Truth Seeker*, April 15, 1922.

15. Ibid.

16. In letters to Queen, Burbank was unstinting in his encouragement. When her lecture "The Rights of Children" appeared in the *Truth Seeker* of July 7, 1923, edited in a manner that distressed her, Burbank wrote sympathetically, "That is an editorial trick to cut out the best part of an article when sent to them or change it to suit their own fancy" (August 4, 1923).

Ironically, the piece that upset Queen may have resulted from W. S. Bryan's attempts to promote her. On July 7, 1923, he wrote to her, "Sometime ago, in a letter to the Editor of the *Truth Seeker*, I suggested that he obtain a copy of your picture and a brief sketch of your life, and print them in the paper; and I am glad to see, in the issue of this date that he had complied with my request, but whether on account of my suggestion or not I do not know."

17. Some controversy revolves around whether or not the ACLU orchestrated the arrest of Scopes specifically to test the law.

18. Much later in life, Queen quoted this specific passage from the transcript of the court trial (incorporated verbatim into the script) in one of her "stock" speeches entitled "Humanities Gain from Unbelief."

19. As quoted from a letter to the editor (Queen) of *Queen Silver's Magazine* 2, no. 3, p. 14. "Evolution from Monkey to Bryan" circulated in another location as well. It was widely distributed at the 1925 International Congress of Freethinkers held in Paris, France.

20. Queen energetically sought backing for a lecture tour on several occasions. In a letter dated October 6, 1923, William Smith Bryan wrote, "If I were a younger man, and had the means to start with, I would be glad to back you in your lecture tours.... You ought to be exactly on the other side of the continent to insure your success. Boston is the place where you should be located. That region is liberal and progressive, and there are any number of large cities and towns within a night's travel of each other.... The Pacific coast is practically out of the world, so far as literary efforts are concerned."

3

Queen Silver's Magazine: *The Early Years* (1923–1925)

*A*S EARLY AS January 15, 1923, twelve-year-old Queen had written to Ethan Allen Gates to tell him of the "small printing outfit... here at home" that she wanted to set up in order to "print leaflets, booklets, poems, etc., and maybe a small weekly paper of our own." Queen was already laying the groundwork to obtain financial support for what many people consider her most significant contribution to the freethought and socialist movements: *Queen Silver's Magazine (QSM)*. Admirers from Gates to Luther Burbank generously donated small sums of money to the planned periodical.[1]

She also solicited advice from veterans of the publishing industry, such as the seventy-eight-year-old William Smith Bryan, who counseled,

> As a rule the newsstand people will not handle anything that the Christian element objects to, and this fact will make it difficult for you to get your magazine in circulation.... The *Truth Seeker* is excluded from the newsstands for the reason mentioned.... When I lived in Washington several years ago there was only one stand in the entire city that sold it.... Christians are the meanest people on the face of the earth, and they imagine they are serving their God when they do anything to weaken or destroy the influence of freethought.[2]

Although he was unable to contribute financial support, Bryan did the next best thing, as Queen later recounted in describing how *QSM* came into being. For years, her lectures had been publicized by magazines and newspapers across the country. The publicity had resulted in numerous requests for printed copies of the lectures, which she was unable to accommodate because she lacked the money necessary to print them up. Then, as Queen explained, "an old-time freethinker, W. S. Bryan, wrote a letter which was published in the *Truth Seeker*, calling upon freethinkers to raise some money to help me publish my lectures."[3] As a result, Queen received seventy dollars, which served as "the foundation fund" for the four-page first issue of *Queen Silver's Magazine*.

Despite outside funding, Queen declared,

> Each issue must pay for bringing out the next number, pay for paper, postage, and the cost of sending sample copies. Any copies left over will be sold at my lectures to help pay traveling and other expenses. ...I have no stenographer, and no one draws any salary or commission on sales or subscriptions.[4]

On October 19, 1923, the *Los Angeles Record* announced: "Girl, Aged 12, Issues Own Magazine" (p. 10). Thus, in the glow of the praise that followed the Einstein and the "Evolution from Monkey to Bryan" lectures, Queen decided to publish and edit her own magazine which she carefully insisted was *not* for children. *QSM* would be an adult-level exploration of rationalism and of political issues that were often too radical for other freethought periodicals.

Each issue was meant to feature a lecture previously delivered by Queen, and her hand was declared to be the sole force behind the editing and publishing of *QSM*.[5] Queen wrote the editorials, and answered letters to the editor. Although most of the brief news items and observations meant as witticisms are anonymous, readers could logically attribute them to Queen. Moreover, *QSM* quickly established the habit of featuring either a photograph of Queen or a cartoon that illustrated one of her lectures on its cover. In short, *QSM* was specifically designed to showcase the talent of Queen Silver, as its name implied.

The first issue of *QSM* appeared in the last months of 1923 as a quarterly issuing out of Inglewood, California, where the family then lived. It began as a four-page periodical, of which fifteen hundred copies were printed. Volume 1, number 1 was apparently sent as a "sample" issue to a wide mailing list, along with a pamphlet entitled "Evolution from Monkey to Bryan."

To the best of my knowledge, no copy of the first issue of *QSM* has survived. All that is known about its contents comes through secondary sources. For example, the second issue of *QSM* declared of its predecessor, "Regarding the Einstein article, published in the *Magazine*. It was written and first published two and one-half years ago" (p. 10). Insight is also provided through the feedback of subscribers. For example, William Smith Bryan wrote of the first issue, "Your picture in the *Magazine* is not good. It does not do you justice. The best I have seen of you is the one where you are reading a book. It is characteristic and shows you to advantage."[6]

Unfortunately, the picture to which Bryan refers was the Haeckel one taken when Queen was eight years old. As photographs of the twelve- and thirteen-year-old Queen revealed, she had become an awkward and mature-looking teenager whose appearance Bryan described as somewhat "hard." Queen's hair no longer fell in curls, but was pulled back and gathered at the nape of her neck in a schoolmarm fashion. Sometimes she wore black-rimmed and unflattering glasses.

In later correspondence, Bryan added, "The best article in your first issue is the one of the Fundamentalists, and I am glad to see the *Herald* recognizes the fact and is not afraid to quote."[7] Surprisingly, one periodical that did not seem to quote *QSM*, or to take serious note of it, was the *Truth Seeker*. Bryan wrote,

> I am sorry that the *T.S.* has not noticed the *Magazine*, but still hope that it will. While he has not the least occasion to be so, Mr. Bowne is

very jealous, and I infer that he is the one who keeps you out of the paper, as he has charge of the literary reviews. But don't let that worry you! Most of the readers of the paper have heard of you and your work through my articles and others that have appeared, and in due time your reward will come. It seems singular that a stupid old man like Mr. Bowne should be jealous of a bright little girl like you![8]

Happily, other periodicals were more responsive. The *Los Angeles Record* of November 25, 1923, while announcing one of Queen's upcoming lectures, stated, "In response to outside inquiries, Queen will start on a speaking tour up the Pacific coast after New Year's.[9] The second issue of her magazine will be out in two weeks. It will be a 12-page journal and will be on sale at city newsstands. A number of prominent men have agreed to contribute to future issues." Socialist magazines also promoted the young radical editor, whom they rightfully claimed as their own. In announcing an upcoming speech of Queen's, the socialist mainstay, the *Industrial Worker*, of November 28, 1923, endorsed the first issue of *QSM*.

As the second issue drew close to press time, the *Los Angeles Record* continued to publicize *QSM*. Under the headline "Girl Issues Second Edition of Magazine," the newspaper proclaimed,

> She leaves soon with her parents for a lecture tour up the coast. She will go as far as Vancouver, B.C., returning to get out her third magazine issue in two months. Twelve thousand copies of the second issue were printed. The number will be increased to 16,000 the next issue. Readers in 38 states are now backing Queen's publishing ventures.[10]

The second issue of *QSM*, volume 1, number 2 (First Quarter 1924), appeared with a cover photograph of the eight-year-old Queen with a bow in her hair reading Haeckel. Somewhat down the page of the inside cover was the headline "A Word from Mother," in which Grace explained the magazine's somewhat antiquated cover.

> The photograph reproduced upon the front cover of this issue is years old. It has been copied and published in many papers and magazines, and has been broadcasted by a newspaper syndicate all over the world. It is published in this issue because so many correspondents have requested the editor to republish it.

Like the first issue, the core of the second was the publication in essay form of a lecture Queen had delivered—this one entitled "Evolution of Brain Power." *QSM* declared, "On Tuesday, October 17, 1922, Queen Silver delivered a lecture before the Popular Science Society of Los Angeles, California, upon the subject, 'The Evolution of Brain Power.' Six hundred people attended, and as many people were turned away" (p. 2).

After mentioning the six lectures delivered by Queen for the London Society of Social Science, Grace commented, "During the past five years, fourteen other complete lectures have been given in Los Angeles, making twenty in all, on as many different subjects, including Religion, History, Philosophy, Science, and Economics."[11]

The twelve-page second issue continued its self-promotion, with Queen stating,

> If this copy of the *Magazine* is marked "Sample Copy," it is an invitation for you to send in your subscription and to induce others to subscribe. If you are already a subscriber, and will send us a dollar, and the names and addresses of six of your friends, sample copies of this issue of *Queen Silver's Magazine* will be sent to them. (p. 2)

The second issue also included Queen's response to correspondence from readers of the first *QSM*, one of whom she addressed as "Dear Comrade." One letter clearly addressed the Einstein article in detail.[12] Queen's response showed a sharpness of tone that was becoming characteristic of her public demeanor. She announced her suspicion that the letter writer was "rather unfamiliar with the theory" and declared herself to be uninvolved with the "mathematical feature" of relativity, only with the "philosophical side." Queen ended by expressing the hope that the fellow she had publicly critiqued would become a subscriber (p. 10).

The next issue (volume 1, number 3 [Second Quarter 1924]) featured a cover photograph of a grinning Queen sitting with Sallie and Billie, internationally famous chimpanzees who were owned by *QSM* supporter Mr. J. S. Edwards. It is the first photo in which the sharply receding chin, about which Queen would be sensitive for the rest of her life, is apparent. Clearly, Queen could no longer rely upon her childish looks to charm people.

As had been announced in the second issue, "Evolution from Monkey to Bryan" formed the core of the magazine, followed by a column entitled "Books on Evolution."[13] In foreshadowing this feature, the previous issue had explained,

> Very few of the first edition of the pamphlet containing the lecture are left and as the author has to reprint the lecture, it seems best to publish it in the next number of this magazine. This lecture has aroused a great deal of interest, and agitators, propagandists, anti-Bryan democrats, republicans, and all others who appreciate a logical, witty, and easily understood lecture upon Evolution should buy and circulate extra copies of this famous reply to William Jennings Bryan's attacks upon Evolution. (p. 2)

A year later, *QSM* 2, no. 3 (Second Quarter 1925) was able to exclaim that, "Twenty-five thousand copies have been circulated....A new edition has been reprinted..." (p. 2). In an earlier editorial, Queen had requested readers to "send money so I can send sample copies of this issue...to the delegates at the Democratic National Convention" which Bryan, as a prominent Democrat, would undoubtedly attend. She asked, "Don't you think my little *Magazine* will help to wake up some of those old fossils?"[14] Apparently she had been successful.

A sense of the fun that Queen was having at the stodgy politician's expense can be shared by anyone who reads the following poem, which appeared on page 9 of the third issue.

No Wonder

I'm tired of being a monkey,
Said the chimpanz to his mate;
I think I'll try to evolute
To mankind change my state.

But why the sudden longing?
Inquired his monkey spouse;
You've been content with monkeyhood
Since Noah built his house.

I know, replied the monkey,
In wild resentment cryin',
But see what they are doing now!
They're classing me with Bryan!

The cover of *QSM* 1, no. 4 (Third Quarter 1924) is a photograph of an extremely mature-looking Queen in a straw hat, wearing a string of pearls. Although she is thirteen, she looks closer to twenty. The sixteen-page issue featured a reprint of her lecture "Pioneers of Freethought."

On page 10, Queen ran the following editorial:

> To my Readers. This is the fourth number of *Queen Silver's Magazine*. It is a year old and I will be fourteen years old next December. It is the only magazine of its kind in the world. Most of its readers and subscribers are ardent boosters, and if a few hundred more subscriptions come in, it will be possible to publish *Queen Silver's Magazine* monthly, instead of quarterly, as at present.

The fifth issue of *QSM* (volume 2, number 1 [Fourth Quarter 1924]) opened by apologizing to its readership for being so late that "some of you may have been worried for fear it would never be published" (p. 2). Queen explained that, with the completion of the first year of publication, many people had "forgotten" to renew their subscriptions. Queen made a vague reference to "other difficulties" as well.

The cover of the tardy issue was an illustration by Frank Espinoza, depicting William Jennings Bryan tightening a vice around the head of a young child. Above the screaming child's head is an illustration of a Chinese girl with her feet bound in the traditional manner. Under the illustration is the caption: "Head Binding in America," and the explanation: "Just as the Chinese formerly bound up the feet of their girls, so that they could not walk properly, so does William Jennings Bryan seek to put the iron clamp of superstition on the heads of American children, so that they may never be able to think properly."

The lecture featured in the fifth issue was one of Queen's most popular, "The Rights of Children," which had been originally delivered at Labor Temple, Los Angeles, on April 11, 1924.[15]

Children's rights and respecting children were issues upon which the young Queen showed a sharp temper. In an earlier issue of *QSM*, Queen had responded to a correspondent who'd expressed the rather innocuous wish that Queen could have a "carefree childhood." She retorted,

> I cannot understand how you, as an intelligent radical, can make the remark.... Do you still cling to the bourgeois idea that to be happy

one must be ignorant? Why do you want a child to spend the best years of its life, before it is fourteen, when its brain is developing, in wasted, useless effort, which gets it nowhere in after life?[16]

Later in the lengthy response which verged on a tirade, Queen declared,

> In my lecture on "The Rights of Children," I took up this matter. Grown people have robbed children of their rights, robbed the whole human race of the possibility of intellectual advancement, just because they wished "to preserve the childhood of their children." The mother looks on her baby, or child, as a sort of glorified doll, and can't bear to see it develop.... When you rob a child of its maximum brain development, you have no means of knowing, nor has the child, how greatly you have wronged him. Children have the right to unlimited knowledge, to get it as early in life as possible, and to have the pleasures and brain development which spring from responsibilities. I wish you would read my lecture on "The Rights of Children."[17]

Going into 1925, the cover of the sixth issue showed a mature-looking fourteen-year-old Queen sitting on a doorstep in an unflattering dress. She is surrounded by chickens that also perch on her lap: presumably, these are the chickens she and Grace raised for their eggs on the half-acre. This issue deviates slightly from the previous one. For the first time, the featured lecture is explicitly and entirely socialist, rather than merely slanted in that direction. "The Rights of Children," for example, had been openly anticapitalist in passages such as,

> I will speak only very briefly of the hundreds of thousands of children in America who are compelled to work in fields and factories in order that their little fingers may produce profits for a few well fed, lazy capitalists. There is not a person in America so ignorant that he does not know that child labor in field and factory is a common thing. It exists because those who make money by the labor of children do not care to give up such an easy way of living, while those who have children at work are for the most part too stupid, or too greedy for the wages of their children, to care how hard they must work.[18]

But Queen had been true to her word and had spoken "only very briefly" on socialism before returning to her main theme. By contrast, anticapitalism *was* the main theme of "Science and the Workers." The lecture was a comparatively later one in Queen's speaking career, having been originally delivered at the Knights of Pythias Hall in Los Angeles on May 2, 1925.[19]

The essay opened,

> The object of the capitalist class is to develop workers who will work for their masters but not for themselves, fight for their masters, but not for their own class, and who will think just as their masters want them to think. In order to accomplish these ends, the capitalist class has secured control of almost all means of education. Newspapers, schools, and churches are owned or controlled by them in order that the minds of the workers, and more especially the minds of the children of the workers, may be controlled. (p. 3)

QSM had become accustomed to advertising socialist magazines and organizations alongside freethought ones in its back pages. For example, it promoted the *Young Comrade* which it described as the "Official organ, Junior Section, Young Workers League of America. A working-class magazine for working-class children." Although such advertisements were more radical than those found in most freethought magazines, the essays featured in previous issues of *QSM* would not have been out of place in those periodicals. Indeed, earlier the *Truth Seeker* had run a lengthy excerpt of "The Rights of Children." With "Science and the Workers," however, *QSM* became a loud and explicit voice for socialism as well as for rationalism.

The sixth issue was distinguished by two other factors as well. First, it ran substantial articles that were not from Queen's own pen.[20] Specifically, the sixth *QSM* included a lengthy reprint of the previously published article "How to Make Your Child a Genius" written by Henry H. Roser.

Second, the Scopes Monkey Trial is mentioned for the first time. Under the headline "Evolutionist Under Arrest," Queen wrote, "J. T. Scoaps [*sic*], a school teacher, was arrested at Dayton, Tennessee, on May 6th, upon a criminal charge for teaching evolution to his biology class at Rhea Central High School." The article went on to give some details of the upcoming trial, including the arrangements being made by the American Civil Liberties Union, to appeal to the Supreme Court of the United States.

The seventh issue of *QSM* (volume 2, number 3 [Second Quarter

1925]) boasted a cover cartoon that depicted the evolution in eight steps of a rather ugly fish into an uglier William Jennings Bryan. The lecture featured was "Evolution of Human Nature," which had previously been announced as "a clinching reply to the man who admits that our bodies came from the animal world, but who still clings to the religious idea that we have a 'soul,' or a 'spiritual nature,' donated to us by a god."[21]

The issue is dominated by another contribution, the previously discussed report by Arthur St. Claire from the scene of the Scopes Monkey Trial in Dayton, Tennessee. Calling the trial "the show of the century," St. Claire provided *QSM*'s readers with a sense of the background against which the drama of the trial was spinning out. Describing the judge as a man who so loved to have his picture taken that he often stopped court proceedings to pose, St. Claire remarked that "no one today recalls the names of Galileo's judges." The judge was also fond of ordering everyone in the court to stand with him and pray for "light" (that is, the conviction of Scopes). The defense attorney Clarence Darrow ignored the command and, instead, sifted through his morning mail while calls to God rang through the courtroom.

St. Claire gleefully informed Queen of the impact her pamphlet "Evolution from Monkey to Bryan" made upon the somewhat cynical city-reporters who flooded the small Bible-belt town.

As she turned fifteen years old, Queen seemed to be poised on the brink of renewed national acclaim, not only as a lecturer but as a pamphleteer; not only as a freethinker, but as a socialist. Reality was to intervene in the form of two events. One would bond the mother and daughter closer together. The other would threaten to tear them apart.

Notes

1. Burbank's support—both financial and moral—continued after receiving the first issue of *QSM*. In a letter dated November 2, 1923, he wrote, "Your extremely interesting magazine received. I wish to thank you for it. It seems to be strictly scientific in every respect and I am sure it will be a success. In order to help you make it I enclose $10 to be used as you think best."

2. As quoted from a letter dated October 19, 1923.

3. Vol. 1, no. 4 (Third Quarter 1924): 10.

4. Ibid.

5. The lectures included, "The Evolution of Brain Power," "Evolution

from Monkey to Bryan," "Pioneers of Freethought," "The Godliness of Ignorance," "God's Place in Capitalism," "Godly Criminals and Criminal Gods," "Science and the Workers," "Evolution of Human Nature," "Rights of Children," "Science versus Superstition," and "Voltaire."

6. As quoted from a letter dated November 1, 1923.

7. As quoted from a letter dated November 12, 1923.

8. As quoted from a letter dated January 26, 1924.

9. The *Crucible* of November 25, 1923, also announced that, "In 1924 Queen Silver hopes to make a lecture tour throughout the eastern states. Comrades and friends who desire dates for their cities should communicate with her in order that arrangements may be made...." In the advertisements run by *QSM*, the *Crucible* was described as "An Agnostic Weekly out of Seattle."

10. From the December 24, 1923 issue. Elsewhere, the figures for the publication run are given as 5,000 copies for each of the issues mentioned.

11. Ibid. When Grace says fourteen different lectures, she must mean fourteen lectures on topics different than the original six delivered for the London Society of Social Science. The original six were delivered collectively at least fourteen times themselves before the date of announcement.

12. Since it was the policy of *QSM* to respond to letters without printing them, the contents of the former must be assumed from Queen's response.

13. "Evolution from Monkey to Bryan" is reprinted at pages 175–91 of this book.

14. Vol. 1, no. 3 (Second Quarter 1924): 12.

15. "The Rights of Children" is reprinted in this book at pages 195–210.

16. Vol. 1, no. 2 (First Quarter 1924): 10.

17. Ibid.

18. As quoted on page 195 of this book.

19. The sixth issue is dated First Quarter 1925. Either the issue came out extremely late due to the tardiness of the fifth issue, which is most probable, or the lecture's date was a misprint.

20. The exception to this is Grace's *Theological Dictionary*—if it can be termed an article—which ran with frequency from volume 1, number 4 onward.

21. Vol. 2, no. 1 (Fourth Quarter 1924): 2.

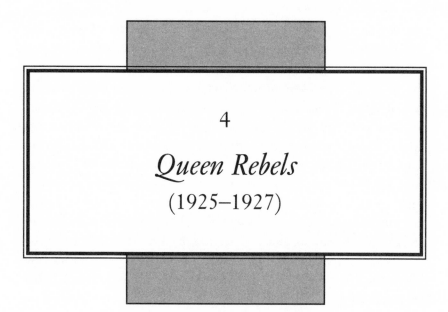

4

Queen Rebels
(1925–1927)

*V*OLUME 2, NUMBER 3 of
Queen Silver's Magazine was
dated "Second Quarter 1925" and,
in all probability, the issue was late
in appearing. More than a year
would pass before another issue of
QSM would be seen. Two remarkable events in Queen's life would
intervene between the issues and
they undoubtedly account for the
gap in time.

Event One:
The Modern Portia

As a speaker, Grace had grown up
in the rough-and-tumble atmos-

phere of Boston Common and the socialist lecture trail, where dealing with drunks and other belligerents in the crowd was a routine matter. In letters to Queen written later in life, Grace matter-of-factly described the violence that erupted at some lectures she delivered. At one street speech, Grace recounted how a fight had broken out around the corner, forcing her to pull the curious and dispersing audience back together again. During another speech, a drunk had grabbed hold of the hem of her dress, and a male friend of hers had to "knock him down." Presumably, this was a service socialist men rendered to their female counterparts. Describing the same speech, Grace related her relief at having taken up the collection at the instant she did. "[A]bout two minutes later an auto went by and someone recognized the driver as a scab worker on the docks and took him out of his car and beat him up." Grace's only reaction to the raw brutality of this scene was, "Lucky for me it didn't happen two minutes sooner."[1] Clearly, Grace was used to and, perhaps, even enjoyed direct confrontation.

Reports of the violent incident that occurred between Grace and the street preacher Jerry Merry vary, but on certain details there is agreement. Queen and her mother—known, then, as Mrs. Henry Roser—had become popular soapbox speakers on Los Angeles Street and later at Los Angeles Plaza, where political radicals and religious evangelists often shouted over each other to attract crowds. Grace and Queen were popular with the radical crowd. But the religious element kept trying, in one way or another, to silence them.[2] Apparently Grace and Queen had been preaching Darwinian theory on a series of Sundays at about the same time that Jerry Merry, a young student at the Bible Institute, had been attempting to bring people to God.

On Sunday, October 25, 1925, Queen was speaking from a soapbox located some short distance away from Merry's own setup. Grace sat in a car parked close enough to hear them both. The events that ensued would lead Merry to sign a criminal complaint of assault and battery against Grace.

According to Merry's testimony in the November court trial, Grace "suddenly and without warning...rushed at him, swinging a piece of automobile skid chain." He claimed that Grace struck him across the face with the chain, nearly breaking his jaw and causing injury to his eye. The *Los Angeles Evening Herald* reported:

Merry was cross-examined by Henry Roser, the defendant's husband, who was once a candidate for governor on the Socialist ticket against former Governor W. D. Stephens.

"Did you turn the cheek when you were struck?" Roser asked the Bible Institute student.

"No," the witness answered.

"Did you receive medical attendance?" the attorney continued.

"No," the witness reiterated.[3]

The *Evening Herald* went on to summarize Grace's testimony:

> She testified that on the Sunday afternoon on which the battery is alleged to have taken place she was seated in a car, a short distance from the place where Merry was delivering his address.
>
> She declared that Merry held up the pamphlet "From Monkey to Bryan," which her daughter wrote, and pointed to a picture of Queen Silver, on the outside cover, between two monkeys.
>
> Mrs. Roser declared that she became so infuriated at alleged remarks of Merry that she seized the piece of chain and rushed at the speaker. A man stopped her, she said, and in the ensuing struggle, she concluded Merry was struck lightly.

Three weeks before the trial, the *Los Angeles Evening Express* of Saturday, November 7, 1925, had given some details about the scuffle that made more sense of the incident. Splashed across the top of its front page was the headline: " 'Girl Wonder' Is Cause of Row over Monkey Trial." According to the *Evening Express*, both Queen and Merry had been lecturing at the Plaza in front of unusually large audiences of several hundred persons. Each speaker became caught up in the energy of the crowds, and they probably began to throw insults back and forth. Certainly such behavior would have been characteristic of Queen. Meanwhile, Grace reportedly heckled Merry from her car, calling him a "funny-de-mentalist" and undoubtedly a few other things as well.

With a surge of enthusiasm, Merry had brandished a copy of Queen's pamphlet "Evolution from Monkey to Bryan" on which Queen was pictured sitting with two monkeys. Gesturing toward the cover photograph, Merry declared to the crowd, "People are known by the company they keep!" Since he claimed to be responding to earlier heckling by Grace, the remark may have been intended to anger her. Grace purportedly flew into a rage.

On the stand, Merry called the assault "sudden and without warning," but in an earlier account he told the *Evening Express* a slightly different story of the attack:

> "You liar!" she shouted. Then, seizing an automobile chain, she swung it at me with tremendous force. The chain landed on my left eye, struck my right jaw, and wrapped itself around my neck. It left two bruises and one large swelling. My glasses shot into the crowd.
>
> I attempted to seize the chain but two men of the rougher element interfered.[4]

In yet another version of the incident, Merry was said to be twisting Queen's arm in a physical attack when Grace began to wield the piece of chain.[5] This version is the most plausible to me. It is not likely that a seasoned veteran of IWW meetings would lose control because her daughter was called a monkey. For one thing, both Grace and Queen were fond of monkeys. But it is very like Grace to have rushed to defend her daughter from a physical assault.

On November 9, 1925, the front page of the *Los Angeles Evening Express* announced, "Modern Portia of 14 Fights for Mother Before Court." Under the headline was a photograph of Grace sitting impassively behind a table in the courtroom, while a bespectacled Queen stands directly beside her, as would an attorney. Queen is gesturing, ostensibly toward the judge. In front of her on the table, notes are spread. She seems to be reading from them. The caption beneath the photograph read, "Queen Silver (standing), 14-year-old authoress, who is acting as defense lawyer for her mother (seated) in assault and battery case."[6] The newspaper continued, "Child authoress expects to win release of parent, accused of battery."

The *Illustrated Daily News* of November 24 announced the verdict in the headline: " 'Not Guilty,' Says Her Honor, as Girl Defends Mother." In the photograph run here, Grace was seated in the witness box staring at an automobile skid chain that was being extended toward her by chief deputy city prosecuting attorney, E. J. Lickley. Slightly in the background and to one side are a smiling Queen and the police judge Georgia Bullock. On a separate page of the same issue, the *Illustrated Daily News* continued, "Long-haired apostles of the Bible and long-haired so-called intellectuals, packed the courtroom, for 14-year-old Queen Silver, the child wonder, who is said to have understood the Einstein theory of relativity when she was but 8...."

The "Modern Portia," as the press had dubbed the fourteen-year-old, had made front-page headlines again. Socialist papers applauded her. The *Daily Worker* of November 20, 1925, ran the headline, "Fundamentalist Gets an Answer to Holy Insult. Calls Cop Instead of Turning Cheek." The article read, in part, "This city of ostracized angels is called the 'white spot' on the map...because this burg of white terror has railroaded more innocent 'reds' to the 'penitentiary' than any other municipality in the country." Identifying Queen as a member of the Young Worker's League, the newspaper praised "Comrade" Grace.

Queen Silver's Magazine must have assumed a low priority during the anxiety and excitement of the criminal trial. And whatever chance the magazine had to get back on schedule thereafter was lost in the turmoil of an event that occurred less than five months later. To understand that event, however, it is necessary to take a step backward and consider the background that made a schism between the mother and daughter inevitable.

Rebel without a Pause

At some point in her career as a girl wonder, Queen started to believe her own press clippings. She seemed to not only believe in her own superiority, but also in the inferiority of others. At least, this is what her behavior indicated. I remember one story Queen liked to tell about traveling with her mother when she was about five years old. Queen was waiting for Grace in a hotel lobby one morning when an elderly man asked in a kindly manner whether she loved God. It was an impertinent question. Queen piped up immediately, "Mister, you must be awfully ignorant to believe in such things." When Grace arrived, the man vigorously protested against Queen's insult. Grace replied, "She's right, you're ignorant."

Queen's passage into womanhood must have been confusing. She had been imbued with the liberal sexual and feminist attitudes of her mother, which contrasted sharply with the society in which she lived. She had been raised to consider herself the superior of not only other children but also of most adults. Great things were expected from Queen. She interpreted Einstein, she challenged Bryan, she issued her own magazine. And, now, newspapers heralded her as a legal marvel.

How could the girl wonder drop by a drugstore with a boy her own age and share a soda with two straws? To whom could Queen confess bewilderment as she moved through her teenaged years?

Yet under the self-confident surface, Queen was vulnerable to the opinion of others and she longed for their approval. William Smith Bryan wrote to her sympathetically about an incident that had obviously hurt her feelings, "…people will regard you as a child, and do or say things that will hurt you, like the lady did to whom you refer. She did not mean to wound you, and yet she did.…[U]ntil you grow older you will have to keep your eyes wide open in order not to get the ill-will of people of that stamp."[7]

Queen once mentioned to me an odd consequence of her upbringing. Although she felt quite comfortable in addressing large crowds, she was painfully shy during one-on-one conversations with people. It was a shyness she never overcame. Yet those who dealt with the teenager must have seen little else but the arrogance, even though it may have been little more than a defensive reaction.

Queen's insolence—defensive or not—did not receive the benefit of the many family and social factors that would have normally served as restraints. For example, she did not have to deal with peer pressure from others her age. There had never been other children with whom Queen played and from whom she learned the minutiae of how to interact in daily social situations. There had been no teenaged girlfriends with whom to discuss all the aspects of maturing into a woman. There were no teenage boys with whom to flirt.

Grace must have considered this isolation from other children to be healthy. In an article entitled "So You Can't Take It!" Grace described her memories of childhood from forty years before.

> Motherless at five, brought up by my peculiarly egocentric father, I was the butt of ridicule throughout my early school years. I got one new winter dress every other year, one new summer dress nearly every year. Lest I outgrow them before they were worn out, they were always too big. I didn't get enough to eat to make me grow much. For years every school day was misery, so I dreaded to be seen in my misfit, often shabby, garments. I was about ten years old when I decided, all by my childish self, to do something about it. I would no longer take the scorn and ridicule of other children.[8]

Grace resolved to become a good enough seamstress to make her own clothing, and she set about convincing her skinflint father to loosen "his purse strings for cloth" in order for her to learn this "necessary womanly art." With better clothing, she was no longer the brunt of jeers, but she "never forgot or forgave those earlier classmates who had once made life unhappy by their cruelly thoughtless remarks."[9]

Perhaps Grace felt she was sparing Queen from painful experiences by keeping her almost exclusively in the company of adults, and admiring ones at that. At the least, Grace would not have thought such a childhood to be harmful. Moreover, as a teenager, Grace had found acceptance and fulfillment by stepping onto the Boston Common to speak. Her joy in seeing Queen applauded as a lecturer would have been more than vicarious: she undoubtedly believed that being a girl wonder would make Queen a confident and happy human being.

Thus, Queen lacked close relatives or adult mentors who were willing to criticize her in a gentle but firm manner. Or, perhaps, there was no one to whom she would listen. Instead of providing her with perspective, the adults with whom Queen interacted treated her with deference.[10]

For example, at eleven years old, Queen wrote to the editor of the *Los Angeles Record* and took him "to task for asserting editorially that 'neither Darwin nor any other competent biologist ever said that the human race descended from apes.'" The editor responded in an article entitled (perhaps with tongue in cheek) "Monkeys and Little Girls."

> We hesitate to contradict a young lady who has achieved national fame as an intellectual prodigy. If our foot should slip, Queen would no doubt run us through and through.
>
> Instead of taking any chances with such a skilled and nimble adversary, we propose to execute, as skillfully and gracefully as we may, an immediate retreat, leaving the field and the glory with Queen....[11]

Mixed with such deference was the outspoken praise of elders toward whom Queen herself should have been turning as role models. For example, William Smith Bryan, author of twenty-one books, wrote to Queen, "We are all interested in you, not because you are a wonderful child—a prodigy—but because you are a great contemporary *thinker*. That is the thing!"[12]

In fairness to Bryan, he did try to counsel Queen. He gently urged her "not to overlook the fact that you are still a little girl."[13] He reminded her "you are still a child physically, and you cannot stand the work a grown person can do. You need time to rest, and sleep, and especially to *play*. Do you ever play? A little girl like you should have her dolls and her playhouses, no matter how much of a philosopher she may be."[14]

Queen must have reacted badly to Bryan's letter. In later correspondence, the elderly man backed away gracefully, but quickly, by explaining that his daughter once had a great fondness for dolls but he understood Queen's response differed. He entirely withdrew his suggestion regarding dolls.

People's deference might have continued indefinitely had Queen remained a child. People forgave insolence in an eight-year-old girl wonder. A diminutive child laughing at William Jennings Bryan could induce an audience to laugh along with her. But the mature-looking fourteen-year-old who wrote, "Some people fail to realize that there is, and always has been, a war between science and religion.... There can be nothing but war—war to the death...," found fewer people willing to applaud.[15] With age, her insolence sounded shrill.

Sympathetic fellow travelers began to offer constructive criticism to the teenager. They particularly objected to Queen's sarcasm and rather vicious ad hominem attacks upon opponents. Over and over again in *QSM*, Queen rebuffed their well-intentioned critiques. In typical editorial fashion, she replied:

> Some readers of my *Magazine* have written to me again pleading with me to be careful of what I say lest I hurt someone's feelings. When will you learn, friends of mine, that it is the very fact that I have never in my whole life cared what anyone might think about my words or actions which has been instrumental in so developing my mind that I was able to publish the first number of *Queen Silver's Magazine* before I was thirteen years old?... In my case, the owner cannot find fault with what the editor says....[16]

Before you could make an effective argument, Queen claimed you needed to hit your opponent over the head with a brick to catch his attention. She wrote of religionists, "In other words, I believe that mental dynamite is more effective than soothing syrup. The shock is greater at the time, but it does not take so long."[17] She insisted upon "using the weapon of ridicule, of sarcasm."

Queen's acid attacks on religionists might have been tolerated by some freethinkers and applauded by others. But, increasingly, Queen's sharp pen was directed not at the enemy but at fellow travelers. One particular issue of *QSM* dramatized this shift. In volume 2, number 2, Queen launched a sustained verbal assault entitled "Telling Lies to Children." The target of her venom was one of the foremost and best-respected of freethought publishers—as well as a fellow socialist—E. Haldeman-Julius.[18] She took him to task in a particularly brutal manner. She attacked his home life and his wife. To be precise, she excoriated him for tolerating the beliefs of his wife and the manner in which his children were being raised.

Apparently, the *Haldeman-Julius' Monthly* for January 1925 had included an article by the editor entitled "Religion—A Pile of Garbage" on one page while, on another, an article by his wife had appeared. Mrs. Haldeman-Julius had explained that she encouraged her young daughters and son to believe in Santa Claus for the great pleasure that such a harmless superstition gave to her children.

Mrs. Haldeman-Julius may have been right or wrong about Santa Claus. Certainly, no one could have justly faulted Queen for writing a personal letter to the woman, stating her disagreement. That is not what Queen chose to do. Instead, in a blast of public criticism that ran in *QSM*, she asked…when the daughter in question was sixteen and encountered a dope peddler in the corridors of her high school, would "Mrs H.-J. sit back and say, 'Alice likes morphine; it gives her great comfort and pleasure; I will not deprive her of the comfort of the hypodermic needle'…" (p. 12).

Queen then proceeded to state bluntly how Mrs. H.-J. was corrupting Alice who, upon discovering the truth about Santa Claus, had entered into a "conspiracy with her mother to let Henry [the younger brother] go on enjoying it till he's bigger…." Queen proclaimed, "Shame on you, H.-J., to allow such crimes under your roof." She concluded,

> The excuse of the dope peddler is that the dope fiend likes his dope, must have it, and that if he does not supply it, someone else will. The excuse of the preacher is that religion is a comfort to people, gives them pleasure, and that they can't do without it. Wherein does the specious logic of Mrs. Haldeman-Julius differ from the logic of the dope peddler and the preacher?

In short, Queen not only personally attacked Haldeman-Julius—a gentleman who devoted much of his life and fortune to the cause of freethought—but also attacked his wife and children publicly.

Even when she may not have meant to be offensive, offense was being taken. In announcing her intention to make *QSM* a monthly publication, Queen advised her supporters that they "will then have the satisfaction of knowing that you helped, by your subscriptions, to start the only illustrated radical magazine of science and freethought philosophy in America."[19] This comment sounds innocent enough until you realize that the *Truth Seeker*—the oldest and most venerated periodical of freethought and science—*was* illustrated and *did* express fairly radical ideas. It was contemporary with her own magazine.[20]

At the same time that Queen was attacking the personalities of enemies and friends alike, her expressed political views were growing more controversial. For example, as a way to end war, she advocated confiscating all the property of anyone who voted for war or went to battle—said property to be used by the military. As for the kings, presidents, congressmen, editors, and preachers who advocated war, they were to be put in the front lines of the military ranks. Moreover, no wages were to be paid to soldiers, sailors, or officers.[21]

Many people had recently lost sons, brothers, and husbands in World War I; they had no patience with such views. Veterans of the war were fiercely patriotic and given to beating up those who were not. Or, at least, those who stated their "treason" publicly. Yet in this atmosphere Queen chose to write an antiwar column and Grace chose to send it out to editors across the nation, hoping for reviews or reprints.[22]

Queen was well aware of the stinging backlash being directed toward anyone or anything radical in America. In an earlier issue of *QSM*, she had written: "The persecution of all kinds of radicals, in fact, of everyone with a new idea, has become a very serious problem.... There are three organizations devoting their time and money to the preservation of such remnants of freedom as are left us. They are: The Citizens' Federal Research Bureau.... The American Civil Liberties Union... The Libertarian League of America...."[23]

The girl wonder had grown into a headstrong and rebellious teenager. Perhaps it was inevitable that she would rebel against her mother.

Event Two: Falling from Grace

No one today would know anything about the dramatic event that followed five months after Grace's criminal trial if Grace herself had not saved three newspaper clippings.[24] Certainly Queen had never mentioned the incident to me or anyone else I know of.[25] One of the clippings Grace had saved was an item from the *Los Angeles Evening Herald*, on which she wrote the date May 13, 1926. The headline reads, "Queen Silver on Cal. Honeymoon." The newspaper continued:

> Mrs. George H. Shoaf, 15 years of age, formerly known as Queen Silver, child orator, was today somewhere in northern California on her honeymoon with George H. Shoaf, 50 years of age, local optometrist and leading Socialist. Mrs. Grace V. Roser, the bride's mother, made this announcement today after revealing that her daughter and Mr. Shoaf had been married a month ago at Tia Juana, Mexico.

Queen had eloped with a man over three times her age and more than ten years older than her mother. Clearly, Grace had not been consulted. Queen had not only eloped, she had left the country so that no one could stop her and no parental consent would be necessary. Upon returning to the United States, Mr. and Mrs. Shoaf did not go to Los Angeles and Grace; they went on a honeymoon to northern California. Although the couple had been married on April 14, 1926, Grace waited for a month before making an emotionally neutral and factually sparse statement to the press.

Indeed, the *Evening Herald* had to research certain facts to flesh out the announcement. It did so in an unsympathetic manner, observing "Mr. Shoaf has been twice divorced, court records show. The groom is reputed to be a man of wealth."

Whatever Grace's response to Queen's rebellion might have been, her reaction to George Shoaf must have included an overwhelming sense of betrayal. He was thirty-five years older than Queen and, thus, Grace's contemporary. He was also a prominent socialist in the Los Angeles area with whom Grace would have associated on a political level.[26] He had probably attended many of the same meetings as Grace, and been a frequent presence at Queen's lectures.

But the betrayal would have run deeper than this. When Queen's eye had been injured in infancy, Grace had taken her daughter to Shoaf, an optometrist, for medical care. Since Queen's recovery had been protracted—extending over the course of years—Shoaf was undoubtedly one of the primary male figures in her childhood, with access to the family home. Grace explained to the press, "Since then...a warm friendship between the child and Mr. Shoaf sprang up, culminating in their marriage." Later Grace would claim that Queen had not realized what she was doing. It was a strange position for her to take, after having trumpeted Queen's self-reliance and independence since the age of eight.

Queen's precocious sexuality should have come as no surprise to Grace, and not only because Queen was precocious in almost every other way. Grace had encouraged her daughter to express this aspect of herself. Among the many photographs of Queen as a child, there are two that may provide insight into this. They appear to have been taken when she was about ten years old. In both of them a naked Queen is standing in the bright sunlight of outdoors, in front of a backdrop of canvas that might be the side of a tent. Her hair is a mass of curls gathered loosely by a bow. Her back is to the camera and Queen grins provocatively over her shoulder at whomever is taking the picture. In the first photograph, Queen is draped only with a feather boa that dangles from her shoulders down to loop across her buttocks. In the second, the boa is absent. At minimum, the photos show that Grace was not disturbed by Queen's early expression of sexuality. Indeed, the two pictures were mixed among others of Queen holding cats, standing on soapboxes, and reading her books.

And, then, there was the seductive correspondence Queen received from admiring males who had a clear romantic, if not a sexual, interest in the girl wonder. For example, Robert F. Hester—a twenty-five-year-old man who was associated with the periodical *The Libertarian*—wrote long, emotionally intricate letters to the eleven-year-old girl.[27] One letter included a poem he had written to a "girl for whom I cared very much." The poem began "Beloved! our mutual joys are past..."[28] In the thick file of correspondence that ensued, Hester asked for photographs, and referred to Queen as a "super-girl" about whom he wished to know everything. He vowed, for her sake, not to "cast a second glance at a statue of the 'Virgin Mary' or the Venus of Milo."[29]

In a letter dated September 7, 1922, Hester responded enthusiastically to the receipt of Queen's photos: "Your photos, besides being otherwise very expressive, are 'REAL CUTE', if you will pardon my use of a common phrase. I don't believe in the gods, but maybe there are GOD-DESSES—I believe YOU are one of the latter yourself!" In another letter, Hester wrote, "To be frank with you, I have almost broken a date that I have with a girlie tonight, writing this letter to you!"[30]

The male admiration must have been heady stuff for an eleven-year-old girl used to being praised primarily for her intellect. And it must have had more immediate parallels among the overwhelmingly male crowds to which Queen lectured. The petite savant with ringlets and a mocking attitude would have been a powerful lure for some men. Although it is entirely possible Grace did not know of the seductive letters to Queen, it is not plausible that she did not notice such reactions from men attending lectures and meetings.

The next information about Queen's teenaged marriage comes from another clipping: a front-page headline of the *Los Angeles Evening Herald*, August 31, 1926. It reads, "Queen Silver's Marriage Annulled." The sub-heading is, "Girl Pastor Free from Husband. 15-Year-Old Evangelist Is Given Marital Liberty in San Diego Court." The front-page article reads, in part:

> Queen Silver, 15-year-old Los Angeles evangelist, today returned to Los Angeles from San Diego—freed from the bonds of matrimony.
> The girl, who was married to Dr. G. H. Shoaf, nearly three times as old as she is, on April 14, 1926, had her marriage annulled yesterday in the San Diego superior court by Judge C. M. Andrews.
> The annulment was granted at the request of the mother of the girl, Mrs. Grace Verne Silver-Roser, who claimed that the affair was a "run-away" marriage in which the girl did not realize what she was doing. The girl separated from her husband last July, it was reported. . . .

Grace's public assessment of Queen's state of mind is difficult to reconcile with a passage from one of her articles entitled "Parents and Sex Delinquency," written over a decade later.[31] There, Grace declared:

> There comes a time in every girl's adolescence when she wants to leave home, even to run away. Wealthy people solve the problem by shipping them away to school. Personally, I solved a similar problem by giving my daughter, even before she reached her teens, a completely separate apartment, a very small allowance, and the privilege of doing all her own housework, her own buying of food and clothes,

and telling her she was free to do whatever she believed right. Of course I have previously developed her self-reliance, cultivated her individuality. She went through the "flapper era" which troubled so many mothers without learning to drink, smoke, or pet promiscuously. Fifteen years after the experiment I can honestly say I am glad I gave her complete freedom at the age when most women try in vain to "control" their girls. She felt so free, so independent of me, that she simply wanted to do her very best to justify my confidence. There was no temptation to sit in parked cars when her home was so much nicer; no falling for the first man who asked because she had a chance to see too many masculine faults....

Queen's annulment continued to make front-page news. The front page of the *Los Angeles Examiner* for September 1, 1926, carried a photo of a preteen Queen, with the caption "Queen Silver Returns, Free." The brief article added no details but claimed that Queen was happy "... in her freedom from the cares and tribulations of a girl-wife...."

Queen's marriage had lasted five and a half months, from April to August, with the couple separating after three. Queen returned to her mother. Indeed, it was at this point that the family moved to what Queen thereafter described as "the half-acre" in Hawthorne, perhaps in order to remove Queen from Shoaf's proximity.

In the many legal papers Grace maintained, there was nothing to indicate Queen's marriage or annulment. The name of George Shoaf does not appear.

Notes

1. Letter from Grace to Queen dated May 28, 1934, from Seattle.

2. For example, in early 1925, the authorities threatened to arrest Queen if she took up a collection at her speeches, because such would indicate exploitation by her parents. Child evangelists were not held to this rule, however.

3. "Free Evolution Woman: Darwin Row Is Bared in Court Hearing: Mother of Modernist Author Not Guilty Is Ruling of Judge," *Los Angeles Evening Herald*, Monday, November 23, 1925, p. 1.

4. "Girl Wonder Is Cause of Row...," *Los Angeles Evening Express*, November 7, 1925.

5. This version comes from a clipping of the *Los Angeles Daily Times* across which Grace has written "Nov. 23 or 24, 1925."

6. Another newspaper clipping in Grace's files, which has no identification to cite, claimed of the trial day itself, "Mrs. Roser was represented legally yesterday by her husband, Henry H. Roser.... Miss Silver also was in court, but denied she intended to act as assistant counsel."

7. In a letter to Queen dated October 12, 1923.

8. From Grace's papers, the manuscript of an article entitled "So You Can't Take It!" which has the notation "published *Psychology*, Feb. 1950."

9. Ibid.

10. In a letter dated July 10, 1922, Ethan Allen Gates stated what may well have been a general sentiment, "The old guard of freethought propagandists are passing rapidly; and the need of coming thinkers to take their place is great." Perhaps in viewing Queen as the hope for the future, adults allowed her too much latitude.

11. *Los Angeles Record*, August 31, 1922.

12. In an earlier letter dated October 28, 1923, Bryan wrote to Queen, "Did I ever tell you that I have written twenty-one books, besides a lot of other stuff for newspapers and magazines? My books have had a circulation of over five million copies. I made a million dollars and lost it, and now I am trying to make another million...."

13. In a letter to Queen dated October 12, 1923.

14. In a letter to Queen dated October 19, 1923.

15. *QSM* 2, no. 3 (Second Quarter 1925): 11.

16. *QSM* 2, no. 2 (First Quarter 1925): 10.

17. *QSM* 4, no. 1 (May–June 1929): 2.

18. E. Haldeman-Julius published one of the most respected series of literature in the history of freethought. Called "Little Blue Books," these over 1,700 undersized booklets dealt with scientific and philosophical works, as well as reprinted classical literature. Among the original commissioned works issued were pieces from Joseph McCabe (121 booklets) and Will Durant. At the age of eighty-four, Queen praised Haldeman-Julius in a lecture entitled "Pioneers of Freethought" delivered March 5, 1995, for the Humanist Association of Los Angeles. She also made favorable mention of his wife in a specific context: When the couple married, Julius adopted his wife's maiden name "Haldeman" as one with which he prefaced his own with a hyphen. This was a rare, almost unprecedented gesture of respect for his wife.

19. *QSM* 7, no. 1, p. 10.

20. Queen had some valid reasons to be irked by the *Truth Seeker*, as revealed in several letters from W. S. Bryan. "Bowne is the reviewer, and I think he is a slow-poke. He is also quite prejudiced, and he may not review your pamphlet at all" (September 18, 1923). "I am surprised that Mr. Macdonald [the editor] thought your lecture on the 'Rights of Children' was too radical in parts..." (October 12, 1923). "I am sorry that the *T.S.* has not noticed you. I don't know what is the matter. They seem to be niffy about something (excuse the slang), but don't worry; they will come round all right" (January 11, 1924).

21. "Our Peace Plan," *QSM* 1, no. 3 (Second Quarter 1924): 12.

22. Grace met with some success. Zoe Beckley's Corner in the April 16, 1924, *N.Y. Evening Mail and Telegram* reprinted Queen's article in full (p. 13).

23. Quoted from *QSM* 1, no. 4 (Third Quarter 1924): 14.

24. Although there were multiple photocopies of most of the other clippings, only the originals of these three were kept. From this, I assume Grace did not circulate the items — as was her custom with other reviews and notices.

25. According to Queen's wishes, I destroyed certain specific papers Queen did not wish to become public, and I make no mention of their contents. I do not know if she realized these clippings existed. I suspect she did not.

26. In an article manuscript entitled "Old Man's Marriage"—on which Grace noted "Pub. *Sexology* Feb. 1936"—Grace had written, "May I be permitted to say that in my opinion the old man who legally and respectably married such a very young girl does her a greater wrong than one who merely seduces, and leaves her?" (p. 1). "When they marry the girls, old men ruin them forever" (p. 6).

27. He was associated with the *Libertarian* in South Carolina, not to be confused with a quarterly of that same name issuing from Los Angeles under the editorship of Charles T. Sprading.

28. In a letter to Queen dated July 17, 1922.

29. In a letter to Queen dated June 28, 1922.

30. In a letter to Queen dated October 23, 1922.

31. As quoted from the original manuscript, pp. 4-6. Grace has written the notation "Published in *Your Body* Jan. 1937 under the title 'Good Parents Make Bad Children.'"

5

Queen Silver's Magazine *Reappears* (1927–1931)

*T*HE LAST ISSUE of *Queen Silver's Magazine* to appear before Grace's criminal trial had been volume 2, number 3 (Second Quarter 1925). It is not clear whether an issue number 4 of that volume ever came out. Queen may have decided to start a new year, 1927, with a new volume number. The possibility is supported by an editorial Queen penned for the re-emerging magazine:

> After publishing my magazine as a quarterly for two years, I was compelled by circumstances over which I had no control to temporarily suspend its publication.

I have now decided to resume its publication, commencing with January, 1927, and to make it a Monthly instead of a Quarterly, as heretofore....

No mention was made of the court trial or of Queen's marriage. Nor did the subjects arise in subsequent issues. The only hint that something had happened during the intervening issues is a shift in address from the city of Inglewood to Hawthorne.

The sixteen-page *QSM* 3, number 1 came out in January 1927. On its cover was a bold black-and-white pen cartoon by the Los Angeles artist Frank Espinoza depicting the hand of Voltaire crushing the snake of Superstition. Its caption read, "Crush the Monster." Appropriately enough, the issue featured Queen's lecture "The Godliness of Ignorance."

On page 2, the constitution of a new organization, the American Association for the Advancement of Atheism, Inc. (the "4As"), was reproduced. The constitution read, in part, "Article 2. The object of the society is to abolish belief in god, together with all forms of religion based upon that belief."[1] After describing the Los Angeles branch of the 4As (called the "Devil's Angels"), *QSM* carried this notice: "The Devil's Angels are also organizing a Junior atheist group, and are about to start a Sunday school class along atheistic lines for young children." The Devil's Angels held public lectures every Friday evening, except for the second Friday of the month when they met together to conduct business. William George Henry was listed as president, and Queen Silver as secretary and treasurer, with her Hawthorne address given as the contact. The notice urged readers to let Queen "help you to save your children from the claws of the church. 'Crush the monster!'" (p. 15).

These were provocative words. In 1927, the word "atheist" was a synonym for "bolshevik," and "bolshevik" was the popular smear word of the day. Next to no one openly identified themselves as "atheists." Indeed, a myriad of words was used to substitute for the more incendiary term. They included: "humanist," "secularist," "freethinker," "truth seeker," and "rationalist." Using the word "atheist" was an act of open defiance. Having atheist *teenagers*, such as the sixteen-year-old Queen, who threatened to spread disbelief among America's pure children was nothing short of a declaration of war. This was made all the more apparent when Queen publicly challenged the extremely popular Rev. Bob Shuler to debate atheism with any member of the Devil's

Angels. Given that all the members were teenagers, the challenge had an insolence similar to the one Queen had made to William Jennings Bryan when she was eleven years old.

QSM 3, no. 2 (February 1927) continued in a confrontational vein. Again the cover was a cartoon by Frank Espinoza, depicting a fat man wearing a barrel labeled "Religion." Standing in front of the surly barrel-wearer were three figures who smiled derisively at him. The figures represented Labor, Science, and the 4As. Labor had a friendly arm around Science, who was poking Religion with a cane, while a grinning 4As gestured as though to say good-bye to Religion. In the background, the sun of "Atheism" rose over the waters of "Superstition."

The featured article was Queen's lecture "God's Place in Capitalism."[2] The essay declared, "In America, the church controls the State and Capital controls both Church and State. Capital finances religion and god sanctifies capital. The workingman is victimized by both god and gold. One steals his brain and the other plunders his body..." (p. 4). The essay concluded, "Man made god and man can and will destroy his god. When he has destroyed his god and remade his industrial and social system, he will have as a result of his labors, a better world than any god ever made" (p. 9).

As with the previous issue, the inside cover page promoted the 4As. It reported on the organization's first annual convention in New York City, with Queen being listed as a member of the National Advisory Council. Charles Smith, listed as president of the 4As, particularly praised the work of the San Francisco, Los Angeles, and New York branches of the 4As "as well as the Damned Soul Society at Rochester University [N.Y.]." He announced a new branch—"The Society of the Godless" in the high schools of Brooklyn, New York.[3] Queen had been unable to attend the convention, but her admiring correspondent Robert F. Hester presented a report written by her, in which she claimed the L.A. branch (the Devil's Angels) had ninety paid-up and "uncompromising Atheists."

The same issue ran an article by William George Henry, president of the Devil's Angels, entitled "What in Place of Christianity?" In it, he attacked Christians with a Queen-like fury: "The orthodox Christian is so small, and mean, and contemptible that he says if he can only squeeze his own dwarfed and runty soul past St. Peter, he doesn't care a whoop where the rest of the family [humankind] goes..." (p. 13). As a substitute, "We suggest decency in place of religion, and humanity as a substitute for Christianity" (p. 14).

But, just as the rhetoric heated to a white flame, *QSM* suspended publication, again, for about two years. There is a time gap between February 1927 and May–June 1929 in the issues Grace preserved.

Decades later and at the persistent requests of the diligent freethought historian Gordon Stein, Queen prepared a brief biographical sketch of herself. Of this period, Queen explained:

> In 1928, I went to San Francisco to deliver three lectures for San Francisco Labor College and after that remained in San Francisco and worked intermittently in a printshop. After I returned home we were able to get enough money to buy a hand printing press which would print a 6x9 page. We resumed publication, printing one page at a time. Published whenever funds would permit....[4]

During her stay in San Francisco, Queen made close contacts with both the IWW and the freethought communities, attending lectures by the celebrated atheist Joseph McCabe. Indeed, a male admirer from San Francisco who signed himself only "Hoppe" wrote to Queen under the guise of keeping her informed about McCabe. But the main purpose of the letter was clearly to nurture or to continue a relationship between them.

Hoppe opened his letter,

> Joseph McCabe gave four lectures, three at California Hall and one at 1254 Mkt St. The one at 1254 was best attended.... [A]t McCabe's lecture Sun night Bill Hinckleman asked McDonald to announce the dance and activities of the IWW but he did not do so. My own opinion of the matter is that Mac wanted to keep the meeting respectable, because at the eleventh hour he had a section of reserved seats guarded for some group of important respectability who sent in a check for reserved seats. I sat or attempted, like a good many more, and was told to vacate. It strikes me, as usual, as evidence of the influence of the goddess gold.[5]

Interestingly, at a lecture on atheism, mention of the IWW was considered unacceptable. "Respectable atheists" did not wish to be tarred with the same brush as socialists.

The Godless Girl

Whatever gap in time existed between issues of *QSM* was quickly filled by a new controversy that revolved around the Junior Atheist League. This league had been organized by the Devil's Angels, the Los Angeles branch of the 4As. The Devil's Angels had decided to target certain Los Angeles high schools in order to spread the message of atheism to America's youth by handing out literature and forming clubs.[6] Or, at least, that was the intention they announced in order to garner media attention. The press rapidly made the connection between "atheist" and "bolshevik."

On June 2, 1927, the front page of the *Los Angeles Examiner* ran the headline "School Atheist Clubs in City Laid to Soviet," with the subheading "Minister, Addressing P.T.A., Tells How Russian Propaganda Perils Youth of U.S." The article began:

> Does the hand of the United Socialist Soviet of Russia reach across the ocean and aim to hold tightly within its grip the youth of this country?
>
> Is there a bond between the atheistic society known in the Los Angeles public high schools as "the Junior Atheists"—a thriving organization—and "The Pioneers" of Russia, embracing all boys and girls from 1 to 17 years of age?

The accusation of Bolshevism was not unjustified. The two issues of *QSM* that had reported on the 4As and the Devil's Angels had both attacked capitalism as the enemy of atheism and the American people. In "The Godliness of Ignorance," Queen had declared, "The capitalist class likes to have the workers exercise the virtues of blind faith...."[7] In "God's Place in Capitalism," she had written, "Capitalism helps to maintain religion; the church helps to maintain capitalism. They are twin exploiters of labor; one exploits the body, and the other robs the brain."[8]

Proudly referring to themselves as "radicals"—then a virtual synonym for "bolshevik"—neither Queen nor Grace had hidden their pro-Soviet sentiments. Indeed, as criticism grew louder, their pro-Soviet stance hardened. Queen went so far as to defend the Soviet political persecution of rabbis and others who practiced religion as "payback" for centuries of imposed superstition.[9] Even if the Los Angeles public school system had been willing to tolerate teenage apostles of atheism roaming high school corridors, they would have never allowed bolsheviks to do so. Even if they had permitted the circulation of pamphlets such as the one entitled "Keep this Jew Scrapbook [the Bible] Out of Our Public Schools," they would have immediately suppressed any Communist material.[10]

In Los Angeles, with Roosevelt and Hollywood High reportedly active with atheist agitation, the school system seemed perplexed but determined to "handle" the situation. The *Los Angeles Times* of June 4, 1927, ran an article that reflected the puzzlement. Under the headline "Atheistic Activities Unverified," the *Times* stated, "no reports of them [atheist activities] have been received at the State Department of Education...." If such reports were filed, the article continued, they would be referred to the local school boards.

Just how such school boards intended to deal with the Junior Atheist League may be deduced from an article in the *Los Angeles Illustrated Daily News* of June 4, 1927, with the headline "P.T.A. Opens Fight on School Atheism." The article read, in part:

> Not only speakers who are slightly "off color" in their views on morality, but those who lean toward atheism or bolshevism, will find no welcome before the state's public school children, it became evident yesterday with the reading of resolutions at the closing session of the California Congress of Parents and Teachers.
>
> The resolutions were interpreted by delegates to be an active step toward combating growing propaganda circulated in the public schools on bolshevism, atheism, and a lowered standard of morals.

By June 10, the *Los Angeles Times* changed the position expressed within "Atheistic Activities Unverified." Its new headline proclaimed, "Atheists in Vain Drive on Schools." The brief article reported that atheist leaflets had been scattered around Hollywood High School and mailed to the assistant superintendent of schools. They invited the public to attend a meeting of the Junior Atheist League.[11] "Postcards inviting young people to join the league, have also been mailed to the homes of boys and girls whose addresses were obtainable," the article went on. "These state that the purpose is to 'combat the disgusting and evil influences of religion in the public schools.'"

Meanwhile, the *L.A. Daily News* of June 11, 1927, reported on an interesting backlash that had been created by the overly aggressive tactics of the Devil's Angels. The *L.A. Daily News* reported,

> First actual efforts to organize a Junior Atheist league local at Hollywood high school resulted in apparent discomfiture for the organizers yesterday.
>
> Almost a score of students assembled in a Spring street rendezvous for the organization, but before... actual formation had been discussed, all but two or three had walked out on the meeting, at which Mrs. Grace Verne Silver, local secretary, presided.

One can only imagine the delight with which the organizers watched what they believed to be an interested crowd swell their meeting. Then, they discovered that the teenagers had come for the sole purpose of staging a symbolic walkout. The fact that the newspaper reported this event means the press was either there by design or quickly informed of the incident thereafter. This alone converted the walkout into a humiliating public protest, especially when the Devil's Angels were so clearly trying to manipulate the media to their advantage.

The *Los Angeles Daily Times* of June 11, 1927, could only have made the situation worse with the headline "Atheist Move Ends in Fiasco." Grace, especially, came off poorly in the column. Christian students were reported to have asked her "disconcerting questions concerning recent scientific proof of certain biblical facts and about the possible effects of unbelief on the code of human conduct, which Mrs. Silver found it difficult to answer." When the students asked her to name any man of national prominence who supported the 4As, Grace looked evasive by responding that such men could not afford to let their names be known because of political reasons.

The June 15 *Los Angeles Times* followed up,

> Investigating the matter... I learned that the organizers had resorted to the stupid method of flooding the immediate territory of the school, mainly, as the leader avers, "Just because it was the only manner by which we could get into the daily papers."... Such an organization is obviously a lot of asinine rot.... The fact is, the organization appears to the writer to be a cousin of the much-discussed red element.

For once the news report was insightful. Mailing unsolicited atheist literature to children's homes was designed to provoke controversy for controversy's sake. And it was "asinine" because it sparked an angry backlash while persuading no one.

In a strange twist of history, the Devil's Angels and Queen received dubious immortality when movie director Cecil B. DeMille used her as a model for his 1929 film *The Godless Girl*.[12] In this motion picture, high-school students, under the influence of a teenaged girl and boy, turn their backs on Christianity to become atheists. One of the "converted" students is killed in a stairway collapse. The godless girl and boy are sent to a brutal reform school, where they receive the harsh treatment that the director obviously feels they deserve.

DeMille was said to be surprised at the popularity of *The Godless Girl* in the Soviet Union until he discovered that projectionists there were playing it without the final reel in which the godless youths are punished.

Queen Silver's Magazine *Reemerges*

Interrupted by a criminal trial as well as by a marriage and an annulment, *Queen Silver's Magazine* had probably lost many of its subscribers and most of its financial support. Moreover, Queen's militantly acerbic attitude had alienated a large segment of the freethought community. The file of clippings maintained by Grace contains nothing to indicate that newspapers such as the *Truth Seeker* were continuing to reprint Queen's material. The fact that *QSM* had incorporated an aggressive socialist and pro-Soviet stance may have also acted to alienate subscribers.

The next known issue of *Queen Silver's Magazine* is the eight-page volume 4, number 1, dated May–June 1929. Its cover boasted the photograph of a monkey swinging one-handed under a banner reading "evolution." On page 2 of the resurrected *QSM*, the eighteen-year-old editor stated,

> This little magazine has had its ups and downs in the four years since it was first started. It has been twice forced to suspend because of lack of financial aid.... The editor is at last in a position to resume publication and wants every one of her subscribers to know that their subscriptions will be continued.... It was forced to suspend the second time solely because it could not raise two hundred dollars—a small sum in the business world.[13]

Queen informed readers that *QSM* would issue as an eight-page bimonthly "for now," but it was not possible to fill orders for the two pamphlets *Godliness of Ignorance* and *God's Place in Capitalism* until $150.00 had been raised. "We have the type all set up for the reprint," Queen explained, "and the engravings which were used in the magazines on hand, and they will be republished as soon as it is possible to spare the money for the purpose." The future of *QSM* clearly hinged on money.

The May–June 1929 issue had a familiar look. On the inside cover, Queen once more felt it necessary to defend herself against readers who believed her style was too harsh. The featured essay by Queen, "Science versus Superstition," opened with a reference to the Scopes Monkey Trial. And the issue ended—as many did—with a new installment of Grace's "Theological Dictionary."

Although *QSM* appeared to be back to normal, changes were occurring. Volume 4, number 2 (July–August 1929) segued into a half-sized format that characterized *QSM* thereafter. Moreover, the issue announced:

> Since the publication of the May–June number, we have purchased a press upon which to print *Queen Silver's Magazine*, also pamphlets and other matter. With our very limited means, it was possible to get a press large enough to print only one page at a time, and it is operated by hand power. We have also bought type, which is set up by hand by Comrade Henry H. Roser, free of charge. The press work is all done personally by the editor, and the folding, stitching, and mailing are done by Grace Verne Silver, with such voluntary helpers as are available. We employ no clerks or stenographers or paid help of any kind whatever. We tell you this so that you will understand that it is not always possible for us to answer all of your letters personally, and still get our other work done. Each page of the magazine represents a day's labor on the press.[14]

Queen was not merely an editor, she was now a publishing concern, producing and marketing her own pamphlets. Each issue of *QSM* continued to promote one of Queen's lectures/essays.[15] This, too, would seem to be a return to normalcy. But some of the essays appear to be a rehashing of older ones and at least one cover is almost identical to that of an earlier issue. Material was being recycled. And it was steadily becoming as much "bolshevik" as it was atheist. The shift reflected Queen's own development.

In *QSM* 4, number 4 (November–December 1929), Queen announced a new group, the Workers' Educational Association. She wrote,
"I have met dozens who could discuss the 'Materialistic Conception of
History' by the hour and quote Karl Marx by the yard, chapter and
verse, but few who knew the history to which to apply the 'Materialistic
Conception,' or knew enough about the economic history of either the
United States or any other nation to be able to apply their economic
theories" (p. 10). The Workers' Educational Association intended to
offer classes in economics, public speaking, music, American history,
and social and physical sciences.

Future issues of *QSM* became more provocative. For example, the
cover of volume 5, number 3 (May–June 1930) depicted a demon
looking in a window at a terrified child. The caption read: "Russian children no longer fear gods or devils." The feature article was not by
Queen. Entitled "Soviet Persecution of Religion," the piece had been
penned by F. C. Oberlaender as a response to the many accounts of
brutal religious persecution coming out of Soviet Russia. (Oberlaender
was identified only as being from Vienna, Austria.) The issue featured
the poem "The March of the Hungry Men."

Oberlaender wrote, "Whereas a year ago the tale of religious persecution emanated from Mexico (where it has since been exploded), it
comes, this time, from Soviet Russia (likewise, to be exploded sooner or
later)." As for churches being closed down and rabbis imprisoned, the
author contended, "Assuming this is true (although of course it is not),
we feel bound to say that these gentlemen get off very lightly..." (p. 3).
After all, "flies must be swatted" (p. 5).[16]

The July–August 1930 issue continued to express pro-Soviet sentiment. An article entitled "Soviet Laws on Religion" quoted extensively
from the Decree of the Union of Soviet Socialist Republics, issued January 23, 1918. The decree, in turn, had been quoted in the fourth annual
report of the 4As. Another article entitled "Labor and Religion" quoted
thinkers such as Leon Trotsky with approval. Interestingly, Queen's
article, "Bootlegging Religion," is uncharacteristically brief.

QSM 5, number 5 (September–October 1930) is remarkable for one
reason: Queen is absent from its pages. Instead, a number of other
writers—including Roser, Ora Vestal, Oliver O. Butler, and Grace—are
represented. Judging from a notice on page 14, *QSM* was again in
trouble:

> We regret the lateness of publication of this number of *Queen Silver's Magazine.* Financial difficulties, and the consequent necessity of doing more than the usual amount of other work, have delayed both the typesetting and press work. Readers inclined to complain should remember that we employ no paid labor.... Readers should also remember that this is an exclusively handmade magazine, and requires fully twenty days of labor to publish.

The following issue, volume 5, number 6 (November–December 1930), featured an essay entitled "The Garden of Eden Myth" by Grace, not by Queen. And, unless several unsigned and brief pieces were written by Queen, the young editor was absent from this issue as well.

Queen reappeared in *QSM* 6, number 1 (January–February 1931) with a short feature article entitled "Religion and Delinquency," but the ensuing issue again showcased a piece by F.C. Oberlaender entitled "Superstition alias Religion." It included a lengthy reprint from the *Arbitrator.* Moreover, for the first time, an errata notice was placed hastily in the issue apologizing for the fact that "pages 13, 14, 15, 16, and 17 do not appear in proper consecutive order." Clearly, something was amiss behind the scenes of *QSM.*

At last, Queen's absence was explained in *QSM* 6, number 2, "Queen Silver Injured in Collision." The article went on,

> The editor and publisher of this magazine, Queen Silver, while riding home in a car driven by a friend, was seriously injured when the car in which she rode was struck by a wildly speeding car at the intersection. She was thrown against the door and out of the car, landing on her head and right shoulder some thirty feet beyond the wrecked auto. The right side of her collarbone was broken in two places and she suffered several lacerations on the head and many severe body bruises and contusions. She is recovering as rapidly as can be expected, considering the nature of her injuries, but it is doubtful if she will be able to write or lecture before August 1st.
>
> Her illness makes it necessary for her mother to run the printing press, in addition to taking care of the invalid and doing her usual work, so our readers must bear all of this in mind and when tempted to complain about the delay in the publication of our magazine.[17]

Because she refused to stay in a hospital, Queen's doctor rigged her to a wooden yoke that immobilized her head and shoulders, allowing her to heal at home. Meanwhile, she virtually disappeared from *QSM.*

Volume 6, number 3 (May–June 1931) reprinted the lecture "God's Place in Capitalism" previously published in volume 3, number 2 (February 1927).[18] In the next issue, Queen seemed to have no presence even in the form of a reprint. It is possible that *QSM* continued beyond the July–August 1931 issue, but Grace preserved no further issues nor is there correspondence that speaks of the magazine's continuing publication.

Queen's youthful words must have haunted her. In volume 2, number 1, she had declared, "*Queen Silver's Magazine* is going to be published as long as the editor lives. I have one subscriber who paid for fifty years before ever seeing a copy—and he never saw me, either. . . . So you see the *Magazine* is a permanent affair" (p. 2).

Seven years later, in 1931, her magazine folded.

Notes

1. The contact address given for the headquarters of the 4As is in New York City, though the organization was reported to have "branches in most of the principal cities of the country. Los Angeles has a branch with eighty-five members." *QSM* 3, no. 1 (January 1927): 15.

2. The essay is reprinted in this book on pages 211–25.

3. In Philadelphia, the branch was named "God's Black Sheep"; at the University of Wisconsin, "The Circle of the Godless"; and at the University of North Dakota, "The Legion of the Damned" with the head of the society being referred to as "His Satanic Majesty."

4. The biographical material comes from a carbon copy of Queen's letter to Gordon Stein, included in her files of correspondence. I do not believe it has been previously published.

5. This material comes, again, from Queen's files of correspondence.

6. Ironically, Queen did not attend high school any more than she had attended grade school.

7. Quoted from *QSM* 3, no. 1 (January 1927): 4.

8. Quoted in *QSM* 3, no. 2 (February 1927): 4.

9. Queen's editorial excoriates Senator Borah for inquiring whether Soviet Russia was persecuting rabbis. *QSM* 5, no. 2 (March–April 1930): 20.

10. The title of the pamphlet sounds anti-Semitic to modern ears. I can attest to the absolute absence of such prejudice within Queen in later life. Moreover, such "anti-Semitic" comments were not uncommon in early twentieth-century writing and do not indicate a deep hostility as they would in present works. The situation is akin to the one Queen describes regarding the word "nigger" in her essay on Mark Twain, printed in this book.

11. Perhaps the leaflets bore the same cartoon as a poster issued by the Devil's Angels: the shoulders of the working class are stooped under the weight of a cross of gold, as the clawed hand of a giant forces them on in their task. The caption on the poster read: "It is not the cross of Christ which you are asked to carry, but the golden cross of wealth in which divinity has no part."

12. Some sources date this movie as 1928. It is one of the DeMille films which has been restored and is available for study at the UCLA Film and Television Archive. An extensive DeMille collection is kept at Brigham Young University.

13. As quoted in *QSM* 4, no. 1 (May–June 1929): 2.

14. *QSM* 4, number 2 (July–August 1929). As quoted from the inside cover which is unnumbered in this issue. The following page is number "1." The reference to Roser as "Comrade" is significant.

15. "Witchcraft" (September–October 1929); "Godly Criminals" (November–December 1929); "Apes and Men" (January–February 1930); "Atheism" (March–April 1930); "Bootlegging Religion" (July–August 1930); "Religion and Delinquency" (January–February 1931). Although I am working with what is almost assuredly the most complete run of *QSM* in existence, several issues are missing, including March–April and May–June of 1930.

16. In taking this stand, the author and Queen fell on one side of a debate within the socialist movement. Many socialists became disillusioned by the brutality and totalitarianism of the USSR—for example, see Emma Goldman's *My Disillusionment with Russia* (1923). Others, apparently including Queen, excused the dictatorial regime.

17. As quoted from *QSM* 6, number 2 (March–April 1931): 11. I assume this notice was written by Grace.

18. On page 2, *QSM* acknowledged that the essay is a reprint and that the pamphlet had been unavailable for several years, thus leading me to conclude Queen never raised the necessary $150 mentioned previously. *QSM* further stated, "The lecture was originally delivered by Queen Silver in Los Angeles five years ago under the auspices of the Proletarian Party. It was addressed especially to those radicals who believe that 'the religious issue will take care of itself.'"

6

The Depression:
Economic and Personal
(1931–1934)

Q UEEN SILVER'S MAGAZINE
was as much a casualty
of the American econ-
omy as it was of the car accident
that injured Queen. On October
29, 1929, a panic selling of stocks
occurred on Wall Street, causing
the market to plunge. Although the
Great Depression did not immediately sweep the United States, by
the early 1930s the economy had
been devastated.[1] In four years,
from 1929 to 1933, approximately
eleven thousand banks failed—
almost one-half of the banks in
America. General production fell
by more than half. The disposable

income of the average American declined by approximately 28 percent. Unemployment rose from 1.6 million to 13 million people. By 1932—the worst year of the Great Depression—approximately one-quarter of able-bodied workers were unemployed in a time when unemployment insurance did not exist.[2] In 1932, Democrat Franklin Delano Roosevelt was elected president, largely because of his promise to control unemployment.

The Depression was particularly difficult for women to endure, because society did not believe they needed a job as badly as men who were, after all, the "heads of the family." This led to widespread discrimination against women in the workplace. For example, most American cities banned married women from teaching positions on the assumption that their husbands were the breadwinners.

In a later article, Grace argued,

> It is curious that married men are not expected to retire and live on their wives...but married women are expected to do just that. It is also curious that a married man is supposed to require a better-paid job than a single one, for his expenses are greater, whereas a married woman's expenses are—very erroneously—supposed to be less than those of a single woman worker. During periods in which work is scarce...married women are deprived of work and income when their husbands are less than ever able to support them, with the result that married men leave home and their families are thrown on some form of charity.[3]

Extra work in the movies had dried up. And even if it had not become dangerous to lecture on atheism or socialism in the Plaza, the working-class audiences didn't have money to put in a collection hat. They were more likely to be found huddled in the shantytowns called "Hoovervilles" as a slap at President Herbert Hoover. Neither Queen nor Grace had marketable skills. Indeed, before working in the San Francisco print shop in 1928, Queen had been employed only in silent movies or as a girl wonder. In short, they found it difficult to earn enough money to prevent starvation and eviction.

Grace later wrote,

> My husband and I lost our ranch, spent all our savings in the first two years of the Depression. Even with strict economy we once reached the point where there was nothing in the house to eat; no money and

no prospect of any; and I was down with a vicious case of asthma. We talked it over and he applied for relief.[4]

The family's poverty was exacerbated by a string of misfortunes. Queen's accident had involved breaking her collarbone in two places, an injury that required the slow healing of bones. And Grace's health was deteriorating. Racked by chronic asthma, she was forced to give up lecturing altogether and to forego the meager money it brought. For this and other "lung trouble," she blamed Roser. In a letter to Queen, she raged, "I told him I was not speaking because I had too much asthma and lung trouble, thanks to leaky roofs, hunger, and exposure in the last three years...."[5]

Roser became dangerously ill, and the strain of nursing him fell squarely upon Grace's shoulders. The bills went to Queen. In a letter to her daughter written years later, Grace expressed a deep abiding bitterness toward her husband from whom she had separated by then.

> We saved his life three years ago when we took him out of the hospital. They [Roser's family] never even offered to help you pay the hospital bill, or Dr. bill, and if I had let him stay in the hospital and used the money to put roofing paper on the kitchen I'd not be having asthma so bad that I almost strangle for two or three hours every night. I have to fight for my breath sometimes, like a fish out of water. And if it had not been necessary for me to have my feet wet for four months three winters ago—never having time to get them dry and the house wet from end to end because the roof leaked, I'd not have the asthma nor this cough.
>
> And if I'd left him to the tender mercies of the county hospital... and I'd still have my home.... They say people are grateful if you save their lives but he never was half human even after I saved his. Next time he gets that way, someone else can save him if they want to.[6]

Queen paid the bills by securing occasional work, mostly as a clerk or typist. Making enough money to stay alive became a full-time pursuit, with any spare energy going into her involvement with the Los Angeles branch of the IWW. In a later speech entitled "The Many Sides of Mark Twain," Queen commented,

> I suppose about a generation ago, he [Twain] would have fitted into that group of young people who said they were out trying to find themselves. In my generation, we were out trying to find a job and we didn't have time to look for ourselves.[7]

Queen was willing to consider any form of employment, even working cleaning other people's houses. Upon learning that she might become a domestic servant, Roser—in the midst of divorcing Grace—urged Queen to come to his hometown to which he had returned, "For god's sake, don't get a job at housework. It is bad enough to do shorthand work. If you get 'stuck,' come to Wellington [Kansas] and I will take care of you."[8]

Roser had received an inheritance that allowed him to make such an offer. He had trained Queen to be a girl wonder; he had taught her Latin and Greek; he had sponsored lectures which made front-page headlines in Los Angeles newspapers.[9] Now he seemed genuinely distressed that the stepdaughter at whom scientists had marveled might be reduced to scrubbing the floors of strangers.

Fortunately, Queen knew how to type and was able to survive without becoming a scrubwoman. By 1928, the financial embarrassment facing both Queen and Grace had become chronic. Displaying an inborn New England practicality, Queen had started to study shorthand on her own, eventually attending evening classes to improve her Gregg shorthand. During the height of the Depression, her typing and shorthand may have saved her life and that of Grace as well. Queen secured brief periods of employment with the Department of Motor Vehicles (DMV), working as a junior file clerk.[10]

Seasonal employment with the DMV was Queen's only reliable source of income but, to secure it and other work, she had to live at boardinghouses in Los Angeles proper. The accommodations were not ideal, as Grace's letters to Queen indicate. In one of them, she counseled her daughter on how to get rid of bedbugs.

Apparently, Queen's efforts at insect control failed, as Grace lamented in one of her next letters.

> I'm afraid you can't get rid of the bed bugs in that house, no matter what you do. Fumigation by an expert is about the only way. They will come in from other apts. Thorough saturation of *all* cracks in floor, wall, molding, bed, stairs, etc., with wood alcohol will do it, but it has to be thorough and must be done twice about five days apart as the first treatment does not kill eggs.[11]

The coming years would be hard ones.

Grace v. Roser, with Queen in the Middle

Meanwhile, Grace's marriage had unraveled. Not one to be placed at the mercy of a man, Grace had assured that all jointly held property was divided in advance of the breakup. In a bill of sale dated September 19, 1933, Roser transferred a Jersey cow named "Bossie" and a flock of Toulouse geese over to Grace in "consideration of the sum of Ten dollars." In a separate document, he also transferred title of "the north half of Lot 114, Tract Number 874, as per Map recorded in the office of the County Recorder of the said County of Los Angeles."[12] Roser maintained possession of the south half of the Lot. The document further provided that "...said Henry H. Roser shall not hereafter become liable for the support of the said Grace V. Roser, or for any bills that may be contracted by her, and...shall not be liable for any alimony, counsel fees, or court costs in any action that may be instituted by the said Grace V. Roser." Similar language was inserted, obviously at the last moment, to indemnify Grace against any claims made by Roser. Queen witnessed the document.

In September 1933, Grace still signed her name "Roser." By May 1934, however, she dropped his name from her signature. In early 1934, they were still sufficiently friendly for Roser to come to her aid concerning her late father's estate. Grace had just learned of his death, which had occurred some years prior. Although Samuel Silver had left most of his property to the Reorganized Church of the Latter Day Saints (the Mormons), his will contained the provision, "My daughter, Grace V. Silver Henry [*sic*], is to be supplied with fifty dollars each year during her natural life."[13] The proceeds of the estate had already been expended by the Church, and an alternative settlement was suggested. Her father had owned a piece of land in Florida, which once had been appraised at $1,500.

In a letter dated March 6, 1934, to the presiding bishopric of the Reorganized Church of the Latter Day Saints, Grace described the property, "The twelve acres include one-third the area of what they call Silver Lake—so the land is half water anyway. The lake for half the year is little better than a swamp good to raise snakes if you like snakes. The orange grove was frozen to the roots in the big freeze of 1898, and the house had been carted away for firewood before my father bought the place. I was present when he bought it. We were living in Vermont at the time. I remember it very well. He paid $100 cash and gave a thirty-dollar cow for the whole thing." Grace stated her willingness to receive the land and $300 plus interest in lieu of an annual payment, undoubtedly because she did not believe such payments would be forthcoming.

The Church plodded toward a resolution, as though slogging through mud, causing Grace to use a phrase that Queen repeated to me several times: "slow as Mormons." But matters did progress, albeit without Roser by this time.

By the summer of 1934, their relationship had dissolved in such an ugly manner that Grace felt it necessary to leave Los Angeles, traveling under an assumed name so that Roser could not track her. For extra protection, she pretended to be visiting back East. In fact, she traveled north and did not stop until Alaska. The journey was a risky one as the Pacific Northwest was experiencing massive labor unrest, which would become violent and hinder travel. As she would later write to Queen, "I never would have left Calif. if it hadn't been for wanting to get as far away as possible from R. for fear some of us would get killed."[14]

In an article written four years later, Grace rendered a sense of how deep the marital bitterness ran:

There was a week when I was intensely jealous, bitter, justifiably angry. I wasn't "seeing" red, but my thoughts were black enough. The more I thought the more angry I became. If thoughts had the power to kill anyone there would have been a death all right! As I walked up and down the floor I said to myself, finally: "If I don't snap out of this, there'll be a funeral for so-and-so and I'll get as much time for killing him as if I'd killed a real man!"

I went out to the garage and got out the pickaxe.... On the next lot to our house—vacant, with an absentee owner—were three neglected, uncultivated, unwatered trees; we had no garden of our own then. The ground was baked as hard as a pavement; the trees were shriveling in the dry August heat. Instead of taking that pick and killing the man I wanted to kill...I used the pick to dig up and turn over that hard soil. Now, I weigh just a hundred pounds, when I'm fat; but I swung that pick high over my head, down and up, up and down, all through one long hot day. Black thoughts kept racing through my head—every bit of injustice I'd endured from that person—and there was a lot!—was rehashed, silently. I thought of all the things I'd like to do to him if I had him on a desert island; I said—aloud, for there was no one to overhear—all I wanted, yet did not dare, to say to him.

Relentlessly, as though *he* were the ground, I swung that pick at him, and it, the two being unified in my mind.

By night I was tired enough to sleep, sore all over—but still plenty mad. The next day was a repetition of the first, except that I borrowed a heavy hoe and started chopping, cutting, all the weeds in sight; occasionally I even forgot to wish I could cut down my enemy as easily. By the third day it was pretty well out of my system. The ground was pulverized, my anger had gone; never did I forget or forgive, for the injury was too great, too often repeated; but I achieved a state of mind best described by the man who said that his enemy "wasn't worth the powder it would take to blow him to hell!" My enemy was not only "not worth killing"; I realized that "life" is a worse punishment than "death"; I'd let him live till he wished he was dead![15]

The specific reason for the violence of the split was never explicitly stated but Roser claimed to have a list of twenty-three men he could name as corespondents in the divorce. Moreover, when Grace went northward, she was accompanied by a man named Mark Kellar. In Alaska, they lived together, sometimes as man and wife, sometimes pretending to be brother and sister. A fellow member of the IWW, Kellar must have been a member of Roser's social circle, and the estranged husband made many pointed inquiries to discover the other man's whereabouts. Whether or not Grace's fear of being pursued by an enraged husband was justified will never be known. Her elaborate plans of "faking" a trip to New England, of traveling incognito and swearing Queen to secrecy, of coaching friends on how to handle inquiries from Roser—all these precautions, and more, might have been warranted.[16]

At the same moment Grace fled to Alaska, however, Roser returned to Kansas to claim a sizable inheritance that made him a man of wealth and of automatic importance in his small hometown. Perhaps his happily changed circumstances kept Roser from pursuing Grace. Perhaps he was just biding his time, as she insisted.

The only reality check on Grace's assessment of Roser is the correspondence that survives between Queen and her former stepfather. Roser was obviously fond of Queen, whom he had helped to raise. But her allegiance was unquestionably with her mother. Grace exhorted Queen to act as a supposedly neutral party. Of course, the interests expressed by Queen always coincided with Grace's own. She advised her daughter to take anything and everything Roser offered her.

On May 14, 1934, Roser wrote to Queen, casually asking when Grace would be traveling back East. A week later, he sent Queen a letter for Grace with the diplomatic request that she forward it to her. Queen and Roser remained cordial on the surface, with Roser apparently trying to protect Queen from "being in the middle" of the breakup, but to no avail. With her mother's power of attorney Queen was left to handle all the paperwork involved with the Church settlement and the ultimate sale of Lot 114. In between discussing legal matters with Queen, Roser sent her small sums of money and items she needed such as a fountain pen, a watch, and some silverware, as well as offering to pay for the repair of her typewriter. He even listed Queen as a beneficiary in his will.

On Queen's part, the letters were chatty, though she politely declined his offer to provide her with a job in Kansas because "I am so tied up with organization [IWW] work here...." Most of her correspondence with him revolved around the IWW and other organizations or causes in which they shared a common interest.

For example, Queen wrote,

> I spoke last night at the Proletarian Party forum on the subject of the New Deal. Everyone said it was a good talk and I think myself that it was fairly good, all things considered. On the first of July I am talking at the IWW Forum (our hall) on the subject of "Technocracy vs. Industrial Democracy." As it is less than two weeks away I shall be pretty busy till after it is over. I have not intended to take on so much at any one time, but on account of another speaker being called out of town and no other speaker available I had to accept as substitute.[17]

In turn, Roser wrote of a stint of street speaking he had done in Wellington, addressing the subject of Sunday laws.

> A Pentecostal preacher...preaches for about twenty minutes on this corner every Saturday evening. I took a big drawer from my store and plumped it on the sidewalk and started in as soon as the preacher got to inviting the people to come to Jesus and also to his church. (He did not claim that Jesus was at his church.) He was quite startled and remained about half an hour and then could stand it no longer. I made great preparations with notes, because I have not spoken from the box for a long time, but when I got up, I was "inspired" and forgot all about my notes in the pocket. The crowd sure enjoyed it and kept getting larger and larger. When I had spoken three-quarters of an hour, I got down, but the people insisted I go on, so I got an encore and talked for half an hour more.[18]

Roser rarely mentioned Grace, except obliquely. For example, in a letter dated August 4, 1934, he made brief reference to the deed to the Florida land, then went on at length about politics. He was especially interested in the labor unrest still sweeping the Pacific Northwest.

> I am keeping posted on the strikes by reading the Wichita papers and also the *L.A. Daily News.* They all publish about the same Press dispatches. It was a great opportunity I think, and probably the rank and file did the best they could under the circumstances. The big-shot scabs like Green and Woll did all they could against the interests of the workers. They are labor Enemy #1 and #2. The Communist Party has been terribly persecuted and may have to go underground again. Well, recovered before and I guess they will again. My impression is that the Utopian Society is a racket.[19] They will collect large sums of money and the clique in power will mainly profit by it. The secrecy feature will be favorable to graft and looting the organization. No radical should join it.

Ironically, Grace wrote to Queen of the Utopians at about the same time and with almost the same perspective,

> This evening's paper carries the news of the formation of a "White Guard" for the purpose of combating communism in all its forms. It is to be composed of three sections, one of which will be uniformed. We also have, as you may have heard, a new organization here called the "Utopians." Some of the radicals are going in for it but I can't see it. You have to join them to the extent of letting them have your name and address before you can attend any meeting and even those who admit that they are members also admit that they do not know what the ultimate purpose of the organization is, beyond the fact that it promises various improvements in the social order. One deputy sheriff has already gone through most of its degrees. The organization is secret and they admit anyone of any class, except that most accounts say they must be American citizens. Accounts in various papers agree in the statement that all members take an oath to uphold the Constitution and defend democracy against any which attempt to overthrow it.[20]

Clearly, Queen acted as middle ground for Grace and Roser. Meanwhile, Grace's letters brimmed over with what might well have been entirely justified anger toward her estranged husband. For example, Grace wrote, "I read of 108 and 110 [degrees Fahrenheit] in Kansas City. Hope Roser likes the climate of Kansas! I suppose having a nice house, care, 'civic honors,' etc. has turned his head."[21] Her next letter speculates about how long Roser will remain in Kansas, perhaps allowing her to return to Los Angeles in safety. "My guess is he will be there some time yet as I think he's getting a swelled sense of his own importance. Big frog in little puddles stuff. I think his main idea in wanting my signature is to find out where I am."[22]

Soon Roser would cease to be Grace's main worry.

The General Strike of 1934

Grace had departed Los Angeles for Alaska via Seattle on May 9, 1934—the same day the Longshoreman's Union began a controversial labor strike in San Francisco. The strike quickly spread to other unions along the West Coast, and ultimately involved more than 100,000 workers. Lasting almost three months, the strike would paralyze shipping to and from Alaska.

Grace's main stop on her flight northward had been Seattle. Seattle was renowned as a radical labor town largely as the result of the General Strike of 1919, which had virtually shut down the city. In 1933, one of President Roosevelt's New Deal programs, the National Recovery Act, had provided that "employees shall have the right to organize and bargain collectively through representatives of their own choosing." A flood of labor-reform activity ensued, and the Pacific Coast became a flash point for labor agitation. At first, only 1,500 Seattle dockworkers joined a coastwide walkout in sympathy with the San Francisco longshoremen. Soon, more followed. Shipping was halted.

In the beginning, the strike caused only minor disruption in Grace's plans. On May 23, 1934, she wrote to Queen from the Governor Hotel, in Portland, Oregon, the city in which she had stopped decades before to give birth to a daughter, "Well, I'm back where I was 23½ years ago. Last time I went south with you when I left. This time I go north without you. It's a queer world." Grace's letter was filled with news about the strike and rumors of it growing more intense. On May 25, she wrote, "Latest report in papers says that all Alaska boats start loading Sat. by agreement with unions on direct orders from FDR. But we went to S.S. [steam ship] office and they claimed they did not know anything about it."

While she awaited passage to Alaska, Grace returned to street lec-

turing. As a young woman, she had gone from Boston Common and followed the socialist lecture trail to Portland and Seattle, perhaps standing
on the same street corners then as she did now. In a separate letter to
Queen, also dated May 25, Grace wrote, "Had a big meeting on Washington St. Climate here is easier on my voice and since I could speak at
night I was not too hot. Got 1.05 (5 cents collection, balance literature)!
Much enthusiasm. I spoke over 1½ hours in spite of some coughing. So
that is that. I have one cent more than the two of us [Grace and Mark
Kellar] spent for meals Wed. night, Thursday, and stamps. In other
words, I have one cent more than when I arrived...."

Later that same night, Grace held a meeting that lasted two hours
and drew a large crowd, including one drunk that Mark had to forcibly
evict twice. For two hours work, Grace made ninety-five cents, all from
the sale of literature that was now gone. "I wish I had brought more,"
Grace concluded.

Two days later and still in Seattle, Grace continued her report,

> I have had three meetings so far—$1.05, .90, and .70. The last was Sat.
> night collection. So you see things are bad here financially. Strike
> makes it worse. The town is "wide open" for gambling, etc. We had
> one fight first meeting and one man had to be knocked out twice
> second meeting. Last night we had no trouble.
>
> All quiet on waterfront. Not the least disorder. No vessels loading
> or unloading except a paper ship containing newspaper stock. This
> the strikers graciously unloaded. I watched them do it. Meals have
> gone up. We now have to pay .15 for dinner.[23]

Grace assured Queen, "You would make a big hit here. I can make
eats here, but probably not room rent too."[24]

On May 29, various strike committees along the Pacific Northwest
voted on a peace plan. Seattle was said to be favoring an end to the
strike, while Portland and San Francisco opposed it. Meanwhile, Grace
commented that her "financial value" was declining. On one night, her
lecturing drew twenty-five cents; on another, she made nothing at all,
although the crowd was large and receptive. Grace sent for twenty-five
copies each of the *Godliness of Ignorance* and *Science versus Superstition*
pamphlets.

She considered going elsewhere to lecture to make a living while
waiting for the strike to let up. "I am told that speaking is free in Port-

land and that meetings are good," she informed Queen. "Fourth and Alder Sts. is the corner. The bus gets in at 11th and Alder. Also that meetings are allowed wherever streetcars do not intersect."[25]

Grace considered a stint of street speaking in Seattle's twin city, Tacoma, as well.

> Also in Tacoma on a vacant lot at 15th and Commerce Sts. One puts up a bulletin board in the morning and the crowd gathers at night. Also at Portland there are said to be good meetings in a park all day Sunday, like the Plaza. We have met lots of people from L.A. here— lots too many. It is unfortunate I have to speak here. It makes me so well known. And lots of people know K. from years ago. I hope R. stays in Kansas till I get out of here.[26]

Grace was still in Seattle on June 2 though she had been forced to move to cheaper accommodations. More and more, her letters dwelt upon financial and health problems: the asthma had returned. She began to worry about whether the strike would make it impossible to sail to Alaska. On June 3, she wrote to Queen:

> Those of the strikers I know seem to think it may last two weeks longer; but maybe not. The communists want to keep it going indefi- nitely but some of the others are getting tired of it. So far the net result seems to be that Los Angeles has grabbed all the shipping— doing more business than ever, they claim. Ocean-going ships now go to L.A. and pass up Seattle altogether. And L.A. may keep the new trade, for while their harbor is not so good it is certainly more modern and better equipped with dock facilities, etc....
>
> There is a rumor now that if the strike is not settled, the Alaska railroad will charter the Alaska ships and run them under Union con- ditions. Nome is without meat (except for a million reindeer more or less!) and other towns are out of meat and have to live on salmon! Ain't it awful? They have more to eat than we ever do, but they think they are starving. A man here says ham and eggs are .60 up in Alaska, but I remarked that we never eat ham and eggs here either so why eat them up there?

Instead of shopping for ham and eggs, Grace bought a rifle with which she and Kellar could shoot small game they could eat for free. On June 6 and still in Seattle, Grace spoke for over two hours and made forty cents. On the seventh, she made twenty-five cents. She told Queen that there had been a very drunk Christian woman in the audience who took exception to Grace's observation that "religion is rotten."

Finally, on June 9, Grace and Mark were ready to ship out to Alaska. The last letter from Seattle filled Queen in on the labor situation.

Seems to be an awful lot of ex-IWWs in the ILA [International Longshoreman's Association] strike here. Seattle has a terrible long waterfront too, as well as San Pedro. But except for the first few days no effort has been made to really load ships here. The police stood by and let the strikers take scabs away from the Alaska line wharf and it is said that when some of the scabs did not like walking down the street between a doubleline of strikers and having their pictures taken, some of them tried to break through the strikers' lines and get away but the police forced the scabs to get back in the lineup! The new mayor may do—or try to do—something drastic—if it is not settled soon. Seattle loses so much by the Alaska tie-up, and Alaska loses a terrible lot.[27]

The long-awaited passage to Alaska would turn out to be more of a curse than a blessing.

Notes

1. For example, the ecological disaster known as the Dust Bowl combined with the Depression to destroy the economy of the American plains.

2. Queen and I differed radically on our interpretation of the Great Depression. She took the more standard approach of blaming the Federal Reserve, laissez-faire capitalism, and the "do nothing" policy of President Herbert Hoover. I take a contrasting libertarian position. Out of deference to her, however, I will refrain from including my perspective beyond this footnote.

3. This article has no notation as to date or placement in a publication.

4. From Grace's papers, the manuscript of an article "So You Can't Take It!" with the notation, "Published *Psychology*, Feb. 1950, pp. 3–4."

5. Letter from Grace to Queen dated August 27, 1934, from Ketchikan, Alaska.

6. Letter from Grace to Queen dated August 21, 1934, from Ketchikan.

7. The lecture is reprinted in this book at pages 259–72.

8. In a letter to Queen from Roser dated July 23, 1934, from Wellington, Kansas.

9. After all, many of Queen's early lectures had been advertised in the following manner: "Henry H. Roser presents: Queen Silver."

10. Her first work with the DMV began on January 12, 1931, and lasted a

little over a month. She was later rehired at a lower salary and laid off when-ever the increased work flow caused by annual license renewals eased. During 1931–1936, Queen was laid off six times. Her first stint of employment at the DMV lasted a little over a month with close to a year of unemployment before she was rehired at a lower salary. Her reemployment coincided with the annual license-renewal period, and the lengths of employment varied from five weeks to two and a half months.

11. In a letter from Grace to Queen dated July 30, 1934, from Ketchikan.

12. Although the couple had "lost" the property, as Grace indicated, the cause had been back taxes, which Queen paid off.

13. The will of Samuel N. Silver, dated September 27, 1927, refers to "Grace V. Silver Henry" perhaps because the alienated father incorrectly remembered the name of her husband, Henry Roser. However, under a photo meant to announce Grace's candidacy (1918) for the Socialist Party for repre-sentative in the Ninth Congressional District, her name is listed as Grace Silver Henry. It would be in character for Grace to protect herself and Queen by using an alias. If she had done so, it might also explain why the estate seemed unable to contact her regarding the inheritance.

As noted elsewhere, Grace apparently used the last name "Henry" from time to time. This lends some credibility to the claim that it was not possible to locate her to fulfill her father's bequest.

In a letter dated March 6, 1934, to the Presiding Bishopric of the Reorga-nized Church of the Latter Day Saints, however, Grace contests their claim. "Neither Mr. Fisher nor his attorney could have ever made any adequate effort to locate me. Publication of notice in any Los Angeles newspaper, or a request to the postmaster of Inglewood, Los Angeles, or Hawthorne (all of which former addresses were known to my relative in Mass.), or a letter to either the chamber of commerce or city police chief of any of the three cities would have brought results. . . ."

14. Letter from Grace to Queen dated July 6, 1934, from Ketchikan.

15. As quoted from the manuscript of an article written by Grace entitled "Working Off a Temper." It bears the notation, "Published *Everybody's Digest,* Feb. 1939."

16. In a letter to Queen dated June 9, 1934, from Seattle, Grace com-mented on how she and Kellar managed to get into the same stateroom. "I told a woman agent he was my brother. . ." (p. 10). In a letter dated June 19, 1934, from Ketchikan, Alaska, Grace advised Queen to buy tickets for *Mr. and Mrs. Mark Kellar.*

In other letters, she carefully instructed Queen on how to address letters so that no one would suspect she was a married woman traveling with a man other than her husband.

17. Letter from Queen to Roser dated June 21, 1934, from Los Angeles, California.

18. Letter from Roser to Queen, dated July 23, 1934, Wellington, Kansas.

19. The Utopian Society became popular with some radicals who felt disenfranchised from the socialist movement. Other radicals were deeply suspicious because the organization required oaths of secrecy to join. Grace independently wrote to Queen about the Utopian Society, "The Utopians seem to have grabbed off my idea of a revolutionary organization of Americans, in a way. Only I would have it very revolutionary, and limit it to native-born Americans. Such a group has a future, if they could keep the reformers out, and the preachers. It is probably a side show for Sinclair to help put him over for Gov. in case he fails to get the Dem. nomination." Letter circa July 13–19, 1934.

Roser later wrote, "Think the Utopians are petering out. It is just another racket. The clique in control will milk the cow dry.... The *Western Worker*, whose plant was destroyed by hoodlums in S.F., has resumed publication. Am reading about the strikes in the *W.W.*, *L.A. Daily News*, and the Wichita papers." Letter dated August 4, 1934.

20. Letter from Grace to Queen dated June 19, 1934, from Ketchikan.

21. Letter from Grace to Queen dated July 21, 1934, from Ketchikan.

22. Letter from Grace to Queen dated July 23, 1934, from Ketchikan.

23. Letter from Grace to Queen dated May 27, 1934, from Seattle, Washington.

24. Ibid.

25. Letter from Grace to Queen dated May 30, 1934, from Seattle.

26. Ibid.

27. Letter from Grace to Queen dated June 9, 1934, from Seattle.

7

Grace: Stranded in Alaska
(1934–1935)

*A*LMOST AS SOON as Grace and Mark Kellar set foot off the boat in Ketchikan, Alaska, Grace began to lament the trip as a disastrous error in judgment. Lodgings were difficult to secure and far more expensive than anticipated. Food cost at least twice as much as it did in Los Angeles, including the cans of salmon that were packed in Ketchikan itself. Fresh vegetables were exorbitant. For example, two bunches of carrots cost fifteen cents, opposed to one cent a bunch in L.A. And Grace—almost immediately plagued by a body-shaking cough, fever, and asthma—felt too sick to gather the salmon berries or other wild-growing edibles to substitute for vegetables. But worst of all, the job at the cannery that Kellar had been promised and upon which they would have relied to pay expenses did not materialize because of shortages caused by the strike.

The longshoreman's strike that had started in San Francisco had spread like wildfire up the coast of the Pacific Northwest. A general strike now directly or indirectly paralyzed much of Alaska's shipping and industry, including the cannery at which Kellar had expected to work. Instead of hiring men, industries were laying them off. Prospects seemed particularly bleak for Kellar who was competing with men half his age for jobs involving hard labor.

Without a steady income, Grace and Kellar could not afford to let a room *and* eat at the same time. Camping outside was out of the question due to inclement weather. (One of the first things Grace noticed was that the wooden sidewalks had eaves extending over them to protect pedestrians from the constant rain.) It poured without cease for the first ten days. Grace and Kellar managed to get their room on credit but Grace wrote to Queen complaining about the cost of their lodgings. It was a better place than she normally would have rented, but nothing else had been available on such favorable terms. And they needed to eat. Everything hinged on whether Kellar could find work.

Usually, under such circumstances, Grace would set up a soapbox on a street corner, with literature spread out for sale. But the steady rain meant that an outdoor meeting would not draw crowds. Moreover, she wasn't certain if the authorities would tolerate her sort of meeting and message, especially with emotions running so high due to the strike. Meetings would have to be indoors. But Ketchikan was a new city, and it was seemingly without a strong radical community with which she could network. Even if Grace had been able to set up her own lecture schedule and rent a hall, a chronic cough made speaking difficult. Moreover, a radical lecture might lead to violence. Grace described the heated situation in Ketchikan: "Some small employer here said the strikers ought to be shot, and somebody burned his place next day. I think sentiment is generally with the strikers but people not involved wish something would happen soon to end it."[1]

As for literature, Grace had sold it all at the meetings in Seattle.[2] She requested that Queen and "Mrs. D." send various pamphlets, including a booklet of atheist poems that always sold well.[3] Grace did not have access to a typewriter on which she could write articles or short stories either. As for seeking out regular employment, "There is very little work for women—except there are Indians for common labor, or blonde Swedish types for clerks, waitresses, etc.... Have to be young, good-looking, and able to stand a lot!"

As she had done upon arriving in Los Angeles decades before, Grace went immediately to the public library. There she found sanctuary not only in the books but also in the warmth of the building. The library allowed her to keep in touch with the rest of the world through the periodicals and newspapers to which it subscribed. But it did not relieve her worries. There or in the rented room, Grace brooded about Roser and her lack of funds as she waited for the strike to end.

In one of her first of many letters to Queen, Grace wrote,

> If I had $50 now, I'm so terribly homesick I'd take the *North Wind* [a boat] down tomorrow if it would take me. I did not realize how far away I was going and I don't think I can stand being so far away from you permanently and I may not be able to make money enough to come and visit you, ever. In Seattle I felt close by. Like I could run down most any time, or you might come up sometime....
>
> I never knew I could be so deadly homesick as I am now. I have not even been able to eat since I left the boat yesterday noon and I've cried so much, in spite of all my efforts, I'm afraid K is scared though I tell him it will wear off, and not to worry about me.
>
> I'm not sorry I made the trip but unless K goes to work promptly I'm going back to Seattle as soon as I have the money to go with, for both of us. I can't leave him up here stranded because it was because I wanted to come that he is here.... The trip was beautiful, but it was a mistake and a waste of money and I'll have to waste some more getting back.
>
> I made so many mistakes and the strike has balled everything up. But I must come back as far as Seattle.[4]

The letter ended with a request for Queen to send money if at all possible. Such requests would become frequent.

Stranded in Ketchikan

At first it seemed that Kellar's cannery job might be delayed by only two weeks. Grace calculated they could manage to eat on "short rations" for that long if meals were carefully budgeted. But soon the trollers were on strike, which dried up the canneries' supply of fish. Only one cannery was fully functioning because it bought fish from nonunion trollers. But, with unemployment soaring, it paid only fifteen cents an hour for labor—the price of two bunches of carrots. Then came the rumor that what was left of the canneries might soon be experiencing walkouts themselves. Two weeks after arriving in Alaska, Grace recalculated the financial situation and informed Queen, "Plenty of fish, but no place to cook them—lots of wood so wet it won't burn no matter what you do with it and I can't yet eat them raw, though in another week I'll have to if you haven't sent money by that time."[5]

Fortunately, Kellar was able to find work in a quarry. He and Grace paid a bit against what was owing on the room, *and* continued to eat. What they ate and how much it cost became a continuing theme in Grace's letters home.

> This town has queer ways, to me. It is impossible to get a small cheap meal at any price; but on the other hand you get a big meal for what you do pay. For instance, the cheapest hotcakes and coffee is .25; but there are 5 or 6 big hotcakes and 2 or 3 cups of coffee with no extra charge. Dinner is always 40, 45, or 50 cents. Same thing varies from day to day. But . . . you get a big plate of meat, two or three vegetables, dessert, and all the coffee you want, and even a second plate of meat if you want it without charge. Something in the "all you can eat for 50 cents" order. I only go in once a day or once in two days and bring out a big sandwich or two for the next meal in my room. K. is working so hard he must eat anyhow. The cook, when he is alone, often gives K an extra meat or egg order. One can't eat cheap here, but if one can spend 1.10 or 1.25 a day they can eat "awful" good.[6]

As June began to approach July, Grace became hungry for information and waited for the newly arrived boats in order to question their passengers and crew. For example, a radical from Seattle who worked one of the steamships told her that meetings were still being held on "her" corner, but seventy-five communists had been arrested at their headquarters. She haunted the public library to absorb every scrap of information she could find on the strike or anything related to it. Still hoping to get back to Seattle, she tried to piece together a picture of what was happening in the city. Among the many businesses and services paralyzed there were the streetcars, which provided transportation for the audiences who came to street meetings. This circumstance, coupled with the mayor's determination to break up the strike by force if necessary, might ruin Seattle for Grace's brand of fund-raising. "If I ever get back," Grace said, "I have to stay in Portland instead."[7]

Her suspicions about Seattle were borne out. A week later, Grace informed Queen, "I see the police teargassed the crowd on the corner in Seattle where I used to speak. They said it was a 'mistake.' I don't know if meetings are still allowed there or not."[8]

Meanwhile, Grace was so homesick and anxious about money she dreamed that Queen visited her bedside and took her to the post office where a money order was waiting. Perhaps if there had been other radicals in Ketchikan with whom she could network, Grace would not have been so lonely. But the only "fellow-traveler" she mentioned in letters was a Dr. Carlson, "which is not his real name," who was an "ex–Natl Organizer of S.L.P. [Socialist Labor Party]." Carlson assured her that Ketchikan was "a bad town" for radicals, where everyone was "scared to death of everyone else." The few radicals who existed were apparently out on boats for the fishing season.[9]

Grace and Ketchikan seemed to be absolutely incompatible. Everything about Ketchikan made her uncomfortable, including the fact that it was an "all-night town" in which there were only three hours of darkness each day. Stores remained open at night and closed in the morning. One store sported a sign "Closed today: open 10 P.M." Grace wrote,

> Whenever it stops raining and the sun comes out up here, it turns cold. "Cold light" is nothing new—they always have it here. There is no warmth in the sunlight. I have had my coat off about an *hour* since I came. I wear my heavy underwear and your khaki dress too.[10]

A thread of thought started to weave through the letters back home: perhaps she should try to walk the distance, or buy a boat and row to Seattle. If she didn't have to go through Canada, Grace declared, "I'd have started to walk back long ago."[11] Walking home was a possibility she kept turning over and over in her mind. "If Canada did not have immigration laws, etc., etc., I'd try to go from here to Prince Rupert and get over on the railway somehow till I got to Vancouver."[12]

By July 9, four weeks after their arrival, Grace and Kellar moved to a cheaper room. Two days later, Kellar got laid off from the quarry. Grace gave Queen an account of their financial situation: "I still have—counting what's coming to him in wages—about $20, of which I owe 2.50 rent here up till next Tuesday, the 13th. He may get other work, or may not."[13] Queen sent what she could, which was very little. Grace's best hope for money lay either in the settlement pending with the Mormons or in Roser buying her half of the previously divided lot. Neither party seemed in a hurry to send a check.

The only other possibility of escape was if the strike abruptly ended, but there was little likelihood of that happening. It was more likely to spread. Grace counseled Queen to stock up on enough food staples—beans, rice, cornmeal, sugar, and flour—to last a month because she believed longshoremen in Los Angeles might go on strike and cause food shortages.

On July 20, she wrote, "The local paper here says strikers in S.F. are split and some have voted to arbitrate and go back to work.... Trollers are back on strike again after a temporary peace, and refuse to catch fish till the price goes up."

About two weeks later she continued,

> The cannery workers all go on strike today or tomorrow. There is much bad feeling here because Filipinos are brought in great numbers to do cannery work, while whites and natives starve, and people who have homes here are unemployed. There is no gov't relief agency of any sort here now. There was one last winter.... I cough so much, along with the asthma, that I get little sleep ... about one night in each week I can sleep.[14]

Grace could not wait for a resolution to the labor dispute. She wrote to Queen, "K. is pretty scared—says I'll croak before R. gets around to pay."[15] Frantic with worry, but trying to appear calm, Queen had written to Roser on July 19, asking him to speed up matters. Through Queen Grace forwarded letters to Roser also urging him to settle with her.

August came. Although the longshoreman's strike was officially settled after over eighty days of work stoppage, the canneries were still closed. Soon the legal fishing season would be over. Unemployed workers were streaming southward in search of work. But Kellar and Grace could not afford the $50 that would secure them both passage. As Queen continued to mediate between Roser and her mother, Grace complained bitterly,

> I think myself he is delaying now on purpose in hopes of inconveniencing me so much that I'll go broke and go back to him. I think that is back of his offering you a job in Kansas. He thinks if you go there I'd be there at least part of the time.... I have to get out of here, even if I risk going to jail to do it. But I'll do nothing desperate as long as there is any hope or anything comes up. I hate jail but I'd just as soon be there as where I am.[16]

Winter was coming, and the strike seemed on the verge of breaking out anew. Grace explained,

> Also, another disquieting factor is this: (1) that the gov't arbitration board ruling in the longshore strike is being purposely delayed because (2) it's going to be against the longshoremen ... (3) that as it is made public (about middle of Sept. is the expected time) there is to be a "bigger and better" strike all over [the] Pacific coast with general reorganization of unions and split with AFofL [American Federation of Labor] (4) that when this comes (within 3 weeks at most, it is expected) even the longshoremen in this town will organize (they are most ready for it now) and also be on strike.[17]

In desperation, Grace penned a letter addressed to Queen but meant to be forwarded to Roser. She warned Queen, "There are things in that letter you would not say to him but he can't blame you for what I say, and if he tries to answer it, tell him I told you not to send on any letters from him."[18] The letter focused on how badly Queen, who would be out of work until December, needed the money which was owed to her from proceeds from the property sale.[19] Grace continued with far less tact than she would later congratulate herself on showing. She informed Queen, "If it was not for wanting to give you the money and having some to start up another atheist magazine I wouldn't sell it to him at all, after all this delay and the inconvenience he has put us both to."

And then she offered Roser a powerful incentive. "You can tell him I'll cooperate about his serving divorce papers if he buys the place first and pays for it. I'll come to L.A. and let them be served on me there, but nowhere else. I don't want people to know I was married."[20]

On August 27, an Agreement for Sale of Real Estate between Grace and Henry H. Roser was executed.[21] Queen signed the document as Grace's "Attorney in Fact."

On September 1, 1934, Grace and Kellar sailed out of Ketchikan on board the Alaska Steamship freighter *Redondo*, on their way home to Los Angeles.

On July 23, 1935, the divorce between Roser (plaintiff) and Grace (defendant) became official. The court papers read, "The Court finds that the plaintiff should be granted an absolute decree of divorce from the defendant on the grounds of abandonment for more than one year...."[22]

A manuscript of a short story by Grace entitled "Old Man's Marriage" captured a sense of Grace's attitude toward Roser and—perhaps—sketched an accurate portrait of him:

> The Old Man was truly old. None of us knew his age, but he had two daughters, and they were both on the late side of fifty. In the good old days of the silent films, before someone invented the talkies and turned the motion-picture business upside down and inside out and stood the actors up in the breadline, he had been a movie extra. He had done old western types rather well and occasionally had done a choice "bit" with the cowgirls. Before he had been a movie extra he had been a broken-down lawyer, and before that he had been a school-teacher and a detective. He had successfully failed at everything, and had been two years on relief when his only known relative, whom he had not spoken to for forty years, died and left him half a million, including a bank and department store. As soon as the estate was settled, and he had his new wealth securely cinched, he applied for and got his fourth divorce.... His fourth wife was glad to be free, even without alimony.[23]

Notes

1. Letter from Grace to Queen dated June 19, 1934. Her return address is "General Delivery," which she asked Queen to use for reasons of anonymity. Although her sympathies were unquestionably with the strikers, Grace joined those who just wanted it all to end.

2. Letter from Grace to Queen dated June 3, 1934, from Seattle. She ran

out of literature after a Sunday meeting: "Sun. night performance is over—85 cents—all out of literature and collections have mostly not worth taking [*sic*]. Big crowd, not so crazy and noisy as Sat. night (Sat. nights are drunk nights—more than usual)." When new *QSM* literature arrived on June 8, she sold out again.

3. I am assuming "Mrs. D." is Mrs. Doughty, an IWW friend with whom Queen and Grace stayed on occasion.

4. From context, the date of the letter from Grace to Queen is probably June 14, 1934.

5. Letter from Grace to Queen dated June 28, 1934, from Ketchikan.

6. Letter from Grace to Queen dated July 3, 1934, from Ketchikan. Grace is writing to Queen so frequently that the letters now bear not merely a date but the time of day they were written. This one is clocked at "3 P.M."

7. Letter from Grace to Queen dated June 23, 1934, from Ketchikan.

8. Letter from Grace to Queen dated June 28, 1934, from Ketchikan.

9. Letter from Grace to Queen dated August 29, 1934, from Ketchikan. Using aliases was just one safeguard Grace employed. She also sealed her letters with thickened canned milk to make the glue more difficult for the authorities to open.

10. Letter from Grace to Queen dated July 19, 1934, from Ketchikan.

11. Letter from Grace to Queen dated July 3, 1934, from Ketchikan.

12. Letter from Grace to Queen dated July 13, 1934, from Ketchikan.

13. Letter from Grace to Queen dated July 11, 1934, from Ketchikan. Kellar did get other work occasionally, but the heavy labor caused his hip so much pain that he could barely walk sometimes. "His hip is worse again and I'm afraid a ligament is torn so that unless he has a long rest and some proper treatment, it will not be better" (letter dated August 31, 1934). Moreover, when Kellar did work, their food expense shot up because, as Grace put it, he got so hungry he needed to eat large meals. She subsisted on a sandwich a day and coffee.

14. Letter from Grace to Queen dated August 2, 1934, from Ketchikan.

15. Letter from Grace to Queen dated July 25, 1934, from Ketchikan.

16. Letter from Grace to Queen dated August 7, 1934. Grace seems to be misreading Roser on this latter point. In a letter to Queen of June 15, 1934, Roser offered her a job as a clerk and stenographer but advised, "I don't think you could stand it here. You would not know what to do with yourself nights and Sundays. There is radical sentiment in this country town of 700, but it is not organized, with exception of the unemployed who have a weak organization.

Elsewhere Grace refers to leaving Alaska as a matter of life and death. She tells Queen that she does not want to die in Ketchikan.

17. Letter from Grace to Queen dated August 31, 1934.

18. Letters from Grace to Roser and to Queen dated August 31, 1934, from Ketchikan.

19. In a letter dated July 31, Grace counseled Queen to make a few badly needed dollars by selling her magazine in the Plaza. "Can't you take your own magazines to Plaza and spread them out like I used to on Sunday and get 1 or

2 dollars for yourself? The Plaza has been without them long enough to be hungry by now."

20. Letter from Grace to Queen dated August 21, 1934. Elsewhere Grace speculates on whether Roser, who was fixing up his house in Kansas, was planning to remarry. If so, he would have wanted to settle the divorce promptly.

Since the letter was still among Queen's papers, I assume she chose not to forward it to Roser, but probably informed him of its relevant contents in a separate letter.

21. The date was filled in on the form as August 27, the notary public signed for Queen Silver as a witness on August 31, as it is dated on the outside of the form.

22. Grace raised Queen to accept divorce as a happy option. In a speech entitled "Women in Freethought," delivered October 29, 1987, Queen recalled a tale Grace had recounted to her. "My mother told me about the woman who got the first divorce in her hometown in Maine. She got her divorce when her oldest child was over twenty-one years old. She had wanted the divorce since the day after she was married. But, because she had no way of paying a lawyer, she remained on the farm and subject to a considerable amount of physical abuse, bearing six more children after the oldest one. When the oldest went away from home, the first money he earned he sent home to his mother so she could go to a lawyer. She got the divorce and the whole town was scandalized. 'How could they do such a thing! They had been married so long.' "

23. "Old Man's Marriage," p. 1. In this apparently unpublished short story by Grace, the parallels to Roser are striking. He was much older than Grace. After retiring from being a lawyer, he did work as an extra on westerns. Because he had been a teacher, he had the certificate necessary to tutor Queen. He had two daughters. He inherited a pharmacy and a jewelry store, after which he immediately divorced Grace, without alimony.

8

The Retreat from Radicalism
(1935–1972)

Q UEEN REMAINED AN active member of the Industrial Workers of the World during the 1930s, belonging first to Union No. 650 and then to No. 670. Queen told me often of how hungry she was during the Great Depression, but the small red booklets representing her IWW membership are filled with colorful stamps that showed month after month of paid dues and other financial contributions. The later booklets are stamped with the word "Administration," lending support to Grace's statement that Queen served as secretary to the Los Angeles branch. "General Convention Stamps" seem to indicate Queen's status as a delegate at various organizing events. Unfortunately, little beyond the membership-card booklets remain to document her activities. Even the identities of those who "vouched" for Queen are obscured in the booklet by being listed by initials or by numbers, such as "17-G6." There is one exception: the name C. Erwin (apparently 17-G6) crops up repeatedly.

Queen's social life revolved around the IWW to which she donated not only her money and energy, but also whatever goods she could spare, including chairs and a typewriter desk for the organization's hall. Alarmed by a growing backlash against radicalism, Grace urged Queen to take remaining copies of the *Queen Silver Magazine* from storage and to either burn them or store them in the hall for safekeeping. The extent of Queen's involvement with the IWW can be judged from one of Grace's letters,

> Mrs. D. said in her letter you were going to make some curtains for the hall [IWW], but did not have the money. . . . I suppose I ought to do something for the hall to help you folks out, while and when I can. If you don't get your curtains before that, and if you want to do so, you can take $10 . . . from my part of R.'s money when you get it and buy your curtains and donate them to the hall.[1]

As it happened, Queen's romantic life revolved around the IWW as well. While Grace made good her flight from Roser, Queen was undergoing a marital situation of her own. Grace's letters were all addressed either to Mrs. Claude Erwin or to Mrs. Queen Silver Erwin, with most of them going to a downtown Los Angeles address at 245 South Flower Street.[2]

Erwin was the same man whose name was listed in Queen's membership booklets for the IWW. Moreover, he was clearly a friend of Kellar. Although there are no existing letters from Kellar to Queen, there is a crudely printed one from Kellar to Erwin, dated June 9, 1934, from Seattle. Kellar greeted him as "Fellow Worker."[3] In a separate letter, Grace commented to Queen about another exchange between the two men, "K. sent Erwin a card with two bears on it."[4]

Whether or not a legal ceremony had taken place, Queen had obviously entered into a second marriage of sorts with a "fellow worker." Indeed, Erwin seems either to have been the main breadwinner of the arrangement or to have exerted great influence over Queen. When Grace advised her to stock up on staples in case the strike spread to Los Angeles, she had added, "If Erwin does not see the importance of this, when you get R's money tell him I want you to buy some stuff and hold it for me for next winter, and if necessary store some at D's house."[5]

In the late 1930s, the Los Angeles IWW seemed to dissolve as much from internal disputes as from a renewed surge of patriotism, under which radicalism never fared well. Of the intraorganizational squabbling, Queen once commented to me, "Mother said that if the revolution were marching with a drum down the street, they [different factions within the IWW] would not have recognized it. Or, they would have crossed the street to avoid it."

A sense of despair permeated the movement in the late 1930s with Europe teetering on the brink of war. This discouragement was well articulated in another letter to Queen, this one written by one of her comrades, Edward E. Anderson, and dated February 6, 1939. Again, it began, "Fellow Worker," and moved quickly onto the violence brewing in Europe:

> This morning's headline states that France and England are requesting a truce in Spain. Whatever the outcome of this request I fear it will be nothing good for the Spanish workers. Still, I sure do hope that the shedding of blood will cease. The wanton destruction has certainly been frightful. And from my personal point of view—looking detachedly from a very safe distance, and with the position of the workers in Russia, Germany, and Italy for background, historically— just what have the workers of Spain to hope for in the line of freedom with communists and their inevitable OGPU in virtual control of government and industry? One dictatorship is as rotten to me as another differing only in phraseology.... So the quicker the fighting stops the quicker the workers will have the chance to take stock of the situation and reorganize their forces accordingly. Just another bitter fight lost and yet not lost.

The letter ends on a note of personal sadness: "I harken back to the pleasant evenings spent on the corner of Second and Hill with you across the table. But them days is gone forever I fear." It is signed, "Yours for OURS."

The extent of bitterness, betrayal, and paranoia gripping radical movements such as the IWW may be judged by a casual letter, dated

March 31, 1937, written to Queen by A. Russell from San Pedro. It began, "Fellow Worker," and thanked her for dropping "them" a line informing them of Erwin's "condition." The letter continued, "I guess maybe you are wondering why we haven't been to see him."

Apparently, Erwin had been hospitalized and his radical friends had not come to visit. They explained their absence. Since "they" had sent a letter to a newspaper, presumably supporting some radical stand, Russell didn't want to compromise Erwin by having anyone see them visit. Several assumptions are implicit in this explanation: the authorities were monitoring the expression of radical political views; Erwin's visitors would be reported to the authorities; and, some action—such as refusing medical benefits—might be taken against Erwin as a result of guilt by association.

The letter continued by asking Queen, "Do you think that we are doing right? If you think that it is O.K. to see him, why just drop a card and let us know.... [I]t seems that everyone is in hospital, first it is Erwin, then Setzer, and now Pachy." The writer added, "... tell Erwin that the fink that had Rude ... kill Ross in his gang is in the hospital with a bad cut in his head. Some lady ran into his car last Sat. nite and he never come to until Easter Sunday nite. I hope he died, the rat."

It is signed, "Yours for the Works."

Clearly the IWW was rife with informers, betrayal, demoralization, and (perhaps justified) paranoia.

Queen had potent political and economic reasons for withdrawing into safe and anonymous employment. There were also personal reasons. By the time Queen received Russell's letter in early 1937, her relationship with Erwin was deteriorating. Queen once mentioned to me a man who was probably Claude Erwin. She said they had broken up abruptly one night when she sat up suddenly and declared, "There's one too many of us in this bed!"

By August 4, 1939, even friendship between the former lovers who were now "fellow workers" seemed to be strained. Writing to Queen from his Los Angeles hospital bed—the city in which she lived and, so, could be expected to visit his bedside—Erwin began awkwardly,[6]

> I do not know why you have not written or visited me, neither do I quite understand why I have not sent you a letter. I have not been quite sure whether you cared to hear from me or not.

I have written five letters to you but none of them were sent. Two of them were written when I did not happen to have a stamp and could not get one here and held them until someone called who would deliver them to the hall but it was a week or so before anyone showed up and the letters were then out of date.

The other three were written at different periods and when a visitor came, they told me of Marsha, Fannie, or someone else asking about me and sending best wishes but nothing about you ever asking any questions about me. I thought perhaps you were not concerned and destroyed the letter.

In fact to date, *no one* has ever brought one word from you verbally or written nor even mentioned you except to answer my questions regarding your health, etc. and they were answered, yes, no, or alright. Bobo and Foster are the only two who ever voluntarily mentioned your name and told me news concerning you.

Erwin went on to discuss the "noble fight" that fellow members of the IWW were waging to keep the meeting hall open. "The organization is in a bad way," he concluded. If anything were to happen to him, he instructed Queen to destroy all organization letters or material in her keeping.

Ten days later, on August 14, he wrote again in response to a letter received from her. After advising Queen about his medical situation, Erwin became more personal.

Now regarding my interest and worry about you. Regardless of how you feel, I shall always look on you as a very dear friend and aside from being a fellow worker I was anxious to hear if you were well or sick. You know you were often not exactly well even tho' you continued to work.

You know our whole social life was closely interwoven with the organization (too much for our own good) so it is impossible to think of local organization problems without thinking of the members connected with it. It is easier and pleasanter to think of you and I knew you in the all too short period when we were away from and could forget organization.

I never asked any questions about your private or personal life. I never done that when we were together.

Foster told me you had moved someplace in that same neighborhood but I did not even ask him where. I thought you would tell me if you wanted me to know.

You mentioned personal implications brought up in my letter. I do not know of having made such implications. I had not intended to.

The letter was signed, "With best wishes," and included a P.S.: "No one has ever asked me one question about you or my married life. You need have no worry about that. I would not be foolish enough to give any information of any kind. Your letter was destroyed after I read it."

If Queen and Erwin were divorced, it was done as quietly as they had been married.

The Personal Is Not Political

In the mid-1930s, both Queen and Grace had made the conscious decision to turn away from the political activism that had defined their lives for decades. In the manuscript of an article she had written entitled "I Don't Want to Be Normal," Grace explained her reasoning,

> I've lived my life, fifty-odd years of it. I've worked hard and long. I've tried not to do anything to harm anyone else; and I've never asked man, woman, or child to do anything for me I would not be willing to do for them, or for myself. I may be a failure, by accepted standards. Maybe I'm an introvert or an extrovert. I care not. In the past my life has belonged to those who needed my work, my love, or care. From now on, it is going to be my life, lived my way. In the few years that are mine I hope to think as I wish, act as I desire (harming no person), and see what happens!
>
> Don't worry—I'm not going on any wild spree of dissipation; I do not want to, for one reason. I do not want to smoke, or drink or dance or skate or stand on my head or play dolls! I do want to spend long hours reading, watching the tiger in the zoo, walking in the mountains or along the beach, or riding a good horse on the trail. I do want to come and go as freely as my daughter has for the last fifteen years! I want time to do all the things I could not do when I had to work so hard to support a family and myself.
>
> And something,—well, I like to think what a century of honest thinking and brave living, particularly by women, could accomplish. I'm too old to have overmuch faith in men, in what they can or will do. Faith in men is a prerogative of young women! One thing only in my life do I seriously regret. I wish I had been brave enough, bold enough, thirty-odd years ago, to have taken the position that I now take....I wish I had been able to realize that in a free country like America each and every man and woman and child must also be free. And I should have known that freedom, like charity, must begin at home....[7]

Tired of being hungry, and disillusioned with the political environment, including the factions within socialism, Queen decided to concentrate on becoming financially secure. In the brief biographical sketch Queen drew up at the repeated prompting of Gordon Stein, she described the next few decades of her life in two sentences. "From 1936–1972 in state civil service in various clerical and stenographic jobs, ending with sixteen years as a hearing recorder. During that period, I was not active, as time and energy taken up with earning a living."[8]

On May 6, 1936, as the Great Depression rolled on, Queen gratefully accepted a permanent job as a junior typist clerk for $70 a month at the Department of Motor Vehicles. She advanced to junior stenographer clerk and then to intermediate stenographer clerk, where she remained until June 25, 1943. At that point, she resigned to take a job in the private sector at 20th Century Fox Film Corp. On a form, she described the job as "Stenographer. Last 2 weeks in Script Dept.; prior to that time in Continuity Dept., taking dialogue and continuity from the screen."[9] After a month and a half, Queen resigned to work for an attorney named Maurice Rose, perhaps because he paid her five dollars more per week than 20th Century Fox. She listed her reason for leaving after only a month as "to take vacation and then reenter State employment." Elsewhere, she omitted the reference to a vacation. Whatever her reasons for leaving the private sector, by December Queen was reinstated as an intermediate stenographer clerk at the California Highway Patrol.

Queen began to work her way meticulously toward the goal of becoming a hearing recorder, one of the best paid and most prestigious civil servant positions then available to women. It was a goal she had considered for a long time. In a letter dated August 4, 1934, Roser had advised her:

> As for court reporter, [I] think you are aiming high. It has become a matter of influence and monopoly. They used to make fortunes out of it. It may be they have been cut down since I was familiar with the matter, but they used to make salaries and fees larger than the judges and other county and state officials, and in a few cases more than the president of the U.S. Go to the information desk in the Broadway lobby (west side, first floor) and ask the man where the office of the secretary of the Superior Court is now. Then go to the secretary, and I think he can tell you all about the court reporter business. It is like getting expert in playing the piano or violin, it takes constant and unremitting practice in shorthand to become expert and speedy.[10]

For a woman without connections or formal education to become a hearing recorder (or court reporter) would be a remarkable accomplishment. Queen committed herself to the goal.[11] The woman who had lectured at the age of eight years to the applause of scientists now took high-school courses to prepare for the entrance exams to a city college. From 1939 to 1943, Queen studied Spanish, American history, algebra, and shorthand dictation at Polytechnic Evening High School. Her shorthand soared to 210 words a minute.

Meanwhile, Grace acted on a decision she had made while stranded in Alaska. "I guess I'll have to get a typewriter when I get the money and settle down in earnest to try to make a business of writing," Grace had concluded.[12] Her asthma and cough had become chronic. Whenever she spoke too long or too forcefully, her throat became hoarse and required time to recover. A career of lecturing was in her past. While in Alaska, Grace had decided, "[I]f I do come back I want to concentrate on writing for sale of MSs as I'm afraid if I speak much, I'll always cough. You know I did make 300 [dollars] one year [from writing]."[13]

Writing was hardly a new pursuit for Grace. Indeed, writing had launched her lecturing career, as it was the prize money from an essay contest that allowed her to buy a train ticket from Maine to Boston at the age of eighteen. Moreover, she had continued to write, contributing material to *Queen Silver's Magazine* as well as to other periodicals.

Her writing ranged from fiction to plays to political commentary. As well as being versatile, she seemed quite sophisticated about the "business" of writing which included keeping track of manuscripts and where they circulated. For example, on the first page of a "one-act playlet" entitled *Virginity*, she noted, "This playlet was written in 1922 and first published in *Droll Stories* early in 1923." She also carefully preserved all motion picture and dramatic rights to the playlet. Her non-fiction was published with some frequency in periodicals such as the *Brain Power Monthly*. Indeed, Queen told me some magazines published Grace so frequently that her mother used a pseudonym to induce them to buy more articles from her. One pen name she used was "Grace Hawthorne," perhaps springing from the period she had lived in Hawthorne.

Over the next two decades, Grace published literally hundreds of articles and short stories in magazines. Most of the articles dealt with "women's issues," especially with sexual topics such as unwed motherhood and birth control. For example, from 1935 to 1936 Grace published the following pieces in a New York magazine entitled *Sexology*: "That Sterile Period" (on birth control), "Birth Control Is Not New," "The Call of Sex," "Men and Marriage," "A Man and His Wife," "Childlessness in Modern Women," "Sex in the Cinema" (on censorship), "Sex and Facial Expression," "The Marriage War," "Love Is Lawless" (on eugenics), and "Free Motherhood and the Modern Woman."[14]

During the repressive 1940s and 1950s, Grace became expert at tactfully exploring graphic topics and at phrasing herself in an explicit manner that was within the bounds of propriety. No wonder she became a regular contributor to magazines with names such as *Your Body, Popular Medicine, Sex Digest, Truth Seeker, Married Happiness, Sex Psychology,* and *Facts of Life.*[15]

Although she was prolific, writing did not come easily. The manuscripts Grace left behind typically have notations scrawled across the first page indicating, among other information, the dozens of times any particular piece had been rewritten and how many times it had been shopped around. For example, the article entitled "The Squaw Has a Word for It!" was finally accepted by *Opportunity* magazine in late 1938, four years after Grace's return from Alaska. Across the first page, she had commented, "This was my very 1st article written after coming back from Alaska. Accepted on about 20th or 22nd time mailed out after being rewritten after 10 trips. Laid in files a year besides."[16]

Grace's gutsy articles on sex and the condition of women made a deep and favorable impression on several editors. One of them was Hugo Gernsback, who is often called the father of magazine or pulp science fiction. As well as publishing pulp fiction, however, Gernsback was the president of Radcraft Publications, Inc. and Popular Book Corporation.[17]

In late 1943, Gernsback made a business proposition to Grace. At the behest of a New York publisher, he was writing a book of between 60,000 to 65,000 words and he wished to enter into what he termed a joint authorship: Grace would produce a manuscript, then he would edit. He would take half the credit, presumably with his name appearing first on the title page. Gernsback said that Grace had occurred to him as the perfect coauthor because the book needed to be "a small encyclopedia of love" and "*not a sex book*." From her articles in *Sexology*, he knew Grace was capable of "innuendo" so that "the reader could read between the lines what the author is driving at without being too outspoken."[18]

Grace jumped at the chance. She stated a price of $300 and requested a period of three months in which to finish the manuscript. Gernsback accepted the financial arrangement, but demanded a time frame of somewhat over a month and a half. To encourage her, he offered to send a $30 payment for each of ten chapters, with the first payment being in advance. Between October 25 and November 28, 1943, working day and night, Grace completed a book of approximately 63,000 words. It was tentatively entitled *What Is Love?*

In a letter dated November 8, Gernsback declared himself to be satisfied with the first three chapters. Nevertheless, there is no record of the book's publication. Instead, the papers Grace left at her death included a full manuscript of the eleven-chapter book with the notation, "Property of Grace Verne Silver to belong to Queen Silver in case of my death." As the $300 was to constitute an outright sale of the book to Gernsback, I assume full payment had not been forthcoming.

As for Mark Kellar, little information on him exists outside of Grace's letters from Alaska. Upon their return, he and Grace seem to have married and happily so. In one of her short stories entitled "All Work and No Play," there is a female figure who is clearly based upon Grace and who finds genuine happiness with a male figure who is probably based on Kellar. The story begins by vividly describing the abject misery of a woman trapped in a loveless marriage with an older and sickly man—presumably Roser. She seeks solace in raising and tending the animals on their small ranch, but a growing hatred toward her husband blackens all other emotions. The woman is finally freed by the passion she develops for another man—a man who satisfies her spiritually and sexually. The final scene is of her lover carrying the woman in his arms to their bed.

Kellar died in the early to mid-1940s. In a manuscript entitled "So You Can't Take It!" Grace described the mourning period.

> [W]hen my husband died, in June a couple years ago, and I let myself give way, and friends tried to rally me...I became so angry I haven't spoken to them since! For just as love offers its own reward to the lover so also does grief offer the only comfort and solace to the griever, for the time being grief sharpens the memory for every loved feature of the dead; for every word and act recalled; while it racks the emotions, it also wears them out, and by so doing, soothes them.[19]

Samuel N. Silver, Queen's harsh and puritanical grandfather.

Grace in her thirties, in costume as a movie extra. Such work was a major source of income for both Grace and Queen.

Queen lecturing in Los Angeles on Los Angeles Street, in the "free speech zone," at age seven and a half.

GRACE V. SILVER

A G I T A T O R

O R G A N I Z E R

ORATOR AND LECTURER WHO IS KNOWN FROM MAINE TO CALIFORNIA AS A FEAR-
LESS, LOGICAL EXPONENT OF INDUSTRIAL SOCIALISM

WILL SPEAK AT

SUBJECT:

"THE WORLD-WIDE REVOLT"

LABOR'S CO-OPERATIVE PRESS ASS'N   439   205 W. WASHINGTON ST., CHICAGO

Poster used to advertise Grace's lectures on the circuit.

Queen Silver, aged 8 years - delivering an address subject "Brains" at a meeting Second and Los Angeles Sts. Los Angeles, California, Oct. 12, 1919

Queen, age eight, lectures on "Brains" with Grace seated to her left. The handwriting is Grace's.

QUEEN SILVER

Twelve Year Old Orator

Philosopher and Scientist

"Pioneers of Free Thought"

Sunday, April 29th, 2 P. M.

...AT...

ODD FELLOWS HALL
220½ South Main Street

ADMISSION FREE

Queen, age eight, reads Haeckel's *Natural History of Creation* in what became her most famous photograph.

The coquettish side of Queen–one of the boa photos –taken when she was about ten years old. Grace encouraged her daughter to express her sexuality.

PRICE 25c

Queen Silver's Magazine

Vol. I, No. 3   Inglewood, California   Second Quarter 1924

—International News Reel Photo

QUEEN SILVER

With Sallie and Billie, famous Chimpanzees owned by Mr. J. S. Edwards

Evolution---From Monkey to Bryan | PAGE THREE

Queen on the cover of *Queen Silver's Magazine* in her second most famous photograph, taken with the chimpanzees Sallie and Billie.

PRICE 25c

Queen Silver's Magazine

Vol. II, No. 3   Inglewood, California   Second Quarter 1925

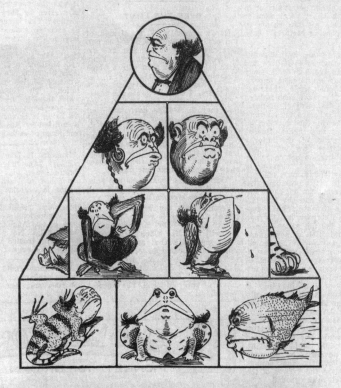

EVOLUTION of HUMAN NATURE
by Queen Silver

Page Three

This cover of *Queen Silver's Magazine* shows a fish evolving into William Jennings Bryan, a leading crusader against evolution. Queen's lecture "Evolution from Monkey to Bryan" received widespread acclaim as the nation focused on the Scopes Monkey Trial.

Queen at age fourteen, one year before her marriage to George H. Shoaf in 1926.

Queen in her sixties. With Grace dead, and having retired from her job as hearing recorder, Queen once again entered the freethought movement.

Queen in her thirties. By now, she and Grace had turned away from the political activism that had defined their lives for decades.

The greatest comfort of all, however, must have been Queen with whom Grace now lived. During World War II, with a severe housing shortage in the Los Angeles area, Queen and her mother lived together in a house they rented from a Mexican family. The family occupied the newer house in the front; Queen and Grace shared the older one in the back.

Queen once related an incident from this period to me. The family had five children. One of the daughters had progressed through the public school system to grade seven without having learned how to read or write. She was Mexican, and the teachers had considered her either unable to learn or not worth the time to teach. The system kept passing her along rather than cause trouble. When Grace discovered the situation, she spent months tutoring not only the daughter but all of the children. Grace was so successful tutoring that the "unteachable child" went from illiteracy to the top of her class.

From Socialist to Civil Servant

When Queen completed a form for the dean of educational services at Los Angeles City College, she filled in the section under "Hobbies" as follows: "No special hobbies. (Too occupied earning a living and preparing for present work.) Like reading (very little fiction), dancing (ballroom and square), shorthand (both as work and outside interest), and cats. Like to sew, but have very little time, as vocation and study occupy time fully." Characteristically protective of her privacy, Queen refused to provide her address or phone number on the form, typing instead, "This information not available for release."

On January 16, 1952, Queen prepared a "psychograph" of herself as part of a psychology course. It provided evidence of her single-minded focus on becoming a hearing recorder.[20] Four pages of self-analysis followed a bar chart aimed at quantifying aspects of her personality, interests, and aptitudes.

She bluntly acknowledged any characteristics that might be a hindrance to becoming a hearing recorder only to dismiss the characteristic as irrelevant or one that she was eager to improve. For example, in commenting on her "General Social Contacts," Queen explained:

There is no doubt that much effort could be profitably applied to widening personal contacts with people. Prolonged necessity for additional training for vocational advancement, plus daily employment which has always been rather strenuous, has left little time or energy for developing purely social contacts. It is hoped that, with release of some of the pressure of earning a living and preparing for advancement, there will be more time and energy available for social contacts, as well as general educational development.

A complicating factor here is that most of the people whom I knew well when I was growing up and in early adulthood were much older than I and are now dead, making it necessary for most of my contacts to be new ones. Difficulties in finding other persons of similar interests, or at least the same degrees of interest, are also a problem.

In August 1954, Queen advanced to the position of hearing recorder at the Division of Appeals at the Department of Employment. In 1960, she achieved another goal. She graduated from Los Angeles City College with an arts degree.

Next to nothing is known about Queen's reaction to the political events of the 1940s or 1950s. Among Queen's papers were pamphlets on the 1944 Socialist Platform and flyers from the Socialist Party of Los Angeles. There were mock ballots with check marks beside Norman Thomas for president and Darlington Hoopes for vice president. The ballots boasted the slogan: "For Full Employment and a Lasting Peace Vote Socialist." But, although Queen clearly did not change her views, the hysteria of World War II and the McCarthy hearings in the 1950s could not have encouraged her to speak out.

Shortly after World War I, a teenaged Queen had published an article entitled "Our Peace Plan" in *QSM*. The article suggested,

Since it has become the fashion for everyone to present to the public a sure cure of world war, we hereby offer our never-fail plan for ending wars of all kinds.

1. Put all of the kings, presidents, and congressmen who advocate war, state and city officials who are in favor of war, in the front ranks of the military forces. Along with them, put all the editors who advocate war, and all the preachers who pray for war.

2. If a referendum on the question of war or peace be put before the people, draft for military service all who vote for war, and exempt all who are opposed to war. Those who want war should do their own fighting.

3. Confiscate for military use, all the property of those who vote
for war, or engage in battle.

4. Pay no wages or salaries to any soldier, sailor, or officer.[21]

She chose to make no comment on World War II. Nor did she go on
record concerning the McCarthy period during which people suspected
of being left wing were branded by a government committee as being
"un-American." As a consequence, many radicals found themselves
blacklisted: under pressure from the authorities, employers refused to
hire them. Queen had maintained friendships with prominent figures in
the movie industry, such as Michael Kanin.[22] As the movie industry was
particularly targeted for investigation, Queen must have had strong
reactions to the blacklisting. She kept them to herself.

I heard Queen mention the McCarthy hearings only once and then
only in passing. During a lecture on Mark Twain, she quoted the author
as having written, "It is by the goodness of God that in our country we
have these unspeakably precious things, freedom of speech, freedom of
conscience, and the prudence never to practice either of them." Then,
she wryly observed, "I wonder what he would have done if he had had
the material of Joseph McCarthy to work his humor on. We could have
used Mark Twain during the McCarthy era."[23]

As a child and a young adult, Queen had experienced the vicious
consequences of speaking out against the crowd. Both she and Grace
had been arrested; they had been verbally and physically attacked; they
had been threatened by the Ku Klux Klan; the stock of Grace's bookstore had been burned three times; they had watched friends and fellow
workers being deported or betrayed to the authorities. Now, in middle
age, Queen stayed on the sidelines. Although she retained friends in the
freethought and socialist communities, she asked them not to call her at
work or mail radical literature to her there. She needed an area of safety.

1972: *The Pivotal Year*

On January 1, 1972, Queen retired. In a letter dated July 18, 1972, to the
California Association of State Hearing Reporters, Queen stated,

I have been more fortunate than most people, I think, in being able to earn my living at work I loved and which gave me great personal satisfaction. It is true I had some routine clerical low-paid jobs in the beginning but after that I had many years in work leading to reporting and in reporting....

...I rather expect that after the first of the year I shall be looking about for reporting work elsewhere. By that time I should have finished the painting and decorating of the house and some other projects I had to put off while working.

It is difficult to reconcile the elder Queen's evident satisfaction at being a civil servant with her youthful disdain for all things respectable. But there can be no doubt that Queen felt fulfilled by her work. After retirement, she spoke of her reporting days often and with fondness.

The respect and goodwill were reciprocated. A thick binder of "Reports of Performance" offers evaluations of Queen's work by superiors: there is not one word of criticism, not one comment to indicate that she experienced or caused the slightest problem in the workplace. The civil service commendations and awards presented to her are carefully preserved in plastic sleeves. *The Grapevine*—a "company" newsletter published for recorders—offered an account of Queen's retirement party:

On January 21, 50 friends and admirers, old and new, met at "Les Freres Taix" restaurant to honor Queen Silver.... Ref [Referee] Anderson surpassed himself as MC and his anecdotes and legends about Queen brought forth avalanches of laughter. Sen Ref [Senior Referee] Evans reflected upon her career—unparalleled and unique in the history of reporters, a perfect example of the rise of a self-made American girl. Sr Ref [Senior Referee] Horn praised her keen, analytical mind and her recommendations and help in training others.... Queen reminisced the good and bad times and mentioned her thousands of unused sick leave hours (hear, hear!)[24] She stressed the fact that her relationship and interest in the office has been more than professional.[25]

Queen had recently moved into a sprawling pre–World War II house in the heart of Hollywood on Seward Street. The front yard was dotted by sunflowers and this, along with an uncommonly large backyard for Los Angeles, offered Grace the opportunity to pursue her favorite hobby: gardening.[26] Queen looked forward to fixing up the house with her mother and, perhaps, easing back into political causes.

On November 19, 1972, less than a month after Queen's retirement party, Grace experienced a mild stroke that required hospitalization for five days. She returned to Seward Street where Queen cared for her with rented hospital equipment. Grace's health deteriorated. On December 14, Queen applied to the Department of Health and Education to have Grace's social security and other benefits placed under her control so she could manage her mother's affairs. Meanwhile, Queen had to constantly reassure Grace who was terrified of returning to the hospital where she believed the doctors would kill her. Queen described one night in particular. Grace had awakened believing that she was back in the hospital. Nothing Queen said could convince Grace that she was home. At her wit's end, Queen finally picked up one of their cats and dropped the animal on her mother's chest. Grace was convinced: no hospital would allow a cat in a patient's room.

At 8:05 P.M., on December 19, 1972—nine days after Queen's birthday—Grace Verne Silver died at the age of eighty-three of cerebral thrombosis. The death certificate listed her occupation as "writer." The blank for "Kind of Industry or Business" was filled by two words— "Women's Rights." The certificate identified Grace as a "widow."

The *Los Angeles Times* announced that the funeral service would be "strictly private."

One of Grace's short stories, "All Work and No Play," is clearly autobiographical. There, she wrote,

> Literature had mattered—she was now too tired to read. Once she had wanted to write—had even sold things occasionally; now the typewriter was rusty, old; she'd have to soak it in gasoline to loosen it before it would write at all. She still had ideas and ideals, but no one else had them, it seemed. She was alone, but it did not matter either. Life is lived alone anyway, unless it is lived with a lover. Any woman knows that, and no man ever learns it.[27]

In another manuscript—a nonfiction article entitled "A Man and His Wife, A Reply to 'Veritas' "—Grace offered insight into her attitudes toward men and life.[28]

> "Veritas" wants to know about my "background," which I think of trifling importance. I may say that my mother died when I was five; till I was eighteen no woman ever was in our house, except for one week out of every other year. I was raised by men, on farm, in machine shop

and mine and wilderness. I have traveled some three hundred thousand miles since then, lived for days and weeks in hundreds of towns and cities, big and little; among savages and civilized, working people and professionals. I learned about men from men; about women from women, and from myself.

He would know "if you are physically attractive?" Modesty forbids a reply; let him ask my husband, or come to one of my lectures, if he can. He wants to know where I've been looking for men? Never looked, always found them without looking!

He implies I must be soured through failure to find a suitable man. How many times I've heard the male make a similar crack? I was brought up to call a spade a spade—when I didn't call it a steam shovel. An old physician warned me, thirty years ago:

"Always trust your instincts; not what someone tells you, if you expect to have any happiness in love or marriage. Don't marry a man you don't know all about. If you are offended, disgusted with anything he does in the love relation, drop him at once. That's what your instincts are for! If you want a child, have it *then*, no matter what your circumstances may be. If you marry, and begin to hate your husband, quit before you're tempted to murder him! Marriage without love is prostitution, no matter how legal or respectable, or financially secure it may be." And much more.

Unconventional advice which will be condemned by people! But if I had a dozen daughters, instead of one, I'd pass it on to them, with additions. No, Veritas, I'm not soured on men. I've got what I wanted because I knew enough to take it; knew how to tell a man by his face and other ways.... I've never been afraid to say what I think, or do what I believe is right, no matter who else may think I am saying or doing wrong. I'm not afraid of life, men, or love.

According to her wishes, Grace's body was cremated and her ashes were scattered on the Pacific Ocean.

Notes

1. Letter from Grace to Queen dated June 28, 1934, from Ketchikan.
2. This seems to have been Mrs. Doughty's address and was, perhaps, a boardinghouse of sorts.
3. One thing is apparent from the spelling, syntax, content, and grammar of this letter: Grace is far better educated than Kellar.
4. Letter from Grace to Queen dated June 29, 1934, from Ketchikan.
5. Letter from Grace to Queen dated July 16, 1934, from Ketchikan.

6. Because so few direct records of Queen's personal life exist, I am quoting almost in their entirety the two letters from Erwin that she preserved.

7. This manuscript was apparently unpublished.

8. A letter dated December 1, 1971, from the California Unemployment Insurance Appeals Board to Queen states, "In looking over your personal history, I note that your employment with the State began in 1931 for the Department of Motor Vehicles." In one of her many Applications for Examination (for advancement within the civil service) Queen listed her work history from January 12, 1931, to March 14, 1936, with the DMV. Her job was junior file clerk, which consisted of filing automobile license records and answering the telephone.

9. Queen gave this description on a California State Personal Board Application for Examination, dated January 31, 1946, on which she listed the job with attorney Maurice Rose as her reason for leaving. On another application form she listed the reason for leaving as "wished to use shorthand more."

10. Queen did *not* become a court reporter, but chose a career as a hearing recorder instead. The two jobs are very similar and require much the same skills, however.

11. The job of hearing recorder offered Queen more security than any other civil service position which she would have been likely to fill. Starting as a junior clerk in 1936, she had made $70 a month. When she retired in 1972, Queen was grossing $1,128 a month as a hearing recorder. Moreover, she was eligible to retire at age sixty-two with annual retirement pay of almost 60 percent of the average of the highest three years' of salary in addition to social security. The medical plan provided through Kaiser was comprehensive.

12. Letter from Grace to Queen dated July 19, 1934, from Ketchikan.

13. Letter from Grace to Queen dated July 24, 1934, from Ketchikan.

14. These are the titles on the carbons retained by Grace and not necessarily the titles under which the articles were published. In one case, for example, the published title was "Sex in the Countenance" instead of the submitted title of "Sex and Facial Expression."

15. *Sexology*, *Facts of Life*, and *Your Body* were all issued by the same editor, David H. Keller, M.D., from 99 Hudson Street, New York, New York. Keller apparently took Grace under his wing, as quite a few of her articles have a written indication that they were done at his request. And his requests seem to have been frequent. A content list of *Sexology* for 1937 has a piece by Grace in every single issue of the monthly periodical.

16. Other notations on the pages of manuscripts indicate yet another way that Grace and Queen supplemented their meager incomes: they played the horses with some success. On the bottom of an article entitled "Working Off a Temper" was the penciled note, "Picked 5 winners in my 1st choices, 5 place in my 2nd choices." Among the many postcards that Queen collected were dozens that depicted racetracks and race horses. Among the ink sketches left behind by Grace were several of horses, some of them with jockeys sitting astride. And

horses were a favored subject in Grace's short stories. For example, there is a fictional whimsical piece dated February 9, 1939, and entitled, "All by Myself I Did It! Or, How I Won the Race without the Handicap of a Jockey." In parentheses beneath the title is the explanation: "The Tale of a Self-Made Horse, as told by REPSAC to Grace Verne Silver."

17. Gernsback's letterhead lists him as a "Publisher of Radiocraft, Flight, Official Radio Service Manuals, Official Refrigeration Service Manuals, Official Air Condition Service Manual, Gernsback Educational Library, and Radio-Craft Library."

18. Letter from Gernsback to Grace dated October 18, 1943.

19. From a manuscript written by Grace entitled "So You Can't Take It!" with the notation, "Published *Psychology*, Feb. 1950."

20. The course was Psychology 21 with Instructor Houghton. The Psychograph included the results of a series of tests conducted from late 1951 to January 1952. The series included: the Otis S.A. Test, the Varnum-Ruhl Reading Test, the Kuder Voc.Int. Test, and the Neyman-Kohlstadt Test. The results were graphed in bar fashion, as well as ranked as a percentage.

21. *QSM* 1, no. 3 (Second Quarter 1924): 12.

22. Among the many scripts authored by Kanin (often with his wife, Faye Kanin) were *Teacher's Pet* (1958) for which he was nominated for an Oscar. He had previously won that award for *Woman of the Year* (1942). Queen once mentioned that she and Kanin had promised each other to live to the age of one hundred.

23. "The Many Sides of Mark Twain" delivered at HALA on November 5, 1995.

24. In what appears to be part of an application form for a home mortgage in 1969, Queen stated, "I have income protection from loss of pay for sickness because I have over 2,300 hours of accumulated sick leave. This, with annual vacation (20 days yearly, plus accumulation), would protect me in case of extended illness."

25. Irene G. Kahn writing in the column, "Los Angeles Referee Office," *Grapevine*, February 1972, p. 5.

26. Grace also took up painting in a serious manner, but her eyesight began to fail until she was no longer able to see the canvas well enough. She gardened largely through touch.

27. Page 13 of the unpublished manuscript.

28. The notation on this manuscript indicates it was published in *Sexology* (October 1936). It was a response to the published query from a reader of another article, "Childlessness in Modern Women," published in the April *Sexology*. The reader preferred to remain anonymous in his query—a maneuver which elicited scorn from Grace who addressed him as "Poor Man-afraid-to-tell-his-name as the Indians would dub him!" (p. 1). Again, the published version may have been edited in a slightly different manner.

9

Queen without Grace: The Personal Becomes Political

(1972–1998)

*A*T THE AGE of sixty-two, Queen found herself alone for the first time in her life. When one makes this statement about an older woman, it usually refers to the death of a spouse. For Queen, it refers to the loss of an equally important partner. Nineteen seventy-two was the first time Queen was without *the* personality that dominated her life: her mother. Grace had carried her daughter toward radicalism since 1910. Queen had been ten days old when Grace had taken the two of them out of a Portland hospital and back onto the socialist lecture trail. She had instilled within Queen the same beliefs that she carried intact to the grave: human beings must rely upon reason for truth; everyone must be free to speak his or her own conscience; the most noble form of human expression is productive labor for which the laborer deserves—and should demand!—just recompense. Another, albeit more subliminal, belief was that a person should never willingly accept abuse from anyone.

Men entered and exited the lives of these two women at seemingly random intervals. While they were present, the impact often resembled that of a tornado. Of course, there were relationships that sustained them as well. Grace found Mark Kellar. In the last decades of her life, Queen found Don Latimer—a freethought activist—who became the love of her life. But most of the men with whom they "associated" vanished, leaving so little trace that Queen's intimate friends had no idea she had been married even once.

Friends also came and went. Over the years, fellow radicals had been arrested, deported, and otherwise silenced. Many of Queen's earlier associates—who had been adults while she was still a child—had died. The radical circles in which she had grown into young adulthood and from which she drew a sense of self had dispersed. For example, the IWW went from spectacular success in the early 1900s to near extinction by midcentury. Where could she go, to whom could she turn to talk about old times? Other than Grace, who knew the person she had been in the old times—not a civil servant, but a shining star?

People and circumstances came and went, but from the first moment of Queen's awareness, Grace had always been there. Grace had been the one constant presence. Now she was suddenly gone.

Queen once expressed surprise and a rare disapproval of me when I confessed to her over lunch that I harbored a desire to believe in God. I desired to believe that there is a unifying and benevolent principle underlying the universe. I just didn't see the evidence for it and, so, rejected the possibility. Queen could not understand my reasoning until I explained one aspect of it, namely, the genesis of the desire. My father died when I was ten years old. If there were a God, then there would also be a Heaven and I would see him again. There were things I wanted to tell him. That fueled a desire to believe in God—but it didn't constitute evidence for belief. Queen suddenly understood my position.

I will not speculate on whether Queen felt a similar need to say something to her mother. Queen drew a thick curtain over the rich psychological and emotional relationship that undoubtedly existed between them.[1] In later years, she constantly referred to "Mother" in both lectures and casual conversations, but it was always in the context of "Mother used to say," or "Mother used to write articles," or "Mother was a second-generation feminist." She never spoke of the emotional bond between the two of them. I never heard her speak the words, "I loved my mother." Discretion was her choice and it should be respected.

After Grace's death, Queen experienced what could be termed a nervous breakdown. The organizing principle of her personal life had vanished: her mother. The job as a hearing recorder, into which Queen had poured herself for decades and which had provided a contact with people, had also vanished. Some radical organizations like the Socialist Party still existed in a weakened form, but Queen did not know the people involved, nor did they know her. Besides, Queen had abandoned radicalism, if not in theory, then in practice. With one important exception, she was no longer intimately connected to a network of fellow-minds who could provide the social solace for which people often turn to churches. Instead, Queen was left alone in the sprawling home on Seward Street in Hollywood, which she had purchased not long before, partly in the hope that her mother could spend days gardening in the unusually large yard.

Or, rather, Queen would have been left alone had it not been for the "one important exception"—the Valle family. Queen and Grace had known the Valle patriarch from radicalism in days long gone. In Queen's own words, the Valles "saved her life" after Grace's death. The family virtually adopted her and, in dealing with their joys and problems, Queen found a surrogate support system. The Valles may have kept her alive for the interim necessary to mourn, but it was radicalism that saved Queen in the long run.

As Queen emerged from over a year of the debilitating disorientation caused by her mother's death, she actively sought the companionship of like-minded people. Those who have experienced the all-consuming passion that can be inspired by a cause know that it is akin to falling in love. Queen returned to the sustaining passion of her life: radicalism.

An impetus behind Queen's plunge back into politics was undoubtedly the heart attack she experienced not long after Grace's death. The attack offered a sense of her own mortality. And she took the episode seriously enough to always carry nitroglycerin tablets with her in an undergarment pouch beneath her armpit.[2] Queen reminded me several times of where the tablets were kept. I presume she did the same with other friends.

After the kindness of the Valles and with the passage of time, Queen began to function once more. Her home base remained the house on Seward Street. But Queen never overcame the trauma of losing Grace. For over two and a half decades, she refused to open the many boxes of documents, photos, and memorabilia Grace had bequeathed her. Indeed, among the papers in Queen's estate was a large envelope upon which Grace had written "For Queen, to be opened at my death." The seal of the envelope had not been broken.

Boxes and boxes of rare periodicals, correspondence, and photographs sat unopened and stacked in what had been Grace's bedroom, or they mildewed slowly in the leaky garage. For the rest of her life, Queen deflected the inquiries of scholars who inquired about any material she might have had relating to the early freethought movement. In all sincerity, she would insist that she no longer had even a single copy of *Queen Silver Magazine*.[3] In reality, she had two boxfuls with many duplicate issues and almost a complete run. Over and over again, Queen lamented the fact that she had no birth certificate and, so, could not travel outside of the United States. In reality, she had several copies of the certificate, including what appears to be the original, all carefully tucked away by Grace. Perhaps, in refusing to sort through boxes, to open closets, or enter certain rooms, Queen shielded herself from losing Grace. She pushed away her grief by not confronting it.

But she did grieve, if not openly, then passively. At the end of Queen's life, I was one of only two people she allowed to stay overnight at her home.[4] Indeed, she allowed very few people through the front door. Whenever someone came to drive her to meetings or for other purposes, Queen met them on the porch because she did not want them to see the inside of her house. She was embarrassed by the cluttered chaos of her home, but it was more than this. Queen was afraid that, on the basis of how dysfunctional her house had become, a visitor might report her to the authorities as being unable to conduct her own affairs. Her fear was not without foundation. Several elderly people in California had been "committed" to senior citizen homes on no more evidence of incompetence than a messy house. For this same reason,

Queen did not hire strangers to do plumbing or any other work that might be necessary. Queen feared strangers and authority, and needed Grace to cope with the world.

The house on Seward Street was relatively spacious, but it was difficult to walk through the rooms due to the stacks of boxes and piles of periodicals. The only way to navigate the house was through open walkways with clutter piled high on either side. After Queen's death, when Don Latimer and I sorted through the stacks, we found an amazing assortment of items tucked into boxes. Kleenexes and dry ballpoint pens lay amid valuables. There was no reason or rhyme to what had been saved, or to the manner in which it had been preserved.

In refusing to deal with—or even look at—the masses of material Grace had left in various areas of the house, Queen had created a psychological monster she could not conquer.[5] All she could do was box it and put it away.

Fortunately for Queen, an outside world welcomed her.

Madalyn Murray O'Hair versus Queen Silver

In a letter dated July 23, 1982, written by Queen to correspondent Warren W. Patterson, she described the path by which she reentered the freethought movement.

> After attending the 1975 AA [American Atheist] Convention in Los Angeles, I attended the organizing meeting of [the] L.A. chapter and agreed to be temporary secretary for a few weeks. The "few weeks" ended up being five years. New officers were elected in 1980 and served to September 1981, when new officers were elected.

When Queen plunged back into freethought in the early 1970s, she walked into an explosive situation not of her own making. At first, it must have seemed disappointingly familiar in terms of the bickering and animosity being expressed among certain people. But the familiarity would have also allowed Queen to be a moderating influence on the bitter melodrama unfolding. She had developed a talent for being the calm voice in a crowd. After all, in the 1930s, she had watched the "4As" (American Association for the Advancement of Atheism) collapse due to infighting. As a child and a teenager, she had seen socialists betray each other.

She now brought this maturity to a freethought community that buzzed with controversy about its most prominent voice: Madalyn Murray O'Hair.

It is no overstatement to say that the two most powerful women in twentieth-century atheism were Madalyn Murray O'Hair and Queen Silver.[6] O'Hair (née Mays) had been born nine years after Queen, in 1919. Her success in the court case *Murray* v. *Curlett*—initiated in 1957 and decided in her favor by the Supreme Court in 1963—resulted in having prayer and other religious practices banned from the public school system. This success propelled her into the position of being the most visible atheist in America. Although the Supreme Court victory had resulted from the efforts of many people, O'Hair blithely assumed all the credit. Her prominence was made all the more secure when O'Hair founded the organization called American Atheists (AA), and headed its monthly periodical, *American Atheist.* For many people, O'Hair became the voice of the American atheist movement.[7]

Without question, the aggressive stance O'Hair assumed in the press and her other forms of activism stimulated a resurgence of freethought in America. But the growth in the movement came at a steep price. O'Hair was notoriously difficult to deal with.[8]

Unless you have been committed enough to a movement or to an ideology to get behind the scenes—for example, sitting on the committees that debate minute issues and often dissolve into personal bitterness over seemingly insignificant matters—the collapse of the American atheist community may seem amazing. For those who have labored behind the scenes, the story will seem familiar. O'Hair's tendency to fling slanderous charges at fellow atheists who threatened her substantial ego spelled disaster for a cohesive atheist effort.

In June 1964, not even one year after the Supreme Court victory, a flurry of protest broke out within the freethought community when the well-respected author Dr. Vitali Negri vigorously protested a slanderous piece O'Hair had published about him.[9] Negri wrote an open letter dated June 3 to "Mrs. [not Dr.] Madalyn Murray" in which he called the charges she had been circulating "a frivolous and irresponsible splattering of manufactured mud."

The next month, Lemoin Cree, president of Other Americans, Inc.

(OA), published a special newsletter devoted entirely to an attack on O'Hair. Or, rather, it might be termed "a defense against O'Hair" as it was written in response to "the slanderous 'Murray Newsletter' dated July 2, 1964."[10] In that newsletter, "the belligerent and unpredictable" O'Hair—then president of the Freethought Society of America—accused her own duly elected board of directors of being agents of the church who were acting against her. In response, the board removed her as president and publicly denounced her for (among other things) pilfering funds. Cree chronicled O'Hair's bizarre accusations against the board, then leveled equally strange-sounding charges. For example, regarding the "friend" of O'Hair's who had reportedly uncovered the plot of the "agents of the church," Cree contended, "The 'true friend' is Mrs. Mae Mallory (known in FBI files as Willie Mae Mallory). She is a militant negro agitator who is touring the East seeking support for negro rifle clubs under her direction. She also openly states that the salvation for the negro is Red China."[11]

The back-and-forth exchanges that ensued between O'Hair and a growing number of her critics made the preceding accusations sound like sweet, cool reason. For example, O'Hair accused the Baltimore police of being agents of the Church, who were attempting to murder her family. Her husband, whom she had earlier dubbed the prophet of a newly established atheist church, was arrested for wife beating. O'Hair seemed to be working hard to earn the popularly ascribed nickname of "mad Murray."

After leaving the continental States in a huff and resettling in Honolulu, O'Hair established the International Freethought Society Incorporated. It quickly dissolved into chaos. O'Hair called the Honolulu police "hulu-hipped dicks." She termed its governor a "whore-thieving nut" who took "millions of dollars from madames and prostitutes, as head of Honolulu vice squad." Such statements could not have endeared her to the authorities.[12] Indeed, by the time the organization's charter had been revoked, O'Hair had found it necessary to flee to Mexico, leaving her brother John Mays in charge as president.

Predictably, the arrangement proved unstable. O'Hair's son William J. Murray, who was the editor of the International Freethought Press, did not take long to publicly call his uncle John Mays "an embezzler."[13] In turn, Mays sent out his own open letter to the atheist community at large, hurling his own set of accusations.[14] The conflict was not merely an internal one: outside authorities began investigating the possibility of fraud having been committed by O'Hair and other freethought leaders. With charges against Cree, Mays, and O'Hair registered with the Fraud Department in Washington, D.C., the atheist community seemed in tatters.[15] Whatever energy the movement had left seemed to be diverted into causing further damage. For example, Cree notified the postal authorities that O'Hair had stolen a mailing list.

Religionists did not need to destroy atheism in America: they merely needed to step back and let atheists destroy themselves. Queen had watched many movements self-destruct. Ironically, the once divisive Queen now acted as a voice of reason. She became one of the few atheist leaders whom all sides respected and with whom all personalities could cooperate. She even had the chutzpah to try and convince O'Hair to be more moderate in her treatment of others. For example, Queen told me she had urged O'Hair repeatedly to pause for just ten minutes before putting a stamp on one of the infamous letters she sent to people who had angered her. O'Hair clearly did not take this advice or, if she did, one shudders to imagine the uncensored versions of letters. Once, when I urged Queen to sign up for an e-mail account so we could stay in closer touch, her response was revealing. She sighed, "It is a good thing e-mail didn't exist in Madalyn's day. Can you imagine if she didn't even have to pause to put a letter in an envelope?"

Instead of taking sides, however, Queen spent most of her time behind the scenes, acting as an officer in various organizations, attending endless planning sessions, getting newsletters printed, and stamping and stuffing envelopes.

In one area alone Queen seemed willing to emerge more conspicuously into the public eye: she began to lecture again, and often at organizations such as the Humanist Association of Los Angeles (HALA), that were critical of O'Hair. Queen often addressed the same subjects as O'Hair. For example, in program 45 of the American Atheist Radio Series entitled "The 'Christianity' of Our Founding as a Nation," O'Hair commented at length upon the repressive laws that characterized colonial America.[16] O'Hair's analysis bore a striking resemblance to passages within Queen's speech entitled "Our Secular Constitution." It also bore a striking resemblance to articles that appeared in *Queen Silver's Magazine*. The similarity between the two women was anything but remarkable. Indeed, it would have been remarkable if O'Hair and

Queen—coming from the same tradition, often using the same source material, and embodying the same approach—did not closely resemble each other on many levels.[17]

Queen once commented to me that she believed O'Hair's need to accuse everyone else of intellectual dishonesty revealed a deep insecurity about her own achievements. Perhaps the insecurity also accounts for O'Hair's tendency to attach "Doctor" to her name even on personal letters and documents. It may also account for her extraordinary sensitivity to offense. This characteristic became her tragic flaw. The stage was set for conflict.

The two women remained on friendly terms into the early 1980s. At the 1980 AA Convention, Queen was still highly enough regarded by O'Hair to receive the prestigious Pioneer Atheist Award. Queen had been personally nominated by O'Hair.

When O'Hair had requested material from Queen to support the nomination, Don Latimer had written back, explaining that Queen could not answer because she "has really been very busy trying to keep up the current Chapter work, banquet arrangements, etc."[18] The hard work paid off. Los Angeles became the largest of the forty-seven chapters of AA in the United States: by 1981, there were eight hundred names on the chapter's active mailing list.

A schism between the Austin home base and the L.A. chapter had been brewing for some time. Again, O'Hair had difficulty dealing with the people involved. The proximate cause of the split, however, was the annual Nativity display in a public area known as Palisades Park, owned by the city of Santa Monica. The chapter argued that the Christian display violated church-state separation: in short, they claimed a religious statement was being made on government property that was sustained by public money. In the end, John Edwards, the director of the L.A. branch of AA, compromised with the city. He erected a competing atheist exhibit in Palisades Park that featured the pagan origins of Christmas.

The response from Austin? "California can ruin everything for atheists," O'Hair told the *Los Angeles Times*. "If we go in (as part of the Santa Monica display), we only add to their right to be there."[19] Other chapters, such as Rhode Island and Denver, were apparently pursuing O'Hair's preferred strategy, namely, to sue the city authorities to remove the Christmas displays. Nevertheless, O'Hair told the *Los Angeles Times* that she did not believe the status of the L.A. chapter would be damaged within the freethought community by its dispute with Austin. The ensuing explosion would be of O'Hair's making.

On December 9, 1981, she and her son Jon unilaterally canceled the crowning annual event of the Los Angeles atheist community: the winter solstice dinner, which substituted for Christmas. In a letter to the L.A. leadership, O'Hair declared, "There will be no Solstice Banquet in Los Angeles and Jon and I have had to call off our trip there because of incompetence, malicious gossip, and an actual attempt to cause harm to Atheism."[20] It is not clear that the Austin group had the ability or authority to cancel the solstice dinner that had been locally planned and funded. But the Los Angeles chapter decided to abide by the decision. The celebration was canceled. The five leaders of the chapter also decided to resign and to channel their energies into a new organization.

Thus, Atheists United (AU) was born out of a bitter controversy with O'Hair. As Queen explained in her letter to Patterson, AU was

composed largely, but not entirely, of persons who were members of L.A. Chapter of AA.... There are some, like myself, who will continue membership in AA and support Austin's efforts as possible but who will support the new group locally. Some others have so much bitterness over personal attacks by Austin that they will have nothing to do with them any more. There will probably be some who were in the Chapter who will not join Atheists United, but will merge into already existing groups, such as Freedom From Religion Foundation, Humanist groups, etc.[21]

True to her word, Queen attempted to maintain both a private and a political relationship with O'Hair, discussing personal matters with her as well as atheist activities. For example, in one letter to O'Hair she wrote about a debilitating injury she had suffered when a man in a pickup truck had snatched her purse with sufficient force to pull Queen off the curb and into the street. She had been dragged a few feet before the strap broke. In the same letter, Queen enclosed a check for $500 to cover a life membership in AA. She also announced that she would be the first speaker to be featured in a series of freethought lectures to be held monthly at the Manhattan Beach Public Library. "It will be a reprise of material I have used at a couple of other groups," Queen informed O'Hair. The title of her talk was "Heroines of Freethought."[22]

In her own fashion, O'Hair attempted to maintain a relationship with Queen as well—but every relationship with O'Hair had to be on her own terms. One of the most interesting aspects of the memo in which she had canceled the L.A. Winter Solstice was O'Hair's unsubtle attempt to woo Queen's loyalties away from the wayward chapter toward the Austin point of view. The paragraph directly following the one announcing the cancellation—the third paragraph in an extremely long letter—stated, "We [Austin AA] have received many communications here which were vicious attacks against Queen Silver and Don Latimer. The theme advanced was that the enemies of Queen and Don within the chapter wanted 'more sophisticated,' 'younger,' and 'more personable' leaders." Of course, anyone who witnessed the respect and affection with which those two individuals were treated by fellow atheists in L.A. would dismiss those accusations as absurd. But O'Hair apparently thought Queen and Don would believe the worst of others.

After four dense pages crammed with accusation and ad hominem attacks, the second to the last line of O'Hair's letter announced, "We are, meanwhile, designating Queen Silver to retain the records and materials of the Chapter."

Perhaps O'Hair did not fully realize how savvy Queen was in the way of movement politics. Queen's response to being so abruptly designated as Austin's representative was: "This is the first I heard of that, and I will not be a part of it!"[23] Queen would pay for her refusal to align with the "correct" side of the dispute. On October 6, 1981, O'Hair had enrolled Queen "as a life member of American Atheists, in recognition of your support of this nonprofit and educational organization chartered in 1963 for diffusing knowledge and promoting freedom of the mind." A scant year later, in correspondence to Queen dated October 30, 1982, O'Hair denounced her as a "damnable liar." As for the personal library Queen had intended to donate to Austin AA, O'Hair commented, "You should shove your meager library up your ass for safe keeping."

The schism had more than a touch of irony to it. O'Hair was demonstrating—albeit to an exaggerated degree—the same sort of behavior that the teenaged Queen had displayed while presiding over her own magazine: namely, she alienated supporters and fellow travelers, she resorted to personal attacks, and she always claimed to be absolutely right. In her later years, Queen displayed the same exquisite patience toward O'Hair that many of her early supporters had shown to her. Of course, Queen had been a willful child when she had taxed the tolerance of others. O'Hair had no such excuse.

Queen's parting words to O'Hair showed how the test of time and circumstance had provided her with perspective without altering her basic determination.

> I have supported and will continue to support any organization fur-
> thering Atheism or Freethought or State/Church Separation, insofar
> as their activities further the principles to which I am committed.
> That support does *not* include allowing any group to dictate what
> other organizations I may support or belong to, what I may read, or
> with whom I may associate. I've never allowed that in the past and at
> this late date I'm not about to change. Calling me names isn't going to
> make any difference but it does say something about the person using
> the epithet.[24]

And, so, the two most powerful women in contemporary free-thought parted ways, never to cooperate again.

The Other Queen

The freethought movement did not begin to contain or satisfy Queen's political and intellectual energy, which spilled over into literally dozens of causes.[25] Two of them ranked particularly high in her priorities: the American Civil Liberties Union (ACLU) and the Los Angeles Public Library.

In later years, Queen's passion for freedom of speech not only led her to be a member of the ACLU, but also to sit on various of its committees, especially the Church/State Committee and Women's Rights. She was particularly concerned about legislation that restricted the discussion of evolution or any form of science. Queen's dedication to the ACLU was motivated by her concern at the growth of the Moral Majority, also commonly referred to as the Religious Right. She believed the Moral Majority to be the greatest threat to freedom of speech and women's rights.

As in all matters, however, Queen drew careful distinctions and definitions. She meticulously pointed out that the Right is not a monolith.

Some on the Right are primarily interested in economic and social issues, others in religious and social issues: there is the "Right" and the "Religious Right." The political position of the "Right" tended to be characterized by policies such as government-spending cuts, a free-market bias, the advocacy of states' rights, a hawkish military stand, and an active anti-Communism. The "Religious Right" might well incorporate all of these policies, but it also included other more religiously based ones. For example, it incorporated an antiabortion stance, the advocacy of prayer in school, and a pro-censorship bias toward graphic sexuality.

In speaking of the Moral Majority, Queen would ask her audience the question, "What can we do?" She would answer, "Be aware." How? People should gather and spread as much information on the Religious Right as possible. She also urged people to learn the mechanisms of government, for example, how laws get passed and how to contact the appropriate government representatives. She ended with the advice, "Get scared and get mad."

In private correspondence, Queen reinforced this message.

> I consider the present threat from the "Moral Majority" and other kindred groups to be so serious that I think it is absolutely imperative that Atheists cooperate with everyone who is fighting the "Moral Majority," whether we happen to agree with them in all other respects or not. In this as in some other areas, I differ from Austin [the AA headquarters and home of O'Hair]. So I am active in and on the board of directors of Humanist Society of Friends in Los Angeles and attend meetings of Humanist Association of Los Angeles. Also attend and am active on ACLU Church/State Committee which meets monthly for action on church/state matters. (Most of the current members are Atheists.)[26]

Queen's admiration for the ACLU was deep-rooted. It extended back to when, as a teenager, she had seen the organization stand up for the socialist radicals no one else seemed willing to champion. In a lecture, she explained the genesis of her affiliation:

> When the American Civil Liberties Union first came in we were in a post–World War I period of hysteria in which left-wing groups were being persecuted. Meetings were being broken up, people were being beaten up. I myself was in a meeting where the entire audience was

arrested and taken away. Half of the people in the room were American Legion men and they systematically arrested the other half. All during this period when the ACLU defended the Socialist Party, the IWW, the anarchists, no radical had anything but praise for them. Then there came a time when other groups were being attacked. The government found out that there were extremist groups on the right just as there were on the left. And they began investigating them and, when their rights were violated, the ACLU stepped in and took their cases. For example, the Jehovah's Witnesses and the American Nazi Party.

Remember that the ACLU started out defending people who were just as detestable, and they were severely criticized for defending socialists and communists in those days as they have been for defending Nazis today. Either you believe in the Bill of Rights as it is in the Constitution—freedom of speech means freedom of speech and freedom of the press means freedom of the press—or else you say I believe in freedom of speech for *me* but not for the other guy, and freedom of the press for *me* but not for the other guy. Well, all I can say is that if you take the latter stand don't come to me and ask for sympathy the next time your rights are violated, because you have brought it on yourself.[27]

Queen's passion for freedom of speech was paralleled by an unshakable conviction that information should be available to everyone, regardless of social or financial status. The conviction translated into a lifetime commitment to public libraries. In the article published by *Brain Power*, her stepfather Henry Roser quoted Grace as saying,

> Practically all of Queen's textbooks during the first three years of her education were procured from the Los Angeles Public Library. I could not have purchased them. She read over one thousand volumes before she was nine years of age, keeping in use the library cards of every member of the family.[28]

The thirteen-year-old Queen expressed her feelings about the profound importance of public libraries in an issue of *Queen Silver's Magazine*.

> Man is the evolutionary product of all his ancestors, and the thoughts, the life histories of all the men and animals which have gone before him go to make up his own thoughts and to form his own mind and create his own life history.

Before printing was invented, and before books were made cheaply, most of the thoughts and much of the experience of our human ancestors died when they died. Now, however, anyone who has an idea puts it down in printed form. The knowledge of the past is accessible to every child who can read. The great men of the world can not waste their time talking to individual children, or to grown people. Through their books they are willing to talk to the humblest and most ignorant....

I can not afford to buy a telescope, but I can buy, or get from a public library, books on astronomy which have the finest maps and photographic plates. I can learn, from these books, in a few weeks, facts which astronomers have spent hundreds of years in learning.

I can not afford a good microscope, or dissecting tools, but from books of geology, biology, and meteorology I can study reproductions of photographs taken with the aid of high-powered microscopes. In a short time, I can gain the benefit of knowledge which some man has spent his life in acquiring.

I can not afford to travel all over the earth, and see strange peoples in stranger lands. But every traveler who has the ability to observe, and to write down his impressions, does so. At the Los Angeles Public Library, fifteen miles from my home, I can get a book about any country which has ever been on a map. It would have cost me many thousands of dollars to have personally visited all the countries I have read about. Besides, in order to learn, from personal observation, all what these writers have told me, I would have to live to be many hundreds of years old.

If you live in a city, and want to get dinner for yourself, you will not raise your own wheat, grind your own flour, or kill your own meat. You will take the products of the labor of many men, in many countries, and from them you will select your dinner.

It is the same with the knowledge supplied by books. Very few people can be original investigators, for they have not the ability, time, opportunity, or money necessary. Anyone who desires can utilize the knowledge discovered by the original thinkers of the world and can make it his own. Anyone who possesses originality of thought can take the knowledge thus acquired from others, add to it the products of his own brain, and, if he chooses, hand it onto others.

Each new invention is the result of some earlier invention made by a previous inventor.

Each new discovery is made possible by some previous discovery.

Each new thought is the product of all our past thinking.

Where, except in books, is the knowledge of other men, races, and societies made so easily available?[29]

Inevitably—as happened with all of Queen's passions—her dedication to public libraries found political expression. In fact, Queen's involvement had been political almost from the start. The *Los Angeles Record* of June 7, 1921, had exclaimed of Queen in headlines, "Educated in Library She Is Bond Booster." Queen later explained to me the incident that had inspired the newspaper account. When Queen had been ten years old, she and Grace had moved into East Hollywood, three blocks from the Cahuenga branch library. Queen haunted the library. She spent so much time there that the librarian jokingly suggested she bring a mattress with her and just start sleeping over.

Shortly afterward, the same librarian asked Queen if she would be willing to campaign in an upcoming election, which included voting on a library bond. The funding, if obtained, would be used to construct a downtown public library. There was a problem, however. Queen explained to me that, despite her ease on public stage, she was painfully shy in dealing with people on a one-on-one basis. Personal conversation was far more difficult for her than speaking in front of crowds of people. Nevertheless, the shy ten-year-old took armfuls of leaflets and went door-to-door to hand them out at every house within a six-block radius of where she lived. She forced herself to explain to everyone who asked why the public library was important to children. On the day of the election, Queen went to her local precinct and continued to distribute literature. The bond passed and the Los Angeles downtown public library was built.

A moment that echoed this history occurred seven decades later during a lecture Queen delivered to a freethought group. She stepped out of character by making what she called a "point of personal privilege." By this phrase, Queen meant that she was momentarily abandoning her usually rigid principle of not telling people in the audience what conclusion to reach, which opinion to hold, or how to vote. On at least one issue, she was willing to break with this otherwise firm policy.

The issue was public libraries. Again an upcoming election in Los Angeles included a library bond. The books in the Los Angeles downtown public library—the same one for which she had campaigned at ten years old—had been severely damaged by an arson fire and by the water used to control the blaze. The bond would be used to restore the books and building. Stepping into a familiar role, the seventy-seven-year-old Queen vigorously urged people to vote for the library.

On August 31, 1988, Queen received a gold-sealed parchment of appreciation from Mayor Tom Bradley and the board of library commissioners in recognition of her unstinting support. On October 3, 1993, at the opening ceremonies of the new Los Angles Central Public Library, Queen joined Mayor Reardon, writer Ray Bradbury, and other notables in a place of honor on the speakers' platform. Her presence was in recognition of an almost century-long effort to preserve libraries in Los Angeles.

Notes

1. From the passionate and intimate letters written to Queen by Grace while she was stranded in Alaska, I assume the two women had an emotionally rich and psychologically complex relationship and that Queen's subsequent silence about this aspect of her mother was part of her discretion and sense of privacy.

2. Queen also carried important papers, such as identification, in the underarm pouch. Over the course of years, she gave me several of these pouches, then ceased doing so when I never used one.

3. In a letter to Gordon Stein dated February 19, 1976, Queen wrote, "A great deal of time has gone by and I have moved numerous times in the past forty-five years or so, with the result that I don't have available any correspondence files or files of the magazine. It is possible that there may be some material in some very old boxes in my garage which I hope to find time and strength to sort out someday, but I really don't know what is there."

4. The other person was Don Latimer, who shared the house with Queen for several years before moving out to assume a burden of family responsibility.

5. I understand that there may have been other psychological reasons for Queen's behavior. Knowing her and the circumstances, this motivation is the one I believe to be true.

6. At various times in the controversy that erupted from the mid-1960s through the early 1980s, Madalyn Murray O'Hair was referred to as either Murray or O'Hair. As other parties in the controversies were called "Murray" —e.g., her two sons—I have chosen to consistently refer to her as O'Hair.

7. The long-lived *Truth Seeker* continued to publish, but the editorship had been assumed by James Hervey Johnson whom many atheists backed away from due to disagreements. For example, he tended to print material that many believed to be racist and anti-Semitic.

8. I use the past tense because Madalyn Murray disappeared some years ago. Most people presume her to be dead. Others within the atheist movement claim she may be living in New Zealand. I believe the evidence overwhelmingly points to the probability of her death.

9. The original attack was published in the April 1964 *American Atheist,* then reprinted. Negri noticed only the reprint and protested its contents in an open letter to Murray dated June 3, 1964.

10. Lemoin Cree, *They Came...As Agents of the Church,* July 14, 1964, p. 1.

11. Ibid., p. 4. The accusations of Murray's pilfering of funds, mailing lists, and other organization records were further presented by Cree in the four-paged *Other Americans Newsletter,* no. 8 (August 1964).

12. From an anonymous circular in Queen's files on Madalyn, which is entitled "Madalyn Murray Convicted by Her Own Words" and dated October 5, 1965.

13. The accusation was made in an undated membership bulletin, signed by William J. Murray, requesting donations from true atheists. Those with a background of involvement in radical causes will be familiar with the phenomenon of shell organizations whose membership may consist of no more than three or four people. I don't know if the International Freethought Press ever produced material beyond the membership bulletin.

14. Some of the viciousness of the dispute may well have stemmed from the fact that family members were feuding on all sides. The April 28, 1966, *Honolulu Adviser* had carried a story detailing Murray's threat to fight her own mother in court. By October 30, 1979, the *National Enquirer* ran an exposé on O'Hair in which her son William Murray publicly accused her of everything from fraud to theft to trying to defect to the Soviet Union (p. 28). William would later find religion and denounce his former atheist activities: he had been a key figure in Murray's appeal to the Supreme Court to ban prayer in public schools.

15. In a letter dated January 25, 1966, a former supporter, A. H. Baumgardt, accused all three of mail fraud and urged an investigation.

16. The program was reprinted in *American Atheist,* July 1983, pp. 26–27.

17. O'Hair was prone to accusing people of plagiarism. For example, in a letter dated November 9, 1981, to Dick James, O'Hair accused Al Seckel, a well-respected member of the Los Angeles chapter of American Atheists of plagiarizing an article on Hypatia apparently on the grounds that, in a popularly aimed piece, he had used data, dates, etc. from a biographical encyclopedia. O'Hair had been apparently working on a similar article. Queen's piece "Pioneers of Freethought" in the first year of *Queen Silver's Magazine* discussed Hypatia in detail and, thus, preceded both of the others in question.

18. The letter is dated February 4, 1979, and signed by Don Latimer, Director, Los Angeles County Chapter. In it, he explains that Queen has nothing more than a scrapbook of clippings that are in poor condition. "She has still been unable to locate complete copies of the magazine," he explained.

19. As reported in the *Los Angeles Times,* December 12, 1981.

20. As quoted from a four-page memo dated December 9, 1981, signed by Madalyn Murray O'Hair, President (AA), and Jon Murray, Director, American Athiest [*sic*] Center. The memo was written on Society of Separationists, Inc. letterhead.

21. Letter from Queen to Warren W. Patterson dated July 23, 1982.

22. As quoted from a letter from Queen to Murray dated September 2, 1981. The letter was in response to an undated letter to Queen from Murray, with an envelope stamped August 23, 1981. Murray's letter stated, in part, "I miss hearing from you. You took damn good care of that chapter when it was beginning...now I feel like I've lost an old friend.... [T]hank you for converting your 'loan' to the Trust Fund to a gift."

23. As quoted by Dick James in "Fact Sheet" dated December 12, 1981, which responded to the Murray memo. Queen later confirmed this statement to me personally.

24. Letter from Queen Silver to Dr. Madalyn Murray O'Hair, dated October 21, 1982.

25. Just a sampling of the non–civil service membership cards that Queen carried in one wallet or another in the last decades of her life includes: Library Foundation of Los Angeles (charter member), Library of Congress Association, Amnesty International, American Civil Liberties Union, Humanist Association of Los Angeles, American Humanist Association, Humanist Society of Friends, Americans United for Separation of Church and State, Skeptics Society, American Atheists, Atheist United (sustaining member), Democratic National Committee, Democratic Congressional Campaign Committee, Democratic Senatorial Campaign Committee, California State Democratic Party, Presidential Trust Fund, The Southern Poverty Law Center, Independent Action, People for the American Way Action Fund, Save the Senate Fund, Americans Against Human Suffering (sustaining member), the National Health Federation, Wildlife Waystation, The Nature Conservancy, Greater Los Angeles Zoo Association (charter member), Tree People, Sierra Club, California Museum Foundation, Ellis Island Foundation (charter member), National Organization for Women, National Abortion Rights Action League, Natural History Museum (Page Museum), The Armand Hammer Museum of Art and Cultural Center (charter member), Friends of the Observatory, Inc., Descanso Gardens Guild, Inc., Hollywood Entertainment Museum, Southwest Museum Casa de Adobe, KCET, Los Angeles County Museum of Art, the Smithsonian Institution, National Council of Senior Citizens, Inc., American Association of Retired Persons, International Senior Citizens Association, Federation of Senior Citizen Clubs of Los Angeles City, and The Boston Computer Society.

26. Letter to Warren W. Patterson dated July 23, 1982.

27. From a lecture delivered on November 25, 1978, entitled "Sense and Nonsense About Equal Rights."

28. *Brain Power Monthly,* p. 55.

29. *QSM* 1, no. 2 (First Quarter 1924): 8.

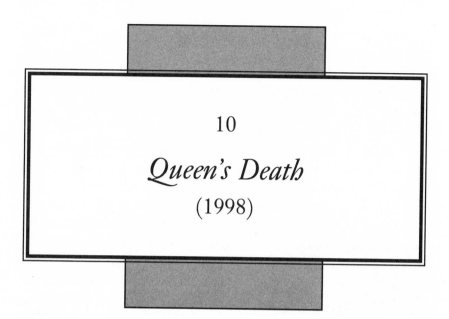

10

Queen's Death
(1998)

QUEEN HAD BEEN a sustaining member of Americans Against Human Suffering since 1987: the slogan on her membership card read, "Freedom of Choice for Physician Aid-in-Dying." She also carried in her wallet a printed quotation from Justice William J. Brennan: "A quiet, proud death, bodily integrity intact, is a matter of extreme consequence." Queen's death did not reflect quietness, pride, or bodily integrity. It reflected the type of medical policy against which Queen had spoken out for decades. Her death reflected our society's opinion that the elderly are disposable.

Queen said that November 10, 1997, began as a normal day. She had two errands to run, and a doctor's appointment on the next afternoon. At some point, she began to throw up repeatedly, which prompted her to call the one person upon whom she most relied, Don Latimer. After hearing her symptoms, Don insisted that she go to Kaiser Hospital and he called there to ensure that the doctors knew she was coming. Sylvia Valle, who lived closer than Don, drove Queen to the hospital.

Queen was diagnosed with pancreatic failure caused by a stone that was obstructing a duct. The stone was eliminated and she was due to be released from the hospital the next day. Queen had started to make concrete plans to move into a retirement home appropriately named Sunset House since it was located on Sunset Boulevard in Hollywood. As Queen described it, the place was a retirement home for old radicals, most of whom were of a socialist bent. There would be no lack of like minds with whom to debate politics and to reminisce. In earlier conversations with me, Queen had wondered aloud whether she would find the pace at Sunset House too strenuous: apparently residents were expected to participate in protests on a regular basis. Or, at least, that was the impression with which I was left.

The location of the retirement home was also attractive. It was on a good bus route, which meant she could still attend all her committee meetings at the ACLU. Queen was adamant about remaining active in old age: indeed, she was also a member of the Gray Panthers. I vividly remember how her militancy about aging with dignity emerged during a bus ride. We were seated near the front, as close to the driver as possible, for reasons of personal safety. An elderly man boarded the bus. The man was soon directing a stream of abuse at the driver who was clearly trying to be helpful. About a minute into the tirade, Queen slowly rose from her seat, planted herself midaisle, and faced the man, now silenced by surprise. "*You,*" she proclaimed, "are the sort of old person that gives old people a bad name." Then she sat down—as did the man.

Queen's plans to move into Sunset House disintegrated in the wake of what happened on the night before her expected release. There are different versions of the story. I intend to relate the facts as Queen revealed them to me.

One fact seems incontrovertible. During the night, when Queen attempted to leave her bed and go to the bathroom by herself, she fell. In response to the fall, the hospital tied her down to the bed although she pleaded with them not to do so. Queen was claustrophobic, and the feeling of being restrained—especially within an institution she had feared almost since birth—terrified her. The hospital's response was to inject Queen with sedatives despite her vigorous protest. The hours that ensued were, in Queen's words to me, "the worst night of my life," including the night Grace had died.

Queen reacted badly to the drugs. Strapped to the bed, and terrified of the hospital staff whom she called "her torturers," Queen watched a television that had been left switched on. According to Queen, a horror movie was broadcast that night. She watched and screamed and called for someone to help her, to turn the set off. No one came. I do not know if the story of the television is accurate or whether the drugs induced false memories. I do believe that she screamed out and no one came. On one visit to the intensive care unit, a friend and I arrived to find that the blood pressure machine attached to Queen was blaring out an alarm. Queen was unconscious. What I assume was a nurse was sitting outside the room, about two dozen feet away. I ran to the woman. She snapped back at me before I could speak, "I hear it. Do you think I'm deaf?" When I demanded something be done, she said, "Talk to a doctor" and would not respond further.

Also according to Queen, no one loosened the restraints on her arms for three days although she pleaded constantly with the staff and with everyone who visited her. Queen intended to sue the hospital—not for money, but for an apology—and the doctors were worried enough to hold a conference of sorts at her bedside a few weeks later to inquire about her complaints.

After experiencing days of terror, Queen had a stroke that paralyzed her left side and left her bedridden.[1] The stroke precluded Sunset House as a possible residence because the retirement home did not accept the severely debilitated. I heard of Queen's stroke on a Saturday night when my husband woke me with the news. At 6 A.M. on the following Monday I was on an airplane from Toronto to Los Angeles. When I entered Queen's room in intensive care, I did not recognize her. Her cheeks looked like the rouged circles you see on the face of a clown, probably because her blood pressure was so high. Everything else looked gaunt and wasted. The first words she spoke to me were, "Get me out of here."

The first thing I said to her was, "Queen, how well is your mind working?" She replied with a slight slur to her voice, "Medium. Like a day without coffee." At that point, I became determined to get her out of the hospital.

Queen told me she had been bound to the bed without release for three days. Because my father-in-law is a medical doctor, I knew that such a practice, if true, violated the law in just about every state. I asked a social worker attached to the hospital how frequently a doctor had signed off on the recurring paperwork that was necessary for the hospital to legally restrain a patient over such a long period. In short, I wanted to know whether the restraint had been conducted in accordance with the law. A doctor became suddenly available and appeared at Queen's bedside to discuss the situation.

Also at the bedside was one of Queen's closest friends, Robert Seeman, a lawyer.[2] He and I had discussed "strategy" while awaiting the doctor. Accordingly I notified my father-in-law that he would receive a phone call from me. (Don Latimer was also at Queen's side, as always.) I have been told that two things are necessary to secure the dignity and rights of a hospital patient: the first is legal representation or the threat thereof; the second is an independent, outside medical authority who shows an interest in the case. Both were lined up.

The doctor arrived. He was intelligent, attractive, and he seemed to truly care about Queen's welfare. But this favorable impression quickly dissolved. He told me—in Queen's presence!—that I was fortunate because I had not been at her bedside a few days earlier when Queen had been raving and needed to be strapped down. With this statement, he absolutely dismissed her statements about being ignored and otherwise mistreated by the hospital staff. He wanted to know what complaints *we*—Don and I—had against the hospital.

Queen began to speak. He silenced her by saying, "I'll hear from *you* last." When he asked me about my complaints, I gave a dry recitation that ended with the observation that if Queen were not released from intensive care her elevated blood pressure would kill her. Don and Bob added their perspective, with Bob mentioning how much he enjoyed cross-examining doctors on the stand. Then Queen spoke. Or, rather, she tried to. The doctor silenced her again. She kept trying to tell her story. At one point, Queen and I made eye contact and I said, "Passive resistance." At this, Queen turned her head away from the doctor, who was giving her a lecture on the hospital's position, namely, she was a patient, and they knew best. Queen closed her eyes and mimicked sleep. To his credit, the man realized something was going on. He stopped speaking for a few seconds. Then he continued, prefacing himself with the words, "I know you can hear me..." Nevertheless, the doctor's lecture now seemed awkward and almost embarrassing to him.

From the phone at Queen's bedside, I called my father-in-law and handed the receiver to the hospital's doctor. As he answered my father-in-law's medical questions, we learned many aspects of Queen's condition for the first time. Bob listened with special care.

When the doctor had first arrived, he had told me there were no regular hospital rooms available into which Queen could be transferred from ICU. A half-hour after the conference at Queen's bedside, a "regular" bed was found. She was out of ICU within twenty-four hours. Her blood pressure immediately sank to and remained at a safe level. But the paralysis resulting from the stroke did not improve. As Don and I observed her from day to day, we came to believe that other, smaller strokes may have occurred. She went in and out of consciousness, sometimes becoming almost impossible to rouse. And, yet, I had the suspicion that Queen was using, at least now and then, the same tactic she had employed with the doctor: passive resistance. She wanted to die.

Queen often told visitors that she needed to "go home." Don wondered if her insistence had anything to do with the quick method of suicide she had arranged years in advance, which awaited her there. All doubt about Queen's state of mind was removed by an exchange that occurred with an employee of the convalescent home into which Queen was transferred from the hospital. The woman asked Don, "Does Queen want to live?" The question stunned him, leaving him unable to reply. She asked the question of Queen.

"Do you want to live?" she asked Queen twice. No response came.

She changed the question. "Do you want to die?"

In the strongest voice Don had heard from her in days, Queen responded, "Yes!"

The remaining details of Queen's death are not pleasant and I doubt she would want me to share them. But there was one evening when she was able to become Queen Silver again for a few hours. It was at the Winter Solstice celebration held by Atheists United. With Don's assistance and a nurse, Queen attended the banquet and her presence drew rounds of sustained applause from the crowd. She began with an anecdote about Charlie Chaplin—a man with whom she felt great affinity and whose movies were included in her very selective video library. Queen recounted how he had received a lifetime achievement award after enduring painful years of ostracism, much of it political. Upon receiving the award and a standing ovation, Chaplin had said, "I can't cope with so much love." Neither could Queen. Overcome with emotion at the palpable love aimed in her direction, she had to pause several times to collect herself.

She died shortly thereafter, on January 7, 1998.

During the days I sat by her bedside at the hospital and at the convalescent home, Queen and I had several conversations. She talked more candidly than ever before. She told me of having had two abortions. She ended by saying, "I have never been ashamed of anything," then turned her face away from me.

Almost sixteen years earlier, Grace's body had been cremated and her ashes scattered on the Pacific Ocean. At Queen's request, her body joined the same waters.

Queen once made the observation,

> We can look back on a period in which hundreds of thousands of people risked their liberty and their lives that we might have the degree of freedom we do. We walk, metaphorically, and sometimes not so metaphorically, in the blood-stained footprints of people before us who did not expect immortality. Their immortality is in the fact that they are in the loving memories of us, and the best memorial that we can do for them is to see to it that the work they did goes on.[3]

Rest in peace.

Notes

1. In my opinion, the stroke was due to elevated blood pressure caused by the terror of being powerless in the hands of the medical establishment.

2. Bob Seeman's kindness and attentions to Queen cannot be overstated—not merely while she was ill, but for many years prior when he went gladly out of his way to make sure she had transportation to meetings and anywhere else

she wanted to go. At the Winter Solstice that Queen attended shortly before her death, she told a story that expressed her feelings for Bob in a typically understated manner. She related her stepfather's (Roser's) favorite joke: Two lawyers are walking in a graveyard and they pause before a tombstone that reads, "Here lies an attorney and an honest man." One lawyer says to the other, "Why did they put two men in one grave?" Queen commented that Bob would need only one.

3. From the question and answer period of a lecture entitled "Pioneers of Freethought," date and venue unspecified on tape.

Part Two
Selected Writings

Evolution from Monkey to Bryan

A lecture in reply to William Jennings Bryan,
delivered at Music-Arts Hall, Los Angeles, California,
on March 1, 1923.

For introductory material, please see pages 53–56 of this book.

NEARLY A YEAR ago William Jennings Bryan, writing in the *New York Times*, said to the defenders of Evolution: "Come down out of the trees and discuss the subject." As soon as I read his challenge, I wrote an open letter to Bryan, challenging him to debate with me upon the subject of Evolution. He has never made any reply, other than to say that he will not debate with anyone who does not accept the story of creation laid down by Moses in the book of

Genesis. In other words, Bryan says that he will not debate with anyone who knows more than himself. I climbed down out of my tree especially to debate with Bryan, and what do I find? I find that this only surviving troglodyte now remaining in America has gone into his hole and pulled the hole in after him.

I have often wondered why man, who is generally supposed to have a brain much superior to that of any other animal, should cling to the superstitions of his ignorant, savage ancestors. The reasoning of some people belongs back in those ages of the world when civilization was unknown. Modern people want automobiles and airplanes, palace cars and great steamships when they travel; and they want fine, comfortable homes to live in. They want the best that modern science can give them in the way of food, clothing, and shelter. Why, then, do they go back to the ages of ignorance and savagery for their thoughts, their ethics, and their religions? I shall try to tell you.

In my last lecture I traced the Evolution of thought, or as I prefer to call it, the "Evolution of Brain Power," from its earliest beginnings in the animal world up to man. In that lecture I showed you how much the animals resemble man. In this lecture I shall try to show you how much man resembles the other animals, especially the ape. It is my contention that man is today far more like the ape than he is like the man he will become after a few million more years of Evolution. Man is not merely a descendant of an extinct species of ape—to all intents and purposes he is still an ape. Both Haeckel and Huxley place man in the same order as the old world apes. Darwin traces man's descent from the ape and the tailed monkey back through the pouched, or marsupial, animals, then back through countless other forms of life to the single-celled amoeba which wraps its whole body about its food in order to devour it.

When I listen to certain people, I am almost convinced that they, at least, have not yet caught up with the ape. For, at least, the ape is always curious, always looking for something new, always ready to acquire new knowledge and to use it; and when man shrinks from a new idea, he voluntarily places himself lower than the ape.

William Jennings Bryan is a fair example of the survival of a primitive mind in a modern body. He travels in a Pullman car, not on donkey back; but he goes back to the donkey-back age of the world for his science and his religion. He would not hire Moses to fix his typewriter, but he goes to Moses for his knowledge of Biology, Geology, and

Astronomy. Bryan says that the theory of Evolution is not reasonable to him; he would substitute for the theory of Evolution the mythical account of creation found in the book of Genesis. He considers that reasonable.

Bryan says he doesn't want any "brute philosophy." He prefers to believe that we came from mud. Mud is sacred—monkeys are not. Bryan wants to believe that his ancestor was made from mud, that his god "breathed the breath of life into him," that is to say he would have attacked Evolution long ago—only, most likely, he never heard of it!

Bryan and his friends propose to suppress by law the teachings of modern science, just as a few hundred years ago, those teachings were suppressed by the church. He proposes first to forbid the teaching in the schools of any scientific facts which may happen to conflict with his particular brand of mythology. Then, after raising up one generation of schoolchildren who will be as ignorant of such matters as were their ancestors a hundred years ago, Bryan figures that there will be enough ignorant voters to get a law passed forbidding the teaching of Evolution anywhere, in school, on the platform, or in printed form. After all this is accomplished, Bryan probably figures that the American people will have no more sense than he has, and will be sufficiently ignorant to elect him president. He will thus achieve his lifelong ambition.

One defender of Evolution went so far as to say, in an attempt to placate the enemies of Darwinism: "Neither Darwin nor any other competent biologist ever said that the human race descended from apes."

Allow me to quote to you, from the greatest writers on this subject, a few sentences: First of all, from Darwin's *Descent of Man*, chapter 6, page 150, of the Macmillan edition:

> Our great anatomist and philosopher, Prof. Huxley, has fully discussed this subject, "Man's Place in Nature," and concludes that man in all of his organization differs less from the higher apes than those do from lower members of the same group. Consequently, "there is no justification for placing man in a distinct order."

Chapter 6, page 153, of the same volume,

> There can, consequently, hardly be a doubt that man is an offshoot of the old world simian stem, and that under a genealogical point of view he must be classed with the Catarrhine division.

This means that Darwin classes man among the apes whose noses point downwards. Some people have the opposite type of nose, however—a real monkey nose.

Chapter 6, page 165,

> In the class of mammals the steps are not difficult to conceive which led from the ancient monotremata to the ancient marsupials; and from these to the large progenitors of the placental mammals. We may thus ascend to the lemuridae; and the interval is not very wide from these to the simiaedae. The simiaedae then branched off into two great stems, the new world and old world monkeys; and from the latter, at a remote period, man, the wonder and glory of the universe, proceeded.

Haeckel says, on page 539 of the *Evolution of Man*: "In his whole organization, and in his origin, man is a true Catarrhine—he originated in the old world from an unknown, extinct group of eastern apes."

The whole of chapter 28 of his *History of Creation* is devoted to claiming the descent of man "from the anthropoid, eastern apes."

It is true that modern biologists do not claim that man is descended from any existing species of ape. The modern man and the modern ape probably sprang from a common and possibly lower type than either. Evolutionists do not stop when they have traced man's ancestry back to the ape; they keep on and show that some of his other ancestors were far less desirable types. A man can't help it, if his ancestors were apes. He does not have to make a monkey out of himself for that reason, nor does he need to turn his children into unthinking little apes—or worse. Do you realize that while man is better able to think than the other animals, yet they always use their thinking powers to the utmost in their daily lives, while man, alone of all the animals, is afraid to think, and afraid to let his thoughts become known through his actions?

In the past the penalty given to a scientist for independent thinking was torture or death. Copernicus dared not allow his great theory to be published till after he was dead. Galileo was compelled in order to save his life, to kneel at the feet of a priest and swear never again to teach anyone that the world was round and that it revolved upon its axis. William Jennings Bryan, if he has his way, will not only forbid the spread of knowledge, but he will make the discoverers of scientific truth afraid to write or speak, lest they be fined or imprisoned. He will make schoolteachers teach lies, or starve them out of their jobs. America established public schools in order to keep religious creeds, dogmas, and superstitions away from children until their minds had developed understanding. Bryan proposes to allow the churches to control the education of the young in the public schools; he would forbid the teaching of any scientific discovery made since Moses wrote the account of creation four thousand years ago. He would plunge the world back four thousand years, and he would do it by legal force. When people like him can not talk others into believing what they want them to believe, they immediately get busy and forbid anyone to believe anything else. Bryan must use force instead of reason because he and his kind are not reasoning beings. He belongs back in the Dark Ages, when ignorance and superstition ruled the world.

One of Darwin's theories was that a species of plant or animal might occasionally, under unusual conditions, develop an individual having certain more or less distinct advantages over its fellows. These individuals, being improvements over others of their species, would naturally have a better chance of surviving in the struggle for existence, and, consequently, the descendants of these improved varieties would ultimately produce other and better variations. Finally, a new species might evolve by means of this process, which he termed "natural selection."

Now, along comes Bryan with the statement: "No species has ever been transformed into any other species." This, if it were true, would be a denial of Darwin's theory of natural selection. You must remember that Bryan holds that every species of animal life, and of plant life, has always been just as it is now, except man, who has been getting worse ever since he was made.

Luther Burbank took a variety of Teosinte grass from the highlands of Mexico, and after seventeen years of selection—without crossing it with any other plant—produced by this process perfect specimens of Indian corn, with ears five to six inches in length. There is one instance showing how one species of plant may be evolved from another species by selection. One alone is enough to prove that *Bryan does not know what he is talking about.*

Burbank accomplished, by seventeen years of brain-directed artificial selection, the same results which nature, assisted perhaps by the Indian planters, required thousands of years to do. If Luther Burbank could change grass into corn in seventeen years, how long do you suppose it would take to change a monkey into a Bryan?

Our common potatoes, two hundred years ago, were no bigger than walnuts; the tomato until seventy-five years ago was only as large as a grape, and considered unfit to eat. Selection and cultivation, guided by man's intelligence, has made them what they now are. Nature working alone might have required thousands of years to reach the same goal.

Another means by which new species of plants and animals have been developed has been by the crossing, and often recrossing, of two or more distinct species. Again, the crossing of two varieties of the same species sometimes produces something entirely different from either of the parents. The thornless blackberry, for example, is the product of much crossing, and selection. All of its parents, however, had thorns. The same is true of the thornless cactus. The shasta daisy is descended from four different daisies—none of which is much like the shasta. Much more experimenting has been done with plants than with animals. If a man should ever do the same thing in the animal world that Luther Burbank has done in the plant world, I think some very interesting discoveries would be made.

It used to be supposed that such crossing would destroy the fertility of the offspring, but we now know that this is not always true. The cattalo is a new animal created by crossing the buffalo with common cattle. There is a new fowl which is half turkey and half hen, which has been developed here in California. Anyone who has studied the history of dogs knows that all the different varieties of those animals have sprung from a common stock.

Numerous plants have undoubtedly been crossed successfully without the aid of man. The loganberry, for instance, a cross between a raspberry and a blackberry, developed spontaneously only a few years ago. Evolution thus made a new berry—one which Bryan's god had never even thought of making. Bryan himself has eaten fruits and vegetables which did not exist a few hundred years ago.

I have explained what natural selection means. Artificial selection means simply putting man's brains behind natural laws, and forcing them to operate intelligently, toward a certain goal instead of blindly. By this means man has developed both the two-minute racehorse and the heavy draft animal from the same stock. The fat modern hog does not look much like his wild ancestors, but if he is compelled to dig his own roots to eat, as he does in Arkansas, you notice that he quickly reverts to his primitive type. Bryan does not look much like a cannibal chief. But if his parents had been stranded on one of the South Sea Islands, and he had grown up in a savage environment, he would have thought no more of eating human flesh than he now thinks of eating oyster stew. That is but another way of saying that while it may have taken millions of years for man to come up from the monkey, he will revert back to type very quickly if given the least opportunity.

Bryan has said that he will not debate the question of Evolution with anyone who does not accept the Bible as infallible authority. So, of course, he will not debate with me. Yet if Bryan believes his Bible, he ought to believe in some kinds of Evolution. Otherwise, how is he going to account for the fact that black men, brown men, yellow men, red men, white men, and so on, have all descended from the same man and woman that were made out of dirt six thousand years ago? Bryan seems to know as little about his Bible as he does about science, history, or statesmanship.

Another point which I would like to call Bryan's attention to is this: How does he manage to account for the existence of his god, without the aid of some sort of Evolution? In other words, Who made your god, Mr. Bryan?

Bryan will have a ready answer to that. He will say, "God always was here—no one made him." But, if he is here, he must have had a beginning. If he was not created, he must have evolved. If no one made god, then he must be the product of Evolution. He must have been spontaneously generated out of nothingness. Now, I would like to ask Mr. Bryan if it is not more reasonable to admit that a single cell of protoplasm, too small to be seen with the naked eye, might spontaneously develop in the warm waters of the primeval ocean, and that from this cell all future life ultimately developed, than it is to accept his theory that an all-knowing, all-powerful god could have spontaneously developed out of nothing, at a time when, according to Moses, there was no heaven, no earth, no light, no darkness—nothing but nothing, everywhere and anywhere?

Bryan says that an amoeba could not develop spontaneously—but his wonderful god could and did do so! Bryan believes in the spontaneous generation of life—as applied to gods, but regards similar ideas as applied to cellular life as absurd.

Scientists do not believe that anything ever originated out of nothing. They know, first, that all forms of matter are subject to constant change in form and structure, but that matter itself is indestructible. The

amount of matter in the world is always the same, whether it be in a
gaseous, liquid, or solid form. They know that this first life cell was not
made from nothing, nor was it something new added to the material on
the earth. Conditions of temperature, moisture, and light became exactly
right at a certain time to develop living cells under chemical reaction.

Dr. E. J. Allen, writing in the *Scientific Monthly*, of Lancaster, Pennsylvania, says:

> Where could the first animals or plants get their food when there was
> nothing on the world but mineral matter? Of late we are beginning to
> get light on the problem. The wall between living and nonliving
> matter is crumbling. Certain sugars and proteins, such as the plant
> forms that we eat, can now be made in the laboratory out of inorganic
> material. Artificial cells have been constructed that grow and crawl
> and feed themselves and stick out feelers and subdivide very much
> like living cells. It has been found that ultraviolet rays, that is, light of
> such short rays that it can not be seen, can convert water and carbon
> dioxide into sugar as chlorophyll does. These short rays are not con-
> tained in the sunshine which reaches our earth today, but it is found
> that ordinary rays may act in the same way in the presence of certain
> substances, such as iron rust in the water. These same rays are able to
> incorporate the nitrogen of mineral salts into compounds like the pro-
> tein of the living cell. So here we see the possibility that the action of
> the sunlight on the sea in primordial periods—or even in the pre-
> sent—might produce sufficient food to give a single cell a start in life
> and enable it to grow and develop into higher forms.

It is possible to understand how a single primitive cell may have
been developed by chemical action from previously existing matter. It is
now up to Mr. Bryan to show us how his god could have developed spontaneously, at a time when, according to Bryan, there was no existing form
of matter—nothing but nothingness everywhere. Bryan's theology is as
illogical as his "science" is ridiculous. He should go back to the kindergarten and learn his elementary lessons over again before he undertakes
to tell the American people what they shall study. His mental development belongs back in the time of the cave dwellers. That is why I always
call Bryan the "troglodyte." His mind dwells in the caves of superstition.
He is what Evolutionists call an "atavism." That is to say, a reversion to a
more primitive form. If he had lived two hundred years ago, he would
have burned witches; if he had lived two hundred years before that, he

would have been a religious persecutor like Torquemada. His mind is so much a part of the past that any new idea is offensive to him. He would have attacked Evolution years ago, only he was so busy talking about grape juice and attending to his duties as an elder of the Presbyterian church that he never heard of Evolution, or of Darwin, until three years ago. Bryan belongs to that class of people of whom it has been said: "Millions now living don't know that they are dead." The worst of it is that he can not rest until everyone is taught to be as ignorant as he is.

"There is not an organ nor a bone in your body which has not been inherited from the ape," says Haeckel in the *Evolution of Man.* Comparison of the various bones and organs of man with those of the gorilla show, in fact, that there is less difference between man and the gorilla, than there is between the gorilla and the other apes. It is not of any great consequence to argue that man did not come from any existing species of ape. We know that he did not, for the apes themselves, as well as man, have been evolving. If it makes you feel any better to think that your grandfather's cousin—but not your grandfather—was an ape, why, all right. People who can't bear to believe that they sprang from the ape have no difficulty in believing that they came from a chunk of mud. As a matter of fact, man's ancestry does not stop with the ape; it goes many million years further back into the animal world. If you are interested in solving this problem for yourselves, I suggest that you get and read Ernest Haeckel's *Evolution of Man.* He will most certainly convince you, if you are capable of simple reasoning, that man is the latest product of the evolution of mammalian life. He will show you that the body of man has evolved from the bodies of the lower forms of life, and that the mind of man has likewise evolved from the minds of the other mammals. Let me quote to you a few sentences from the last chapter in the *Evolution of Man.*

> The resistance to the theory of descent from the apes is clearly due in most men to feeling rather than to reason. They shrink from the notion of such an origin, just because they see in the ape-organism a caricature of man, a distorted and unattractive image of themselves; because it hurts man's aesthetic complacency and self-ennoblement. It is more flattering to think we have descended from some lofty and godlike being—and so, from the earliest times, human vanity has been pleased to believe in our origin from gods and demi-gods. The church, with that sophistic reversal of ideas of which it is a master, has succeeded in representing this ridiculous piece of vanity as "Christian Humility,"

and the very men who reject with horror the notion of an animal origin, and count themselves "children of god," love to prate of their "humble sense of servitude." In most of the sermons that have poured out from the pulpit and altar against the doctrine of Evolution, human vanity and conceit have been a conspicuous element. Just as most people prefer to trace their family back to some degenerate baron or some famous prince, rather than to an unknown peasant, so most men would rather have as the parent of the race a sinful and fallen Adam than an advancing and vigorous ape. It seems to me that it is a finer thing to be the advanced offspring of a simian ancestor, which has developed progressively from the lower mammals in the struggle for life, than the degenerate descendant of a godlike being, made from a clod, and fallen for his sins, and an Eve created from one of his ribs.

It may not be pleasant to think of your monkey ancestors; but neither is it pleasant to think that some of your ancestors may have been cannibals or stolen sheep or been members of Congress. We are going to make our descendants whatever they will become—we are not to blame for what our ancestors were. If we do not want our descendants, as well as our ancestors, to be apes, we had better see to it that William J. Bryan does not have charge of their education! Bryan is making monkeys out of a whole lot of people.

Until a very short time ago, our knowledge of the gorilla, the closest living relative of man, was very limited. Even now we know but little about the gorilla. Two gorillas have been studied in captivity, and the amount of intelligence which they have displayed is not unlike that of a deaf and dumb child of similar age. John Daniel, who died when he was but five years old, was brought up by Miss Alice Cunningham, in England. She says that John was just like any child of similar age, liked to romp with children and play with children's toys, was mischievous, and sorry for being naughty—just like any little child. He attended to his own toilet, opening and closing the bathroom door, turning on the water, and turning off the faucet when he was through washing himself. He would wash his own hands and face, and comb his hair. At night he would get into bed and pull the covers up over him. He could laugh and he could cry. When he was sent to a museum in this country, he missed his mistress and soon died. Most people think he died from a broken heart. Miss Cunningham says gorillas require constant company—either that of another ape or a person. John Daniel was allowed to sleep in the same room with a human being, and to eat at the family table. His table manners were better than those of the usual child of the same age. He seemed to understand many things which were said to him; and also things which were said about him.

Miss Cunningham says:

> One day, when I was going out, I was sitting ready dressed, when John wished to sit on my lap. My sister, Mrs. Penny, said, "Don't let him, he will spoil your dress." As my dress happened to be a light one, I pushed him away and said "No"; he at once lay on the floor and cried just like a child for about a minute. Then he rose, looked about the room, found a newspaper, went and picked it up, spread it on my lap, and climbed up. This was quite the cleverest thing I ever saw him do.

Miss Cunningham is now caring for a very young gorilla named Chula. She is treating him like a little child, and hopes to develop him in the same manner as she did John Daniel. Many people think that Chula may learn to speak a few words if he is always treated as a companion by his caretaker. The late Dr. Alexander Graham Bell, inventor of the telephone, said there was no organic reason why even the dog should not speak words, and that the only reason the dog could not be taught to speak words was because he could not be taught to properly control his throat muscles. Bell, when a young man, used to manipulate the muscles of his own dog's throat, so as to make the animal pronounce certain syllables. He says the dog would try to repeat the trick of his own accord, but without success. It is certain that all of the apes have a language of their own, consisting of many different syllables, with which they communicate with one another. Professor Garner said the chimpanzee had forty words. Many dumb people possess all the organs necessary for speech, as did Helen Keller, but as they do not know how to use their throat muscles, they can not speak words. The parrot, and some other birds, learn to imitate the words which they hear; it may be that some time some of the apes may be taught to speak our language. As it is, most likely the gorillas wonder why we do not learn to talk their language. As we are so much more intelligent, we ought to be able to learn their methods of communication, whatever they may be, much more easily than they can learn ours. Probably John Daniel said to himself, "Why does not Miss Cunningham, who is my friend, learn to talk as I talk, so we can understand each other?"

All animals and birds have a means of communication with each other. Most of them use definite sounds for certain ideas. They have no difficulty in understanding each other, but when they try to communicate with humans they have as much trouble making themselves understood as you would if you were talking to the Chinese.

The microscope has shown us the most startling proofs of Evolution. It has made possible what is called embryology, that is, the study of the growth of life before birth. The microscope shows us that there is a time in the development of such widely different forms of life as a man, a dog, a rabbit, and a fish, when they all look alike. It has shown us that there is a time in the development of a bear when he has rows of scales like a fish, and that at one time in the development of the human animal it is entirely covered with hairy wool, and has a tail as long as a gorilla at a similar stage of development.

You know that tadpoles have tails, but that as the tadpole grows into a frog, its tail is absorbed within its body, till finally it is all gone. It is that way with the human being. Every human being has a rudimentary tail under his skin which he keeps all his life. The gorillas, like men, have no visible tails after they are born. Both men and the tailless apes lose their tails before birth, while the tailed monkeys always keep theirs. It will shock Mr. Bryan terribly to know that he once had a long tail, and still has a short one, but we can't spare his feelings in the matter. He also has an appendix, unless he has had it removed, and this appendix the apes also have; but, like man, they have no use for it. Apes and men no longer need the appendix, because that is a relic of those ancestors of man which chewed the cud. It was an extra stomach which the ape and man can no longer use. Perhaps, if the girls chew gum for the next million years, the appendix may resume its former function in the anatomy.

Why does man count up to ten and then start all over again? Why do we have the decimal system? Because man has but ten fingers, and man learned to count things by counting his fingers. He has ten fingers because his ancestors had ten claws. At one time all the horses had five toes on each foot. Gradually the extra toes, not being needed, fell into disuse. Whenever an animal has no need for an organ it gradually becomes useless and disappears. Now, a horse has one toe on each foot and the rest are rudimentary. The organs of the body flourish with use. If you do not use your hand for six months, you find that you can not use it. If you do not walk for a long time, you find that you can not walk.

If you let someone else do your thinking for you, you will find that you can not think, and if you think for your children, you will make them so that they can not think. That is the trouble with Bryan. He lets Moses do his thinking for him, and he himself wants to do all the thinking for the whole human race.

The subject of embryology contains proof enough for anyone of the evolution of man from the lower forms of life. In addition to that, we have the evidence of anatomy. There is not a bone in man's body but that there is a similar bone in the ape, the dog, the horse, or the other mammals, which serves a similar purpose. Then we have the evidence of chemistry, showing how the evolution of the most primitive cells took place in the warm waters of the ancient ocean. We have the evidence of geology, showing how the various forms of life correspond to the sort of stratum in which their remains are found. A geologist reads the earth as we read a printed page. The chemist examines the shell on the inside of a mastodon's skull found in a cave of France, and tells us it was used as a cooking pot 300,000 years ago, and that the Neanderthal woman who used it had not washed it out; and he tells us what she had for dinner just before she fell over the cliff and left her skull in the river sands far below. In the waters and on the land are yet to be found surviving relatives of even the most ancient creatures. A lizard six inches long is the last survivor of the giant reptiles of the past. Moss, jellyfish, and starfish are all relatives of very ancient forms of life.

Man gets his brain from the first creatures which had a nerve cell, and many of his ideas go as far back. People like the rhythm of music and poetry, and dancing, because a hundred million years ago the clams beside the ocean were dependent for their food on the regular, rhythmic ebb and flow of the tides. They clap their hands together when they are pleased because for untold ages the nursing young of the mammals have pressed their forefeet and later their hands against their mother's breast to make the milk flow freely. The sensation of pleasure in the infant in getting its food is transformed in the older child and in the adult into pressing the hands when people shake hands with each other, and into clapping the hands together when people are pleased with an idea.

The human baby creeps about on all fours because some remote ancestor walked all the time on four feet. Man does gymnastic exercises in order to counteract the effect of always remaining in an upright position. Man's organs are not yet completely adapted to thinking. Man thinks only when he is forced to do so by circumstances. After another million years or so, man may evolve to a point where he will have a brain, and a body, to be proud of. Man, as I said in my last lecture, is far more like the ape than he is like the man he will sometime become. He is on his way from apehood to manhood, but he has not yet arrived.

People like Bryan are trying to retard man's upward progress. While they deny that man came from the monkey tribe, they want him to always remain an ape. While denying that man ever came from a fish, they want him to remain a sucker all the days of his life. Only by keeping the children of the present in ignorance of scientific facts will it be possible for the priests and politicians of the future to control their minds and their votes when they are grown up.

No form of superstition can stand the light of a scientific investigation, therefore it is to the interest of those who make their living and get their power from the ignorance of the people to keep them from knowing the latest discoveries of science.

Bryan is opposed to Evolution. More than two hundred years before Christ a king of Egypt measured an arc on the earth's surface, calculated the circumference of the earth, and proved by astronomy that the earth is round. For fifteen hundred years after Christ the church punished people with death or torture for the crime of having in their possession the books of the ancients dealing with scientific facts, and no one dared to teach that the world is round. They were like Bryan in their desire to suppress knowledge. They had the same motive which he has. The rulers of that time knew that they could not master the people if the people should use their brains, so they sought to keep them in ignorance. The rulers of our time know that an intelligent people who are accustomed to think for themselves will be hard to manage, and Bryan knows that such an intelligent people would never give him a job. The people who pay Bryan to lecture—the people who give him five hundred dollars a night for telling fairy stories to his audiences—know that it pays to chloroform the minds of the people and they hire Bryan to do the job. There are laws against selling people poisoned food, but any man is allowed to go around and fill the minds of the people with thought-destroying dope, and paralyze their brains with intellectual poison.

Moreover, the man who tells the truth to the people does not always have enough to eat, while the man who bunks them is always stuffed with the good things of life. A certain novelist has made half a million dollars out of his silly effusions, but Madame Curie, the famous discoverer of radium, has had difficulty in procuring the bare necessities of life. A certain dancer is paid a thousand dollars a week for showing her heels to the people. Did you ever hear of a scientist or a philosopher, or a great benefactor of mankind who was paid that much? The reason is simply that the people who have a great deal of money do not care to spend that money in spreading knowledge in the world. They want the people to have healthy bodies, so they can work hard; but they are willing to think for us so we can work for them. Only a short time ago, the president of Dartmouth College said: "Too many people are going to college; we must restrict the higher learning to a selected class." He went on to explain that the benefits of this so-called higher learning should be "restricted to the ruling class, who would know how to make proper use of it."

After all, there is no reason why a man like William Jennings Bryan should have been ashamed of having come from a monkey. As Darwin says, at the conclusion of his *Descent of Man*:

> He who has once seen a savage in his native land will not feel much shame, if forced to acknowledge that the blood of some more humble creature flows in his veins. For my part, I would as soon be descended from that heroic little monkey, who braved his dreaded enemy in order to save the life of his keeper, or from that old baboon, who, descending from the mountains, carried away his young comrade in triumph from the midst of the astonished dogs—as from a savage who delights to torture his enemies, offers up bloody sacrifices, practices infanticide without remorse, treats his wives like slaves, knows no decency, and is haunted by the grossest superstitions.

Even Bryan will admit that at one time our ancestors were savages. There is much more to be admired in monkeys than there is in the mud that Bryan thinks he came from. There is intelligence in monkeys. Bryan is a living proof that there is no intelligence in mud. There is progress in monkeyland, but no progress is possible if we admit that the brain of man is made from mud.

I might even say that the monkeys possess some virtues that man appears to have lost. Did you ever hear of a monkey putting other monkeys to work picking cocoanuts for him? Every monkey picks his OWN. Did you ever hear of a monkey robbing another monkey of what he has gathered for himself? Monkeys do not require jails and police to keep them from robbing and murdering each other. Did you ever hear of a big, fat, lazy baboon who was so lazy and so degenerate that he put all the little child baboons to work for him? There is no child labor in monkeyland, but in our own country two million little children are working to furnish profits for a few hundred big, fat descendants of baboons. Does William Jennings Bryan lift his voice in protest when the Supreme Court decides that the Congress can not pass any law to stop the slavery of little children? He does not, because his employers pay him more for telling the people they came from mud than they would pay him for helping to set those children free from work in order that their brains might have time to develop.

Monkeys would not do the things which Bryan thinks are all right for human beings to do. Did you ever hear of monkeys storing up food in warehouses to keep for the big and strong ones, while the weak and little ones went hungry in the midst of stored-up plenty? Why, the monkey has not yet developed to a point where he can corner food and starve his fellows. When the monkey gets to be a man, he will do these things. Did you ever hear of a monkey mother being ashamed of her baby, and leaving it on another monkey's doorstep? No mother ever did that till religion taught her to be ashamed of her motherhood. Monkey mothers do not even know enough to tell fairy stories to their children. The human mother is the only one who tells her children things which she knows are not true.

A man like William Jennings Bryan ought to be proud to trace his family tree back to the apes. It is probably the most respectable ancestor in his whole line. It is lucky for Bryan that the monkey can not tell him what he thinks about his grandson, however. Do you suppose the apes would be proud of their descendants, if they knew how badly some of the humans are turning out?

Several hundred years ago, when the printing press was made, the world of superstition united to destroy it. Today, William Jennings Bryan would destroy science, by making it impossible for the children of the country to have access to scientific facts. Bryan's brain is a relic of the past. He is to be pitied, but not blamed, if he really believes the stuff he says he does. Evolution explains why Bryan's thought processes are those of a caveman, just as it explains how his body came from that of the ape-man. Bryan's body has evolved; he looks like a man, not like an ape. His brain has not evolved, his mentality has not developed, beyond that of his superstitious, savage ancestors.

I am not making a personal attack on Bryan. I do not care in the least whether he is a good man or a bad man. I do not care whether he is honestly and sincerely foolish, or whether he talks as he does because he thinks all the people are fools. Those things do not concern me. Bryan's ideas, if carried out in laws, will deprive the children of America of the right to learn the truth, and after a few generations of Bryanism the people will have degenerated to Bryan's level. It has taken thousands of years, and the loss of millions of human lives, and the torture of millions of human martyrs, to gain what freedom and knowledge the world now has. Let us not allow the Bryans of the world to take it away from us.

The Rights of Children

*Q*ueen Silver's Magazine 1, number 4 (Third Quarter 1924) stated, "The lecture, which takes issue with conventional views of social status of children and which has aroused great interest, will be published in full in the forthcoming issue of *Queen Silver's Magazine*, Vol. 2, No. 1. It was delivered at Labor Temple, Los Angeles, on April 11, 1924." Queen was thirteen at the time.

The lecture was indeed reprinted in the subsequent issue. But Queen's advocacy of children's rights extended far beyond one lecture. Part of her commitment may have sprung from the fact that, on at least one occasion, the authorities tried to remove Queen from her mother's guardianship. Moreover, she was prohibited from speaking in public several times because she was underage. In response, Queen attacked the California child-labor law that required a child who wished to lecture or otherwise entertain in public to obtain permission from the authorities. California, she pointed out, was the same state that allowed children to do back-breaking agricultural labor in the fields with no limit on hours worked and no permission required. Apparently only children "engaged in artistic, professional, or scientific work" needed legal "protection."[1]

Queen Silver's Magazine often contained commentary on children's rights. For example, volume 2, number 1 (Fourth Quarter 1924) quoted a passage from the *Libertarian* with which she traded copies. Queen accused the editor of supporting child labor.

Volume 2, number 3 (Second Quarter 1925) included a long letter written by Queen to the International Congress of Freethinkers being held at Paris, France, August 15–18, 1925. In it, she appealed to the attendees to focus more attention upon the proper education of children. She accused "freethinkers of the past generations" of failing "in their duty to the children about them." One of the results of this failure was that "[i]n America anyone who attends a gathering of freethinkers will immediately notice that most of them are past fifty, that very few women are interested, and that young people who take a serious interest in the cause are very rare"(p. 9).

Queen's message seems to have been crystallized and well expressed in one of the brief reflections that *QSM* routinely offered. She wrote, "Women suffragist leaders used to say, 'Men have made a failure of governing the world; give the women a chance.' I say, both men and women have made a failure of government, of education, of religion. GIVE THE CHILDREN A CHANCE."[2]

Notes

1. *QSM* 2, no. 2 (First Quarter 1925): 10.
2. *QSM* 1, no. 4 (Third Quarter 1924): 11.

The Rights of Children

I will not attempt to discuss all of the rights of children in this lecture, for it would take too long to do so. I merely want to call your attention to a few of the ways in which children are victimized by their parents, teachers, and by society. I want to show you how well-meaning people destroy the minds of their children. I want to show you how the genius of intelligent children is killed out by those who profess to have the welfare of children at heart. I want to show you how professional educators paralyze the brains of the children they are hired to teach. Perhaps, when I am through, you will understand better why the really great men and women of this country have been men and women who did not enjoy the so-called advantages of careful home training and modern educational methods.

I will speak only very briefly of the hundreds of thousands of children in America who are compelled to work in fields and factories in order that their little fingers may produce profits for a few well-fed, lazy capitalists. There is not a person in America so ignorant that he does not know that child labor in field and factory is a common thing. It exists because those who make money by the labor of children do not care to give up such an easy way of living, while those who have children at work are for the most part too stupid, or too greedy for the wages of their children, to care how hard they must work. The worst cases of child labor are those on the farm, and in the home sweatshops of the cities, where children work directly under the supervision of their parents. Parents who have children working for them expect more from them than do strange overseers and no strange overseer would ever dare to punish a child as severely as do its own parents. In the beet and onion fields, and in the cotton fields of the south, live hundreds of thousands of children who work all day long in the hot sunshine. No law protects the child whose father or mother is its boss. A manufacturers' journal of Michigan has recently objected to the protests of those who seek to do away with this form of child slavery. This journal says the work is healthful, and keeps the children out in the fresh air, and that, anyway, most of them are children of Europeans, and that they might as well be there as anywhere else.

We are accustomed to think of child labor as something which only modern peoples will tolerate. The savage had no work for his child to do. No animal ancestor of man ever lived off the labor of his young ones. But, as soon as man began to be civilized, he began to make slaves of all those who were weaker than himself. He made slaves of his prisoners of war; then he made slaves of his womenfolk, and lastly of his children. For a long time only female children were enslaved by their parents, for everyone wanted the boys to grow up strong and healthy, so they might be good fighters.

Three hundred years ago the Puritan girl was compelled to sew as soon as she could hold a needle. Hour after hour she worked, sewing tiny pieces of cloth together to make quilts, or embroidered "samplers" with religious mottoes, such as "God bless our home." As soon as she was tall enough, when about five or six years old, she was taught to spin wool and flax into thread, while her older sister of nine years stood on a three-legged stool to make herself tall enough to work the heavy looms. The New England people had always worked their children, from the age of five upwards, at spinning and weaving (at home) in the days of the hand loom. When the power loom was invented, they thought it perfectly right to send them away from home to work at carding, spinning, and weaving at the great mills. When other people objected, and limited the ages at which a child might work, these New England parents felt that the law was very harsh upon them. My mother's mother went to work in a cotton mill when she was eight years old, and she worked sixteen and eighteen hours a day, from half past five in the morning till after ten at night. So did all her sisters.

The Puritans worked their children all day, every day, six days a week, and on Sunday sent them three miles to church, to listen to long-winded sermons by cruel, witch-torturing bigots, about the most merciful god who sends all disobedient children to hell and roasts them forever. When a Puritan child sat at the table, it was never allowed to speak to its parents without first receiving permission. It was not allowed to take part in any conversation of its elders, nor to laugh in their presence. The brightest of the Puritan boys, as soon as they grew up, left home and went forth into the wilderness as pioneers, preferring the society of Indians to that of their bigoted human companions. The weaker ones stayed at home and helped to hang witches.

I do not intend to take up your time with stories of the industrial slavery of children, however. Our political masters have for the most part decided that it is not wise to work a child when it is little, for if you do, it may die before it is big enough to do a full day's work. They have decided that it is neither wise nor profitable to stunt a boy's body when he is little; if you do, he may not be big enough to make a good soldier when he grows up. It is now recognized that while boys have an industrial value as children, they have a greater value on the slave market if allowed to first grow up into men. Also, our wise statesmen have concluded that one good soldier, well trained and big enough for the opposing army to shoot at, is much more profitable to the government than one half-starved, overworked son of the slums who has toiled in a mill ever since he can remember.

The aim of society at the present time is to develop children with big, fat, husky bodies, full of muscle and energy, so that they may work, and fight, efficiently for their employers, and for their government. They want these children to have enough intelligence to work at the machines for their masters, but not enough to work for themselves. They want them to have strength to fight for their masters, but not brains enough to think for themselves. To raise up men and women with strong bodies and no brains is the object of present-day society. Train the body and starve their mind is their motto.

I maintain that children have a right to grow up free and intelligent, that they have a right to develop their reason by using it, and to develop their sense of responsibility by being independent. I also say, that the only way you can expect to have free men and women is to concede to the children a right to equal freedom. The American Indian wished his son to grow up to be brave, so he never punished him. He wanted his daughter to be submissive, so he allowed even his son to punish his little sister whenever he felt like doing so. The Puritan said, as soon as his child was born, "We must break its spirit," and he used every means short of inflicting actual death to do so.

The Russians, for hundreds of years back, had a proverb, "Break the spirit of a child and kill the man," and travelers have said that nowhere in the world were children allowed so much freedom by their parents as in Russia. Perhaps that is one of the reasons why those children, when they grew to be men, finally overthrew their government. It has been frequently said that the Russian university young men were the most radical young men in the world, and that the reason for their radicalism was largely the fact that, when they went away from home to the university they left the freedom of their homes only to come in contact with police and military restrictions. It is easy to keep in slavery a child that was always a slave; it is just as hard to make one who has always been free become a slave.

About the first thing which the average mother teaches her child is fear, to be afraid of something. Long before a child is able to talk, he is afraid of many things. He can never get over his fear of thunder and lightning, or of the dark, or of goblins and ghosts and demons, until he develops sufficient reasoning power to realize that his fears are the products of someone's ignorance. In many cases, the sense of fear planted in the child prevents the development of the mind to the reasoning state. The mother seeks to make her child good by teaching him to become a coward.

The biggest fear of all implanted in a child's mind is usually the fear of a god. Whether the mother be a Christian, a Mohammedan, a Hindoo, or a Zulu from Africa, she is equally certain to teach her child that there is some god or other to be afraid of. She is equally certain to teach her child that there is also some god or other which will deal out rewards to the child if the god is first given suitable bribes, presents, or sacrifices. Cannibal savage and civilized Christian mothers thus unite in teaching their little ones to fear the wrath of an angry god and to buy the goodness of a corrupt, bribe-taking god. Neither mother ever saw the god she tells her child so much about nor did she ever see anyone who did see him. But if the child should say, "Mother, how do you know that what you tell me is true?" her only answer would have to be, "Because, when I was small, and ignorant, and incapable of reasoning, someone told me about this god, and I believed him because I knew no better. Because I know no more now than I did then, I am handing on to you what they told me, and I do not stop to question whether or not they told me the truth."

No child ever had a fear of god, or a sense of the existence of any sort of godly being, till after someone had told these religious fairy stories. I think I was about four years old when someone told me that the mountains at the headwaters of the Missouri River, in Montana, at which I was looking for the first time in my life, had been made by god. I shocked him very much by saying, in reply, "Mister, you must be very ignorant if you believe that stuff."

Very small children believe everything which anyone tells them to be absolutely true. They can not discriminate between fact and fiction. They can not tell the difference between history and mythology, or between superstition and truth. Little children do not reason as well as many animals do. An ape, a dog, or an elephant which is three years old is capable of understanding much more than is a child which is just learning to speak the language of its parents. Little eleven-month-old Sallie [a chimpanzee], which Mr. Edwards has on exhibition at Seventh and Spring Streets, understands a great many more of our words, and behaves better, than any eleven-month-old baby would do.

When children are born, they know nothing at all. They have brains which are waiting to receive knowledge, and which absorb every idea with which they come in contact. Most people have noticed that a baby puts everything it picks up into its mouth, because it has found that its food goes there. It does not discriminate between what is edible and what is unfit to eat. It is the same way with its brain as with its mouth. It can not discriminate between knowledge which is good and false teachings. It absorbs it all. Modern psychologists tell us that every moment of a person's life is spent in learning something useless which is not spent in learning something useful. A child spends just as much energy, and taxes its brain just as much, in listening to the story of how the earth was made by god in six days out of nothing, as it would have to use in learning the true, scientific story of the earth. It uses just as much time and strength learning about Santa Claus coming down the chimney as it would use in learning about Isaac Newton and the Law of Gravitation.

When a child's mind is open, waiting to receive knowledge which is true, can not you see what a crime the mother and the teacher commit when they fill that mind with a lot of nonsense? You hear people say, especially when they are talking about me, "That child ought not to be allowed to overtax her mind." Can not you see that a child's brain is working all the time, and that the only question is whether you will compel your child's brain to work at something useless or whether you will allow the child the right to use his brain and his mental energy upon the things that are useful to him?

Little children do not know how to reason with their brains, but they do know how to store up facts in them. The brain of a little child is a warehouse into which it puts all the facts, all the myths, all the evil, and all the good with which it comes in contact. It stores away all these impressions, without reasoning, without thinking about the matter, without any conscious effort of mind or body. If you will allow your child to store up a lot of lies, fables, mental trash, you will find that as it begins consciously to study and learn for itself, it will prefer the useless trash, such as has already filled its warehouse, to more solid information. He will have a light mind, unfitted for serious study. If you will see to it that he comes in contact with valuable information, that you protect him from fairy tales, myths, and superstitions, till he develops reasoning capacity, then you will find that he has a desire to add to his mental storehouse more and more of the sound knowledge of the world. You must concede to your children the right to store their minds with useful knowledge.

In still another respect a child's brain is like a storehouse. It takes up, and keeps, through its memory, everything which it may need in after life, everything which may help it and everything which may injure it. The child has a right to use the best years of his life when his sense-perceptions are the keenest, and his memory the most active, in storing up facts and impressions so that he may have his mental warehouse filled with them by the time he grows up. To compel a child to waste his time storing up trash is a crime. To compel him to spend half his schooltime in telling some teacher what he has learned is to compel him to waste much of time which he might better use in learning something else. A child has the right to study what he wants to study, when he wants to study it. It is his brain that is being developed; he alone can develop it, and no one has a right to tell him what floors he must put in his warehouse. His teachers and his parents have a right to help him learn what he wants to learn, but they have no right to compel him to learn what they want him to learn.

You expect children to study under circumstances in which no man or woman could do brainwork. You put children in a room with fifty more children, some of whom are their friends and some of whom are their enemies, yet you would not expect a man to sit down and write a book with fifty of his friends and enemies around him, in the same room. You, if you are reading an article in the newspaper, do not like to be interrupted, but whenever your child, in school, is reading something which interests him, he must drop it whenever the bell rings, or the teacher thinks it time to change the subject. I have heard of a man who was given a dictionary by a friend. Later when asked how he liked the book, he replied that it was "very interesting, except that the author changed the subject too often." When you read a book, you like to finish it before you start another. But your child must read three pages of history, and a page and a half of geography, and a couple of pages of something else. He never has a chance to get interested in anything. His continuity of thought is hopelessly broken. Why does a schoolboy find a detective story interesting, and his history dull reading? Simply because he can read the first all through at once, but he must spend a whole year on the history. By the time he gets to the end of the book he has forgotten what the first half of it was all about.

The other day a woman came up to me at Fifth and Broadway, and began to ask me questions. With my answers, they were about like this:

"Where do you go to school?"

"I don't go to school—I have a private tutor."

"Why don't you go to school?"

"Because I don't want to lose all the brains I now have. If I went to school, I would not have any time left to study."

"How many hours do you study?"

"Oh, about eight or nine—sometimes longer—all I want to."

Then she said, "I think you study too much."

First, she was worried because I was not in school, and then she was more worried because I studied much. She asked to see my books. I had five library books with me, and was on the way to the public library at the time. She looked at the titles and said: "But those books are too old for you."

I told her that while they might be too old for her they certainly were not for me and invited her to attend my next lecture. She said she came from the department of compulsory education, and went away firmly convinced that something ought to be done to keep me from knowing so much.

When I read a book of history, I read it as some people read their novels. I read it for hours at a time. Frequently I read a whole volume in a day. I may forget some parts of the book, but I am sure I do not forget nearly as much as does the child who takes a whole year to read the same book. I seldom read the same book twice. I get another one by another author, upon the same country, and read that in the same way. In that manner, I get the impressions of different writers dealing with the same subject and I am much better informed than if I had depended on one writer to tell me what I want to know. Another thing—when I am studying history, I do not stop and study arithmetic or languages, unless I want to. I have the right to study the things I want to study when I want to study them, and if all other children had always had the same right, they would all like to study just as well as I like to study. You can not expect a man to like his work if he is not interested in it; but you do expect your children to like their studies when their teachers make it impossible for anyone to be interested in them. If I had had to do as other children do in school, I am certain that I should never have become sufficiently interested in any subject to desire to study it, or lecture upon it. The reason I can do what I do is partly because I have never attended any school, except to give lectures, or as a visitor.

If you have had children of your own, you must have noticed that they seemed very bright and said many clever things when they were between two and five years of age. Newspapers and magazines frequently publish some witty or clever sayings of little children. It is well known that many little boys and girls ask questions which their parents can not answer. Now, the first trait indicates quickness of wit, and the ability of a child to ask a hard question shows ability to reason and to understand a correct answer. When children are tiny, they are sometimes allowed to be as clever as they please. When they are four or five years old, parents and later on schoolteachers punish them for being smart and clever, so that in a very short time the child's fear teaches it to keep its cleverness to itself, and before long it becomes almost if not quite as stupid as its parents and teachers want it to be.

A "good" little boy or girl is almost always a stupid one. One of the reasons why I can give you these lectures is because I have never, in all my life, been afraid to tell anyone what I thought, at any time. I am not afraid of expressing my opinions on any subject at any time. I have never been compelled to keep my thoughts to myself, for fear someone might punish me for being too clever. I have never been compelled to respect other people's opinions just because they were older than I, or because they were related to me. I have never been associated with the kind of people who consider it necessary to be hypocritical in order to be polite. If I meet people who are offended by what I say, I tell them exactly what I think, and if they do not like it, they can do me no greater favor than to keep out of my way. I do not like people who are afraid of ideas, anyway. I have met many old women who have tried to convert me and save my soul and ruin my brains, and most of them have been so badly shocked that they have never tried it again. I see no reason why I should pretend to believe what I do not believe, in order to associate with intellectual hypocrites with whom I have no desire to associate anyway. It seems to me that society is founded on hypocrisy, and that the second lesson which a child learns, after it has learned to be afraid, is to BE A HYPOCRITE.

Parents tell a child to be honest, and then compel him to be dishonest with himself and with them. They tell him to be truthful, and then compel him to lie in order to avoid scolding and punishment. In all of this perversion of the brain, in all of this teaching of cowardice and hypocrisy, the parents come first. Then comes the schoolteacher with her rules which must not be broken, and her machine process of paralyzing intelligence. She will either make the child fit the school system, or break the child in the attempt.... The Sunday school teacher's business is to make the child want to give his heart to Jesus and his brains to the holy ghost.

First of all the child is denied the right to think for itself, and then it is prevented from learning how to think. Finally, if it should happen to possess so much originality, so much natural genius, that no one can crush it out, it is at least prevented from expressing its thoughts aloud, by fear of some sort of punishment. By the time a child has endured ten or fifteen years of such treatment, it is not likely to have any great ability to do anything. Whatever genius it possesses is crushed out, and it is fit only to be a good working slave all the rest of its life. That, I believe, is the object of the system under which we live.

Our educators want to keep a child's mind occupied with useless, or worse than useless, activities so that it will have no desire to be any different from its fellows. I once talked to a ten-year-old girl who was going to school in this city who had never heard of grammar, and who did not know what the word "history" meant. The object of the capitalist class is to produce a new generation of good slaves who will work, but not think, fight, but not strike, and who, after spending six days making profits for their masters, will be satisfied to spend the seventh day down on their knees giving thanks to god for the prosperity which they do not possess. They want to raise up a generation of voters who will know as little as possible, and who will be too cowardly to stand up for their rights as American citizens. Millions of dollars are spent in this country for the purpose of keeping children from knowing what they ought to know.

If our school system were to be introduced among the ignorant people of the South Sea Islands, it would possibly be an advantage over any previous educational systems which they may have possessed; but if it is ahead of the primitive methods of the savages, it is equally far behind what it really ought to be.

The proof of this is in the fact that our educational system turns out failures. Any system of education which takes sound, healthy children and turns them out into the world to make failures of their lives is in itself a rank failure. According to figures furnished by the United States Navy department, in one of its circulars, more than 95 percent of the men who live to be fifty years old have no means of taking care of themselves. Probably most of the other 5 percent are also failures in the sense that they have not been able to do the things which they really wanted to do.

An educational system which is really worth anything would at least turn its students out with brains enough to make a living for themselves. Even the savages can do that. The savage is better equipped to struggle for his existence in the jungle than the modern man is to make his living in the capitalist system. An educational system which is worth anything ought to be able to turn out its students with brains enough in their heads to devise a social system without so many jails, and a political system without so many wars, and an industrial system without so many hungry people, as we have today.

The United States Draft Board is authority for the statement that the average mentality of all the drafted men examined during the last war was that of a thirteen-year-old boy. Those three and a half million drafted men were supposed to be the healthiest and best in the country. If their mental age was thirteen and one half years, then the mental age of all the people can not be more than twelve. Some scientists maintain it is less than that. Now, what can be said in defense of a system of home training, church training, and public and private school education which, after spending many millions of dollars on so-called education, turns out its victims with their brains so stunted, and their intelligence so paralyzed, that the American government itself, after examining three and a half million of the best of them, says they are like thirteen-year-old children? What can be said in defense of a system which, with all the scientific knowledge which the world now has, with all the knowledge there is available in books, with all the experience of thousands of years to draw from, has reduced the intelligence of the majority of the American people to that of an average child a dozen years old? Is there any wonder that 95 percent of the people are failures and that a few people have most of the wealth of the world in their hands?

Why do schools and colleges use up from eighteen to twenty-one years of a child's life in order to turn it out, old enough to vote, but with no more sense than it had when it was twelve? Because the master class do not want to put the child to work till it is full grown, and they must kill time for a few years so it will not know too much. I, myself, working at home, with the use of only one of my eyes, did as much work in six months as is done in the primary schools in four years. In some lines I did much more. In one and one half years I learned to read any book published in English as well as my mother could read them. When I was eight years old I was reading such books as Haeckel's *Story of Creation* and many of the works of Darwin, Huxley, and other scientists. I have seen a number of high school, and some college, students, who could not read as well, after all their so-called education, as I could read when I was eight years old. They are unable to read aloud, with intelligence, a single page of a scientific work. Men and women of college training, who have had what is supposed to be the best of educational advantages, make mistakes in grammar which I would have been ashamed to make when I had been studying for only two years. Thomas Edison says that only about one college graduate in a hundred can pass the intelligence tests which he gives applicants for work. The highest percentage of correct answers ever given Mr. Edison was given by a man who had never attended school since he was a small boy. Do you think Abraham Lincoln would have become the great man he did if he had had the advantages of a modern college with its football, baseball, girl flappers, and he-flappers?

The right of a child to develop his mind is absolutely denied him at the present time. Any child who rebels against the system will be crushed out in some manner, unless it has radical friends who will protect it from its enemies. In this state, the school law distinctly states that any child having home instruction from a qualified private tutor is exempt from attendance at a school. This law is intended to protect the children of the rich. Wealthy people want your children to lose their brains, but they do not intend to submit their children to the same paralyzing methods. I understand that the new law passed in Oregon takes away even this privilege, and compels every child to attend a public school. If I had lived in Oregon, it would have been necessary for me to leave the state as that law would have been used to prevent me from learning so much. Even here, some people occasionally feel that they must interfere with my education. I was once offered, when I was eight years old, a free scholarship at a fashionable boarding school for girls. I had given a number of lectures, and I suppose they thought it would be a good thing to get me into their school before I learned any more. I know of two people who would be willing to pay for a college education for me, but when I suggest to them that I would prefer to have the money which they would spend upon a college course to buy the latest scientific books to study at home, they lose all interest. They are willing to spend a thousand dollars on a college course, but they are not willing to give me so much as the price of one book so that I may continue my education in my own way. Women of the Juvenile Protective Association once informed me that I should not earn money by giving lectures, and that my mother must not give me money earned by her lectures for the purpose of buying books, or for any other purpose. In the last six and a half years I have read over two thousand books, which I have secured from the public library in Los Angeles and from the county library. I have also bought nearly two hundred books with money which I have earned in my lectures. My mother has bought several hundred more, so that I may have them to use. A friend has only recently sent me his library of historical and freethought works, over three hundred volumes, so that I may have them to use. Whenever I can, I buy more, and read them, and keep them for reference. During the last ten years so many new scientific discoveries have been made, so many new and valuable books about them have been published, that I find it very difficult to get enough of them to keep properly informed as to what is going on.

One of the very important rights of children, which few parents are willing to concede to them, is the right of a child to determine for itself what it wants to do, and what it wants to become. It is not necessary for a child to grow up in order to do this. If its mother had any sense, she would know, by watching it till it was four or five years old, what line of work it was adapted for, and if the child was allowed to study only what it wanted to study, its adaptability to its chosen line would become still plainer to its parents. All a teacher has any right to do is to help a child to learn for himself the things which he wants to learn. One reason why there are so many people in the world who are unhappy, and who have not made successes of their lives, is because parents, and teachers, have compelled them to waste their time upon lines of study, or work, for which they were not adapted. A man sometimes thinks it would be fine to be a lawyer, so he compels his son, who ought to be a musician, to study law. A woman wants her daughter to be a good cook, so she makes her do housework when the child ought to be studying something she likes. There are many judges who ought to be hod carriers, school-teachers who ought to be working in a laundry, and poor farmers who might have been good mechanics. The desire of parents to regulate their children's lives is responsible for most of the misfits of society, and for much of the crime.

People are not willing to treat children as human beings. They treat them as property, or as toy walking dolls, and they feel that they have a right to use their own property, or plaything, as they see fit. At one time it was legal and right for a father to put his child to death. At another time, and for many thousands of years, it was lawful for a father to sell his child into slavery. In our own times, it is lawful for a parent to take from a child all his earnings, if he works, and in many states a father may compel a child to go to work and to turn over his wages to himself. Everywhere, parents still have the right to control the minds of their children, to dictate what they shall think, how they shall talk, and what they shall eat and how they shall be dressed, and how long they shall sleep. The fact that some parents are too intelligent to exercise their lawful rights is the only thing which prevents all children from being slaves to the grown-up people of the world. The fact that most children are still slaves to their parents is one great reason why most men are slaves to their employers.

All religions of the world have inculcated as one of their first precepts, in some form or other, the command, "Honor thy father and thy mother." It did not matter to the founders of religion whether the father might be a criminal and the mother a degenerate; their children were supposed to honor them just the same. Children were told to accept without question whatever was told them by their parents, so that they might accept without question, when they grew older, whatever was told them by the priests. They were told to obey their fathers, so they would be obedient slaves to their king when they were older, and they were taught to have reverence for their fathers so they would have reverence for their gods. They were trained to be slaves to their parents so they would be good, contented workmen when they grew up. Children who are slaves cannot grow up into free men and free women.

Another point which I wish to make is the right of every child to be economically independent, as far as its parents are concerned. All the people of a city or state unite to provide schools for the children, so why should not all the people also unite to provide pensions for every child, before the time when it is old enough to earn its own living? Then, when it is of working age, it will, in its turn, help to support the young children of the community. This might be stated in another way: the right of a child not to be an economic burden upon its parents. Parents can not love children very much when every child means an increasing amount of work, and poverty, for themselves. Neither can they properly feed and clothe all their children under a system where each additional child which is born becomes an additional economic burden. Under the present system, the more children there are in a family, the less food and clothing and educational facilities there are for each child. Each additional child helps to take away from the older ones the things which they ought to have, until finally there is not enough of anything left for any child.

A child has a right to its own responsibilities—to its own judgment as to what is right and wrong, and to the management of its own life. Most of all it has a right to its own brain, and to determine what shall be put into its mind, and to choose its own occupations. Unless you concede to your child those rights, it is only your slave. If you concede to all the children these rights, you will raise up a generation of free men and free women, with real ability to . . . raise the intellectual level of the whole people when you concede to the children the same rights which you want for yourselves.

At the present time Russia is making some remarkable new educational experiments. In many places thousands of children have been left orphans by the famine. Colonies of these children, numbering several hundred, have been established. There are few teachers in Russia, so the children are being taught to teach, and to govern, themselves. Palaces which formerly belonged to the czar and his friends have been confiscated and transformed into children's homes; while in other places villages of children have been established. The children have committees selected by themselves, from among themselves, which take charge of the library, workshop, classrooms, and to select the studies. Teachers are with them only to assist them in their work. The children may vote to dismiss their teachers, if they desire.

Books of mythology, fairy tales, and books which teach respect for kings and priests are not allowed to circulate, nor will any more of them be published. There are so few pencils that one or two must do for a whole class of children, and there are few books, and paper is almost unobtainable. They are handicapped in every way by lack of materials with which to work, and with insufficient clothing and food. But the people in Russia have decided that they will at least give their children freedom, and that they will not allow their minds to be poisoned by false teaching. No teacher is permitted to teach a child any religion, and no priest or monk or nun is permitted to teach a child any subject whatever. Such persons are considered unfit to have the care of children. The people have decided that children's minds shall be protected from superstition until after their reason has been developed, and they are able to protect themselves. They protect minor children from church influence, just as the American government protects them from the evil influences of poolrooms and cigar stores. The Russian experiments are in their beginnings. No one can say just what they will lead to, but one thing is absolutely certain, and that is that Russian children will have a great deal less respect for religion, and will know a great deal more, than did their parents. They are to enjoy the responsibilities of freedom, as well as its pleasures.

Parents frequently resent the fact that their children know more than they do. It seems to me that a parent who can not educate a child so that the child will know more than he does is not a very successful sort of a parent. An educational system which does not give the present generation of children greater knowledge than was possessed by the past generation is a failure. New discoveries are being made all the time. A child of ten ought to know more about the laws of gravitation than did Sir Isaac Newton, and more about the geography of the earth than did Christopher Columbus, and more about electricity than did Benjamin Franklin.

The supply of knowledge is being added to every day, and if the present generation does not know more than did the last, it will be because of the paralyzing system of education devised by the master class of our time. The children of today ought to know more than did the wisest men five hundred years ago. If your son or your daughter does not know more by the time he or she is fifteen years old than you knew when you were thirty it will be because you have not properly developed the child's brain, because you have not trained it to enjoy responsibilities of its own, and because you have not allowed it to have the freedom which it should have had. If your children are not greater than you are, it will be your own fault. And if they are not greater than you are, the world will begin to slide backwards, instead of going forward.

It is a crime to waste the time of a child. After the age of thirteen or so, the human skull begins to harden and to press in upon the brain. It is therefore far more difficult to acquire brainpower after one is thirteen than it is before. To waste the time of a child under thirteen with useless, or worse than useless, masses of misinformation is to deliberately seek to prevent that child from properly filling its mental storehouse with useful matter. It makes it just that much harder for even a talented child to make a success of his life.

We have condemned the Chinese, because for hundreds of years they were accustomed to bind up the feet of their little girls, so that they could not walk properly. That was very cruel, and modern Chinese no longer do it. But here in civilized America it is customary to bind the heads of little children with bands of superstition, stronger than bands of iron, so that their brains will not grow, and so they will not know how to think properly. Men like William Jennings Bryan are striving to make these bands tighter and tighter. Only a few people like you and me are trying to increase the knowledge of the world, and promote its freedom of thought. Let me tell you, that if we do not succeed in freeing the minds of other people from the chains of superstition, they will turn around and make us their slaves.

God's Place in Capitalism

"**G**OD'S PLACE in Capitalism" was first delivered in 1926 in Los Angeles under the auspices of the Proletarian Party. The lecture was Queen's answer to those radicals who believed that religious matters would be automatically cured once socialism had been implemented. It was first printed in *Queen Silver's Magazine* 3, number 2 (February 1927), then later reprinted in volume 6, number 3 (May–June 1931).

Anticapitalist comments were common in *QSM*. For example, *QSM* 3, number 2 (February 1927) stated:

211

In the year 1924, twenty-two great capitalists...donated $11,526,334 to various religious institutions. Approximately a half-billion dollars more was donated by other great and small financiers in the same year.

This does not include fifty million dollars for the YMCA, or other vast donations to the Knights of Columbus, the Ku Klux Klan, Salvation Army, YMHA, and the Catholic Welfare Conference.... These men of means are very "tolerant" and quite willing to finance any religion, for they know that all religions serve the interests of the dollar god. (p. 16)

Queen's attitude toward what she considered to be the partnership between capitalism and religion was crystallized in an article reprinted by *QSM* entitled "Aimee's Gospel Dope for Workers."

Although the love affairs of Aimee Semple McPherson are now ancient history, there are other things about her which have never been brought out. Mrs. McPherson has played a very important part in keeping the minds of the workers inactive. She is a member of the Chamber of Commerce, and is one of the greatest allies that big business has locally. Her religion is one which has proved very effective in keeping the workers contented and satisfied. It will probably continue to be effective for this purpose for some time to come. By enticing the slaves with the message of future rewards, Aimee Semple McPherson, along with other theological fakirs, has proven a great help in keeping the thoughts of the people away from their present existence.

Fixing the thoughts of the workers upon the mansions in the sky which they hope to receive after they are dead, religion—of which Aimee is but one representative—serves to keep the workers satisfied with their filthy lodgings here on earth. By teaching them to take no thought for the morrow, religion keeps them from worrying about their empty stomachs and the fact that they may starve to death soon. Religion teaches them that "the greater your sorrows in this life, the greater will be your reward in heaven." So the slaves believe that their exploitation in this life is but a stepping-stone to a higher and greater life beyond.

The worker, if he believes Aimee, believes that even if he starves to death tonight it will be simply a rapid method of transporting him to the heavenly beyond, to the new Jerusalem. Also, Aimee is a striking example of the inconstancy of evangelists. She preaches the ideas of six thousand years ago—the ideas of the donkey-back, ox-cart age of civilization, and she uses every scientific device known to make known her doctrines. She opposes every form of scientific investigation, and she uses the radio, the most modern result of scientific research to preach her doctrines. While trying to induce the people to adhere to the ideas of from two to six thousand years ago, she preaches in a temple built and decorated by the latest achievements of the builder's art. When she travels, she makes use of all the means which can possibly contribute to her comfort. Even when coming from her recent trip to Mexico she came on the train, not on donkey-back. Altogether, Aimee is merely like others of her creed, strong on preaching, but mighty inconsistent when it comes to carrying her doctrines to their logical conclusions.[1]

Note

1. Originally published in the *Daily Worker*, November 3, 1925. Reprinted in *QSM* 3, no. 1 (January 1927): 13.

God's Place in Capitalism

When I speak of god, I want you to realize that by the word "god" I refer to that particular sort of supernatural being whom you happen to worship, to your idea of god. Religion teaches that god made man, but I say that each man makes his own god, and that god is made in the image of man, not man in the image of god. Man makes his god according to his ideas of what he himself would like to be. He wants to be strong, so he makes a powerful god; he wants to oppress the weak, so he makes a cruel god; he longs to be rich, so he makes a wealthy god. Sometimes he makes a loving or merciful god, to correspond with the gentler sides of his own nature. Man frequently makes goddesses, evidently concluding that the gods might be lonely in heaven if there were no women about. Some religions also have child gods, but the worship of child gods has mostly gone out of fashion, for the capitalist class long since discovered that it was more profitable to put children in a factory to work than to put them in a heaven to be worshiped. Some men have made gods of stone and wood, and bowed down before the products of their own hands; others have created intangible spirit gods, and worshiped the product of their own imaginations. Some have created gods part human, part animal; others have made them all beasts of degenerate form and character. Every act performed by a human being has at some time or other been symbolized by a god created for the purpose; every phenomenon of nature has its own godly representative; every human emotion has been incarnated in a god or goddess.

You must realize that when I mention a god I am not necessarily referring to any particular brand of god, not a Jewish god nor a Gentile god nor a pagan god, nor to any of the thousands of other gods which have been created by crafty men and worshiped by foolish ones. When I refer to god, I am talking about the god idea—the conception of god which is in your minds and in the minds of the rest of the people. There is not, and never was, a god; therefore no god can either help or harm us. It is the idea of god which causes the mental corruption and perversion of reason, not the mythical god itself. Ignorant and fear-ridden men, superstitious and stupid women, crafty and unscrupulous priests and others have created an unlimited number of samples of the god idea and turned them loose on the world. We can not destroy these gods, because they have no existence. Against the theory of god, the idea of godly existence and interference in worldly affairs, we bring our logic. The subject of this lecture should really be "The God Idea in Capitalism." But three weeks ago an address was given here on "Man's Place in Nature," and so it occurred to me that a lecture on "God's Place in Capitalism" would be in order.

I think you will all agree with me when I say that, the chief object of the capitalist class is the production and accumulation of wealth. No matter what radical group or organization you belong to, you will also agree that in order to accumulate wealth the capitalist class must control an abundant supply of raw materials and must also have an unlimited supply of cheap, efficient, and contented laborers. You will also agree with me when I say that cheap labor is of more importance to capitalism than cheap raw materials, and that it is by cheapening the cost of labor that profits are more readily increased. Even the cost of the raw material is largely determined by the labor cost of making it available for use in manufacture. Cheap labor is absolutely essential to the maintenance of any sort of industrial system based on profit. Efficient labor is necessary, otherwise much time is lost and valuable material is wasted. Contented labor is of vital importance, for dissatisfied workers disrupt production, unsettle markets, and more or less disorganize capitalist society. Capitalism must find ways and means of keeping labor contented, while forcing the workers down to the lowest possible standard of living. The god idea offers to the capitalist class the best possible means of keeping the workers satisfied and contented with their condition. The capitalist class did not invent the god myth, neither did it create gold or silver. The god myth was so much raw material, and the masters were not slow to discover it and turn it to their purposes. They used god as a bribe, and they used him as a threat of punishment; they found that the more they drove god into the heads of the workers the less room was left for brains. The fear of god kept the slave on the job; the wrath of god kept him from growling when he was out of a job; and when he got hungry the love of god kept him from crying about his empty stomach. The worship of god kept what little mind the slave had so busily employed that he had no time to think about a raise in pay. He was so busy worrying about where he was to spend eternity that he didn't object when the landlord threw him out for nonpayment of rent. He was so scared of hell that he didn't mind going to jail in the least and so sure of wearing a golden crown in the next life that he was quite willing to be broke in this world. He was eager to catch hell on this earth in order to secure a taste of heaven in another world; anxious to work himself to death in this life that he might have a chance for eternal rest in the next. They told him that only the poor could enter the kingdom of heaven; so the poor idiotic slave said to himself, "Let the rich man get all he can out of me now—he's going to hell later, anyhow, so he deserves all he can get out of this life." The capitalists, of course, were quite happy to let the workers have everything they wanted in the next world. The workers may have heaven and all there is in it; the capitalist class wants the earth and all that there is on it. Capitalism helps to maintain religion; the church helps to maintain capitalism. They are twin exploiters of labor; one exploits the body, and the other robs the brain.

In certain European countries the State controls the church. In America, the church controls the State and Capital controls both Church and State. Capital finances religion and god sanctifies capital. The workingman is victimized by both god and gold. One steals his brain and the other plunders his body.

America, alone of any civilized country, concedes to priests and ministers of any organized church or faith the right to perform a legally binding marriage ceremony. In every other modern country, while a religious ceremony is permitted, it is not binding upon the parties concerned unless preceded by a civil contract. The civil contract alone is legal.

America opens its legislative assemblies with prayer, and the politicians, after they have been properly sanctified, proceed to pull off more crooked work than is done anywhere else in the world.

America appoints priests and ministers as chaplains in each military unit, and in order to compel respect, gives them the rank and privileges of commanding officers. Every bullet goes on its way to kill with the blessing of god behind it; every machine gun has a holy mission; every cannon booms with the will of god.

America has gradually been putting god into the schools. From a third to a fifth of all the songs published in the school songbooks teach religion to the children. They tell of god, Jesus, and his mother. Some Jewish children living near me learned all about god, Jesus, Mary, the "Holy Night," and "Santa Claus" from their kindergarten teacher within a few weeks after they commenced attendance at a public school maintained by Los Angeles County! In their first year at school they also learned that rabbits lay eggs and that Jesus rose from the dead. They were shown, in the classroom, by a teacher paid by the people, pictures of the virgin and child, and when the Rev. Aimee McPherson held a revival in our midst the schoolteachers distributed in the classrooms circulars advertising her meetings and asked the children to take them home and give them to their mothers. While the children learned all this junk in their first year at school they did not learn to read, write, or do any useful thing. They did not even learn the alphabet.

In most of the states it is customary, and even compulsory, to open the school day with a prayer and a chapter from the Bible.

In a number of states, children are required to attend classes in religious instruction three times a week, during school hours. The parents are permitted to designate whether the instruction shall be Protestant or Catholic; but they are not permitted to demand that their religious instruction shall be Jewish, Mohammedan, Buddhist, or atheist. The government recognizes but two religious groups, Protestant and Catholic, and denies the right of the child to receive antireligious, or even anti-Christian instruction during school hours. The church is determined to control the education of the children, subvert their morality, and pervert their reasoning powers, for by so doing the religious leaders will be enabled to dominate social and political life. The capitalist class desires the church to pervert the education and destroy the intelligence of the children in order that they may become cheap, efficient, and contented workers when they are grown men and women.

At the very lowest estimate, five billions of dollars are contributed to the cause of religion each year. The capitalist class would not pay out five thousand millions of dollars annually unless it expected to get a still larger amount back in profit and security. There is not a church that could survive and pay its ministers a salary if it was entirely dependent on collections taken up in its congregation. The Christian workingman or woman is induced to contribute as much as can be gotten out of him or her, and the ruling class supplies whatever else may be necessary to keep the wheels of religious superstition turning.

The man who worships a god has no confidence in himself. He lays his troubles on godly shoulders because he is not brave enough to assume responsibility for his actions. The man who fears a god is also afraid of any man who occupies a higher or more powerful position than his own. The man who would trust a god would also trust any crooked politician. It is very desirable from the capitalist point of view, that the working class should worship their masters, fear their bosses, and put their trust in the crooks who rule over them. The Christian religion tells you to "become as a child . . . knowing neither good nor evil," to trust those who injure you and love those who hate you. They tell you that you must be born again, I suppose because when you were born the first time you knew nothing at all, and when you are born the second time you will know still less. No wonder the capitalist class can afford to spend billions of dollars trying to convert you to Christianity.

Every religion has for its object the pacification of a restless people. Whatever the origin of religious belief may have been, the only excuse that modern religion has for organized existence is the ability of religious leaders to control the masses. For that they are paid in proportion to the efficiency with which they can exercise their power.

Christians talk everlastingly to the effect that "Jesus died to save us," but a hundred million people, and more, have died that you and I might have what little freedom we now enjoy. They say that "Jesus died upon a cross," and forget that hundreds of thousands of rebellious slaves have died upon crosses, died fighting for their freedom. They want us to forget that the Christian church has burned, crucified, tortured, starved, and slaughtered uncounted millions whose only crime was harboring an idea different from that accepted as true by their ignorant, brutish, fanatical neighbors. They want us to forget that human progress has been an eternal struggle between the men who have property and the men who have only muscle, between the men who have power and the men who have brains, between the men who use their intellect to enslave their fellows and those who would use their reason to set free the human race.

Since religion is based on delusion, it follows that the bolder the delusion the more successful the religious organization is likely to be. Religion flourishes with emotionalism and dies in the white light of reason. The various religious fathers have boldly put forth the most absurd claims, told the boldest lies, and promised the most impossible rewards. The wilder the tale, the more ridiculous the claim, the more followers that religion acquired. There is no limit to the credulity of the people when once they have accepted faith as their guide and discarded reason. It is quite often said that the letters "D.D." which a minister puts after his name stand for "Doctor of Delusion."

Mohammed said the moon came down from heaven and entered his right coat sleeve, passed over his back, and came out the left sleeve. He went to heaven—to seven heavens, to be exact—came back and described all that he had seen. He performed hundreds of other marvels and miracles. The Christians said that Mohammed was a liar and of course he was. But the lies of Mohammed have more followers and believers than those of Jesus and all the Jewish prophets put together.

Joseph Smith put forth another wild tale and founded a highly successful church on what was written as a work of fiction.

Mother Eddy started to found a religion by denying the existence of all material things, and millions of her followers deny all matter— save money. Truth goes begging for hearers, while falsehood calls forth special editions of the largest and most powerful newspapers in circulation. Fiction has news value; truth has not. A religious fanatic can always get more followers than a labor agitator. People like to be fooled, and love the man or woman who deceives them. They would rather listen to a happy-sounding bit of illusion than to the soundest and truest philosophy ever uttered. The churches know this. Just as the peddler of dope undertakes to supply the demand of his client for drugs—just as the bootlegger supplies the market for liquor—so does the Christian preacher attempt to supply the demand for myths, fairy tales, miracles, and delusions of all sorts. Competition between different religious groups is keen; hence new delusions are continually being invented by new religious sects. Spiritualists, Holy Rollers, Theosophists, sun worshipers, and a thousand minor cults rival each other and compete with the established and conservative churches in their attempts to capture popular fancy. There are fashions in religious delusions, as well as in clothes. Each and every one helps, however, to keep its followers contented and satisfied. Mayor Cryer summed up the religious attitude when, in a thanksgiving proclamation a year or so ago, he called on all good citizens to "go to church, to join a church." He went on to say that they should join any church, just so they affiliated with some religious group or other. That is the attitude of capitalism. Join any church—send your children to any Sunday school; any religion will serve to keep you in subjection on earth and none will count either for or against you hereafter. All religions are loyal servants of capitalism.

The man who feels certain of eternal peace and glory in the next life has no particular interest in this one. The man who has a "house not made with hands" fronting on a "street paved with gold" is not seriously worried by the fact that he is a homeless vagrant in this life. He will live and suffer a few short years in this life in order that he may enjoy endless glory and happiness in the next few million years. The capitalist system will see to it that he earns his future reward by giving him adequate suffering in his present existence. The church will console him by saying, "The greater your sorrow in this life, the greater will be your reward in heaven." The slave will turn a deaf ear to the labor agitator who calls upon him to awaken from his dope-filled dreams and claim the reward of his toil here and now. The slave will be contented; the church leaders will pocket the money given them by grateful capitalists; and the master class will gloat over "what fools these workers be."

While capitalism enslaves the bodies of the workers, its schools stunt the brains of their children. Its churches chloroform young and old into mental unconsciousness. The glory of heaven blinds them to their class interests. The prayers of the priesthood prevent them from demanding more wages, the threats of hell hereafter and jail here and now keep them submissive to the will of their masters. Capitalism uses its wealth to increase the power of the church. The church uses its religion to bless the exploitation of labor. Capitalism has armies and courts, clubs, guns, and jails to enforce its will. The church has angels, demons, and gods at its call. Capitalism causes the workers fear of the present; religion curses them with the fear for their future. Capitalism condemns them to suffer want and hunger and cold here, and when they are noisy and complaining the church threatens to send them to a hotter place next time. The worker is cursed by capitalism in this life, and haunted by gods and devils in the next. If he is a good servant, works hard, raises ten or more children to become slaves; is contented with his station in life; if he never eats, drinks, or sleeps too much; if he never steals, begs, strikes, or thinks; if he does what the church tells him to do in all things, then at last he will reap a glorious reward. He will have about one chance in a million of going to heaven, provided there is a heaven, provided the sky pilots are able to find the way for him, and provided also that his soul does not burn up while hurtling through space between earth and heaven.

The savages made gods because they feared nature—all the phenomena which they could not understand. Capitalism keeps gods and devils on hand to inflict fear on the workers, to punish and reward them at its command. Capitalism has two great arms which reach out to strangle the human race. One arm is represented by its economic power, by the control of wealth and labor. The other arm consists of its control of religion and education, of all the mental activities of the people. From the lowest kindergarten to the highest university god helps capital and capitalism helps god to muddle the minds of the masses. God and capital together control every institution from our great daily newspapers, our courts and legislative bodies, to our asylums for the insane and our homes for the feebleminded. ·

If the god idea was not useful to capitalism, then the gods would long since have been scrapped, just as capitalism abolished the wooden plow, the hand spinning wheel, and the birch bark canoe. Capitalism discarded all the tools of production invented by our savage ancestors because it found them clumsy and inefficient. It discarded their weapons of destruction because they could not kill enough men with them. It discarded their methods of dressing, eating, and of housing people because it found them crude and unsanitary. But capitalism kept the savage gods, the barbarous mythology, the sanctified but unsanitary prophets, the silly heaven and brutal ideas and devoted them to its own uses. It did this because the capitalist class soon found that it had a place and use for god, and all godly matters in its scheme. Capitalism adopted the Jewish god, the Christian god, the Mohammedan god, and took all the gods and goddesses under its protection.

Of all the gods which have found a place in its system, however,

Capitalism prefers the Christian god. He is the most efficient, the most helpful, the most easily adapted to the needs of the master class and the most useful in keeping the working class satisfied and contented. Capitalism can with the utmost satisfaction quote the teachings of Jesus to "Turn the other cheek," "Lay not up treasures on earth," "Servants, obey your masters as ye would the lord himself," "If a man take thy coat, give him thy cloak also," and countless others of like character.

All religions have the same purpose, but since we live in a Christian country we have to pay more attention to the destruction of the Christian religion than to any other. We have to free the brains of the workers so they will want to free their own bodies. Many radicals are of the opinion that the religious issue will take care of itself. It will not. Capitalism is taking care of it now, to the great injury of the workers. It is up to the radical groups to take care of it, expose its power and its fallacy, in order to free the slave brain from the insanity of religious faith. Do you doubt that religion is a form of insanity? We confine in an asylum the man who says that he is Napoleon, and we let the man who sings "I'm going to be an angel" live freely in our midst.

The gods and god worshipers and the capitalists who finance both should either prove the existence of their gods or consign them to oblivion. It is up to the believers in a supreme being to prove there is one. They have never done so. They accept on faith what no one has ever demonstrated by fact to exist. Moreover, it is up to any being who wants to be accepted as a god to prove his own claims to divinity in such a manner that no one—child, savage, or scientist—can possibly misunderstand. If your god is omnipotent, he should have sufficient power to demonstrate his own existence. If he is merciful, he should desire to do so, that religious dissension may be prevented. If he is a jealous god, then he should do the same thing for his own glory. The world is several hundred billion years old. As we have waited all these billions of years for proof of the existence of god, we are likely to wait some time longer. No god ever did anything to demonstrate his own existence.

The religionist's position is the positive. The atheist's position is the negative. No court of law requires the proof of a negative. It is up to the gods and the god-worshipers to prove their positive position. No man, for example, can prove that he is not guilty of murder, theft, or any other crime. The law presumes him innocent until he is proven guilty. When the jury brings in a verdict of "not guilty," they do so simply because the prosecution has failed to prove his guilt, not at all because he has proven his innocence. No negative can be demonstrated; every positive can be. If a positive statement can not be demonstrated, then that of itself proves the negative to be the correct and truthful position. No god has ever been proven to exist, therefore the atheist takes the logical position that he does not exist.

The agnostic straddles the fence, either through a fear of public opinion, family troubles, or through a sneaking fear that there might be a god, and if there is one, he wants to stand well with him. In other words, the agnostic is still obsessed by the remains of the religious fear implanted in him while he was a helpless child.

Capitalism has no use for atheists who come along and destroy its gods and upset its ethical creed. It knows that if the man or woman who scoffs at gods and hells and heavens is allowed to go freely about inspiring others to do likewise, the god idea will soon fall into disrepute. The KKK has already announced that speakers for the American Association for the Advancement of Atheism will not be allowed to talk in certain states. It may be assumed that the Klan is prepared to use violence to prevent atheist meetings, or, as in the present case, debates between atheists and theologians, as there is no legal means of doing so. A movement to put the Bible into the schools of California and other states which do not now compel religious instruction is well organized and heavily financed. Other religious groups, also well supplied with money, are organized for the purpose of controlling the leisure time of the people. Capitalism, not being able to force people to attend church services by direct legislation, has with the aid of the holy ones of god devised laws and regulation which make it illegal to go anywhere else, or engage in any amusement or useful occupation on Sunday. By such means they hope to enforce church attendance. People like to go somewhere on the only day when they are not working, and the godly believe that they will go to church if all other attractions are closed to them. Capitalism has been careless in this matter for a number of years, and church attendance has steadily decreased. But in a very few years, if that class has its will done, there will be no place to go on Sunday except to a church, and a few years later they will make it illegal to stay at home.

Capitalism has unwittingly defeated some of its own objects in this matter of church attendance. Henry Ford, for example, is anxious to see religion flourish. He is a very religious man himself and expects everyone else to be also. Yet the Ford factories have made and sold over twelve million cheap cars, thereby giving millions of people something else to think about than the hereafter, and furnishing them with a means of taking their families to the open country on Sunday. The motion picture and the radio have done more to keep people away from churches and to weaken religious influence than any radical propaganda.

Capitalism realizes this. Hence the Sunday closing laws, the government and church monopoly of the radio, government censorship of the films, and other restrictive legislation. Having already secured control of the education of the children, of the press and other agencies of news, capitalism, with god at its side, is now assuming control of art, music, the movies, radio, book publishing, and all other means of disseminating information to the adult mind. Having already secured economic and political control of the earth, they are determined to secure brain control—to own the minds of the people from birth to death.

Not only does the ruling class propose to put the fear of god into the minds of the workers and their children; not only does it finance religious propaganda more liberally than ever before, but it is doing more than that to insure the future ignorance of the American people. Money is withheld from educational institutions which teach more science than theology. Teachers who show the slightest tendency to develop an individuality of thought, either in themselves or in their pupils, are being dismissed from service. Already in a half-dozen states laws have been passed forbidding the teaching of that branch of science which most openly clashes with all religious faith. Evolution has been made illegal as a subject for discussion, and some states expressly state, in the laws intended to suppress scientific instruction, that "nothing shall be taught which conflicts with the story of creation as told in the Book of Genesis." As two conflicting stories of creation are set forth by Genesis and as nothing shall be taught which conflicts with either one, the Tennessee lawmakers and others have forbidden the reading of Genesis, as well as the teaching of Evolution. A strict interpretation of the law would find teachers who read Genesis to their pupils as guilty as John T. Scopes.

This bold and open effort to suppress the knowledge of the modern scientific world and in its place give to the youth of our time the myths and legends of the ignorant, unwashed, half-naked barbarians of from two to five thousand years ago is well financed and thoroughly organized. A dozen or more states will be asked to pass similar laws during the next year. The old battle between Science and Religion, which some of you had thought over and won by the scientists fifty years ago, is to be refought in the twentieth century. Ideas that belong to the oxcart age of civilization will be broadcast over the radio. Arguments that were discarded before printing presses were invented will be revived and published in modern newspapers. Miracle stories which were disbelieved by all the contemporaries of the alleged miracle workers will be remodeled and taught in the schools in place of geology. Your children will be studying the map of the New Jerusalem in place of astronomy. History will be taught with special reference to the acts of the apostles. Physiology will be revised to teach that rabbits lay eggs, that the hare has not a divided hoof but chews the cud, and that the bat is a bird. Geography will have to revise its maps in accordance with the flat-earth theory held by all the sanctified sons of god in past ages.

You may say that all this is absurd, and that not even the most ignorant preacher is so stupid as to believe that he can thus turn back the intelligence of the world four thousand years. But they do believe it is possible to thus force their ideas on the public. They have passed many laws toward that end. They are prepared to wage a battle in every legislature in every state to attain their ends; and they expect to be victorious. They may not carry their teachings to such absurd lengths as I have indicated. They may not burn people at the stake or hang them as witches because they are teaching and publishing scientific truths. But they will blacklist them, starve them, and cut them off from the opportunity to use their knowledge for the benefit of humanity.

As soon as man ceases to depend on a god to help him, he begins to devise ways and means of helping himself. As soon as he learns that there is no god to hurt him, he begins to lose his fear of priests and politicians; as soon as he realizes there is no god to reward him for his sufferings, he desires to abolish suffering and reward himself. When man rids his mind of the god idea, he has a cleaner brain, more courage, and a greater hope of making something of himself and of the world he lives in than he ever had before.

Man has done countless things which no god ever thought of doing. Man's hands and feet were insufficient to do the bidding of his brain.

Therefore he invented the machine. He was not satisfied to stay on dry land, so he made a boat. He was not satisfied to stay on the surface of the water, so he made a submarine. He was not satisfied with the speed of the horse, so he made the automobile; when his mind outgrew that, he made the airplane. He has made machines to make his clothes, build his houses, transport him from place to place, do his writing, and carry his voice over the earth with the speed of light. He has made dry land out of the ocean bed and turned the desert into a fertile garden. He has taken the wild animals and made them better and more useful. He has taken scrawny vegetables and made them large and pleasant to the taste. He has taken sour and bitter fruits and made them large, sweet, and luscious. He has made machines to think for him. There is no limit to the desires of man, therefore there is no limit to what he may sometime accomplish.

We are told by the book of Genesis that god worked six days, pronounced his work good, and rested. He was satisfied. Man, the man related to the ape, is never satisfied, never content. He never rests but is always making improvements. Man, himself the product of evolution, is now directing the further evolution of all useful forms of life, and providing for the elimination of the unfit. He is helping organic evolution by putting his brains behind the forces of nature.

Only the mud-men and the gods are ever satisfied.

When man can do more than the gods could do or would do, why should he any longer depend upon them? Man made god and man can and will destroy his god. When he has destroyed his god and remade his industrial and social system, he will have as a result of his labors a better world than any god ever made.

Witchcraft

*T*HIS ESSAY constitutes an early investigation of what has become an enormously popular theme within contemporary feminist scholarship: the political reevaluation of witchcraft and its suppression. Featured in *Queen Silver's Magazine* 4, number 3 (September–October 1929), pages 3–12, the essay was followed three pages later by an article entitled "Witchcraft, Saintly and Biblical":

> "Thou shalt not suffer a witch to live" (Exod. 22:18).
>
> "There shall not be found among you anyone that make

either his son or daughter to pass through the fire, or that useth div-
ination, or an observer of times, or an enchanter, or a witch, or a
dreamer, or a consulter with familiar spirits, or a wizard, or a necro-
mancer" (Deut. 18:10–11).

"To obey is better than sacrifice, and to hearken than the fat of rams.
For rebellion is as the sin of witchcraft" (1 Sam. 15:22–23).

"And he [Manasseh] caused his children to pass through the fire in the
valley of the son of Hinom: although he observed times, and used
enchantments, and used witchcraft, and dealt with a familiar spirit,
and with wizards" (2 Chron. 33:6).

"And I will cut off witchcrafts out of thine land, and thou shalt have
no more soothsayers" (Mic. 5:12).

"A man also or woman that hath a familiar spirit, or that is a wizard,
shall surely be put to death; they shall stone them with stones: their
blood shall be upon them" (Lev. 20:27).

See also Gal. 5:19–21.

Said John Wesley, the founder of Methodism: "Giving up witchcraft
is, in effect, giving up the Bible" (*Journal,* 1768).

Said Sir William Blackstone (father of English jurisprudence and
patron saint of modern lawyers): "To deny witchcraft is at once flatly
to contradict the revealed word of God in various passages of both the
Old and the New Testaments."

Said Martin Luther (father of the Reformation): "I should have no
compassion on these witches; I would burn them all."

Indeed, Queen's political reassessment of witchcraft from a feminist
and skeptic's point of view is the earliest of its kind I have encountered.
Perhaps the "witch hunting" of socialists that she personally observed
and experienced left her especially open to reconsidering the persecution of witches in the past.

Witchcraft

It is my intention to take up in this lecture some of the less widely known features in the history of witchcraft which are usually overlooked in the recounting of historical facts concerning the witchcraft delusions and persecutions. Most of us are familiar with the more recent history of witchcraft, and the trials of witches, during the fifteenth, sixteenth, and seventeenth centuries, but the earlier history of witchcraft is not so well known, although most interesting.

There has probably never been a belief more widely held by mankind than the belief in witchcraft. It appears in nearly all races and nations, from the African savages to the American Indians. For a number of centuries it was universally held amongst the Christian nations, and that belief caused the death of from three hundred thousand to several millions of persons, according to various estimates.

A logical consequence of this belief in witchcraft was the fear of the results which might be obtained by it, and the development of a vast store of information as to the best methods of escaping from the ill effects of charms cast upon one. Many of these charms are commonly believed in at the present time, among the more ignorant portions of the population, and among savage tribes.

Due also to this fear of witchcraft, the penalty for its practice has been very severe among many peoples; those convicted of it meeting with a horrible death at the hands of the tribe. Among some tribes of American Indians, it was not customary to make a distinction between the two classes of magicians, that is, those who produced good results and those who produced bad results. The tribal medicine man acted as both good and bad witch doctor on occasions, sometimes meeting the penalty of death if he failed to cure his patient. In other tribes, especially among the Indians of the plains, a person upon whom a charm had been placed had but one recourse: he could go to another medicine man and try to get a more powerful charm, but to kill a medicine man for casting a spell upon anyone was unthinkable.

Records of prohibition against witchcraft and magical practices are found as far back as the Greek and Roman empires, before the alleged birth of Christ. These prohibitions, however, were only occasionally enforced, and usually without severity.

Early Christianity adopted the several courses of tolerating heathen rites; of adopting them into her own practices, to destroy the influence of heathen practitioners, and of suppression of unauthorized and unorthodox magicians.

Most prominent among the beliefs of the early Christians are two things: belief in the actual existence of the pagan gods and goddesses (whom they considered as devils), and belief in the efficacy of magical charms and remedies for disease. Ferguson (*Philosophy of Witchcraft*, page 41) quotes the following charm prescribed by the church for the chills:

> Against chills at all hours of the day, write on a paper and bind with a cord on the neck of the patient in the evening the following, "In the name of our Lord, crucified under Pontius Pilate, by the sign of the Cross of Christ. Fevers or quotidian chills or tertian, or quartan, depart from the servant of God. Seven hundred and fourteen thousands of angels will follow you, Eugenius, Stephanus, Protacius, Sambucius, Dionisius, Chesilius, and Quiriacus." Write these names, and let the patient carry them upon him.

Another charm (page 42) is for the removal of bone in the throat: "Look at the patient and say, 'Come up, bone, whether bone or fruit, or whatever else it is, as Jesus Christ raised Lazarus from the Tomb, and Jonah out of the whale.'"

Many other charms, equally amusing, were in use, but space forbids their quotation at this time.

Persons wishing to be cured of an affliction could consult the witch, the doctor, or the church. All would use the same or similar methods in their cures. For a disease such as osteoarthritis, for example, which was very common in primitive life, the witch would use oil, warmth, and the chanting of pagan incantations. The priest would use oil and warmth and Christian invocations (or incantations, as you please to call them). The doctor would use oil and warmth and possibly both kinds of supernatural influence, thus giving the patient an extra chance for recovery.

In an effort to win the people over from paganism, the church, not as yet powerful enough to compel belief, adopted many of the customs, rituals, and symbolisms of the earlier pagan religions. Temples previously devoted to the worship of gods and goddesses of fertility, love, and general nature deities were sprinkled with holy water and thus transformed into Christian churches. In order to render acquiescence doubly easy, the church adopted the festival days of the pagans, attaching new names to them. In this way, the birth of Christ, after having wandered over most of the calendar, became fixed at or near the twenty-fifth of December—a concession to earlier sun worship. The date of his so-called resurrection was given to another such festival day, and we have the feast of Easter, which is now celebrated by so many millions of people. In addition to these concessions, the church adopted, in its ceremonies and in the garments of its dignitaries, the symbolism of the nature cults, often without change and occasionally with minor changes. Christian practice contained within itself a curious mixture of ritual and worship, gathered from many religions.

In other words, the primitive church, in order to discourage heathenistic rituals and charms, adopted them and made them its own. It discouraged the belief in magic—except when the magic was exercised by a priest or other orthodox person, when it was considered not to be magic. It discouraged the use of charms in the cure of diseases—except in the cases in which the priest pronounced the charms or sold the amulets. For the heathens to display emblems of phallic worship in their ritual was a most reprehensible practice, but the same emblems, in a house devoted to Christian worship, suddenly became sanctified!

Side by side with the development of the early church, there developed a religion in opposition to Christianity. Some writers have been in the habit of explaining away the witchcraft delusion by various means, attributing the testimony given at the trials to imagination, exaggeration, hysteria, etc. There seems to be no doubt that there was a ritual of witchcraft, and that for many centuries there existed a very real witch cult or demon worship.

This witch cult, which we are led to believe had a strong organization and spread all over the civilized world, seems to have fallen heir to the practices and ritual of the early nature cults, with many additions through the ages. Parodies and reversals of Christian practices were common at witch gatherings. The recital of the Lord's prayer backwards, the "Black Mass," and similar practices were common.

These witches understood such medical knowledge as existed in their time, and possibly some things not known to those who called themselves doctors. They also understood the practice of magic and charms; incantations, also, were in common use among them. It is not necessary to attribute any supernatural power to the witches in order to account for the results they achieved, any more than it is necessary to do so to account for the power of any medicine man, priest, or minister. A careful study of their methods will reveal the natural explanation of their achievements.

Originally (as far as is known) mainly beneficial in their efforts, the former priestesses of the pagan religions turned their attention to the malicious possibilities of their vocation. They developed their knowledge of herbs and poisons, and their successors, the witches, showed their knowledge of the use of poisons upon numerous occasions. We find that witches, of whatever tribe, have not hesitated to make use of purely natural means when their efforts to invoke the supernatural failed. A savage, informed that a spell had been cast upon him, and that he would die within a certain time, might reasonably be expected to give in to the power of suggestion; but if he failed to waste away within the stated time, the witch would be likely to use poison to hasten the effect of the charm. More civilized witches have used similar tactics upon occasion. However, with a very ignorant and superstitious person, whether savage or civilized, the suggestion would usually be sufficient.

Witches were supposed to be in league with the Devil, and to worship him in their ritual. That groups of witches did meet and go through a prescribed ritual is well established. They worshiped a being whom they believed to be the Devil, regular meetings being held, at which worship took place. Any disaster, from a thunderstorm to the sudden cessation of a cow's milk, was attributed to a supernatural power, usually to the Devil, and to those supposed to be his assistants. Hence, old women and young girls were occasionally accused of causing storms by pulling off their stockings, and by similar mysterious means.

By what is termed sympathetic magic, the witches were believed to be able to cause damage to any person to whom they took a dislike. Image magic, that is, the making of an image of the person upon whom the spell was to be placed, was practiced frequently. This type of magic has been in common use among some Negro tribes, and references to it during the witchcraft delusion are frequent. An image of wax or clay would be made, usually containing some part of the person to be bewitched (such as eyebrows, hair, fingernail parings, etc.). The image might then be stuck with pins, either all over the body, or in the particular place in which one wished the pain to be centered, or it might be buried, or burned slowly over a fire and then buried. Among some savage tribes, a clay image of the person to be killed was placed in a river, where the current of the river would gradually dissolve it. The person being bewitched was supposed to waste away as the image dissolved. Many other examples could be cited. Similar beliefs are entertained even at the present time in the less-educated sections of this country. Fear of witches is also common among some groups of people.

The ecclesiastical crusade against witchcraft, which lasted for several hundred years, and which is said to have caused the death of from three hundred thousand to several million persons (according to various estimates), may be said to have had its beginning in the bull issued by Alexander IV December 13, 1258. This was followed in the fourteenth century by a bull issued by John XXII, and on December 7, 1484, Pope Innocent VIII issued the bull entitled *Summis desiderantes affectibus.* By the authority of this bull, inquisitors were appointed, among them one named Sprenger, who five years later assisted in publishing the work *Malleus Maleficarum,* or *Hexenhammer.* This book served as a textbook of procedure in trials for witchcraft, especially in Germany. It described the means by which a witch could be detected and much other information. The author held that witchcraft was more natural to woman than to man, because of her inherent wickedness.

Previous to the decrees mentioned above, there had been minor attempts to discourage witchcraft, but with little success. The earliest ecclesiastical decree is supposed to have been that of Ancyra, 315 A.D., which condemned soothsayers to five years' penance. In canon law, soothsayers were subject to excommunication as idolators and enemies of Christ. The decrees, however, did not lead to wholesale persecutions; neither did they discourage the practice of witchcraft.

After the bulls issued by Alexander IV and John XXII, and especially after that issued by Innocent VIII, there were many trials and executions for witchcraft. The penalty in practically all countries was death by being burned alive. In the trials in Salem and other parts of colonial America, for some reason or other, the condemned witches were hanged instead of burned, although the statute specified the penalty of burning. However, many were burned after being hanged.

It is practically impossible to arrive at an accurate estimate of the number executed. Various estimates have been given, ranging from three hundred thousand to several million. We are told that in Nancy, France, one judge put to death eight hundred persons; that in Toulouse four hundred were executed at one time; and that in the city of Treves upwards of 7,000 were killed during the period of persecution.

Witnesses not admissible in ordinary cases were allowed to testify against the accused in a trial for witchcraft because of the seriousness of the offense. Such witnesses were not permitted on the side of the accused, notwithstanding the fact that the "witch" was in danger of losing his or her life!

An accusation of witchcraft proved to be a very easy and effective means of doing away with persons whose continued existence was believed to be inconvenient. Therefore, people who possessed considerable property found themselves accused of witchcraft and were executed for the benefit of their accusers, and their property confiscated.

It is impossible to take up even briefly the history of witchcraft in the various countries in which these persecutions were carried on. Suffice it to say, that the trials were conducted all over Europe, in England, and in America. Since the American trials are nearer home, and are fairly representative of the trials as a whole, it may be worthwhile to sketch briefly those carried on in Salem, Massachusetts, during the years 1691–92.

As we have all been told in our history textbooks, the Puritans came to American shores seeking religious liberty for themselves. Immediately upon reaching their new home, they began to compel everyone within their settlements to adhere to their religious beliefs under penalty of banishment and various horrible punishments. Much capital has been made by some persons of the fact that certain blue laws have been discovered to be fictitious, but the real blue laws were in force and frequently they crop out at the present day. The Puritans set out to regulate the morals of the entire community. Infractions of the moral laws, however trivial, were made the concern of the city or state, and usually punished publicly. Their lives were severe to the utmost, both as to clothing and their habits. They changed their names in order that they might continually be reminded of their duties. Their children were named in accordance with this idea. The following jury list was filed in the year 1688, and is said to be in the museum at London: Killsin Pimple of Whitham, Standfast Stringer of Crowhurst, Be-Faithful Joine of Britling, Fly-Debate Roberts of Britling, Weep Not Billings of Lewes, Fight-the-good-fight-of-Faith White of Elmer, Meek Brewer of Okehan, Safety-in-Heaven Snat of Okefield, Search-the-Scriptures

Martin of Sollburst, Fight-the-Devil Richardson of Southton, Shall-Hope Briggs of Rye, The-Peace-of-God Knight of Burwash, Seek Wisdom of Worden, Much-Mercy Crier of Worden, Peaceful Harding of Leevas, Gift Weeks of Culkfield, Increase Weeks of Cruckfield, Faint-Not Hurst of Heathfield, Be-Thankful Maynan of Britling, Be-Courteous Call of Herensey. (Source: *The Salem Witch Trials* by William Nelson Gemmill.) It is logical to suppose that people bearing such names, like the vast majority of their contemporaries, were grossly superstitious and extremely ignorant.

At the time of the Salem witch trials, the city had a population of about 1,700 persons. There were no public schools, and a few private schools endeavored to teach some of the children how to read and write, as well as various religious matters, such as the Lord's prayer. Disease was believed to be a visitation of the wrath of God. Insanity was believed to be evidence of possession by an evil spirit.

Prior to 1692, there had been about twenty trials for witchcraft and several hangings in New England. The most prominent persons of the colony believed in witchcraft. Governor Winthrop, Governor Endicott, and Governor Bradshaw presided at the trials of witches and gave their approval of the executions. In 1691, the charter of the Massachusetts Colony was revoked by the English king, and the laws of the colony were thereby abrogated and the statutes of James I were substituted for them. They provided the death penalty for witchcraft. The governor appointed by the king, William Phipps, found the jails of the colony full of persons accused of witchcraft and appointed a court for the trial of the cases. Among the inhabitants of the colony was a West Indian slave girl, by name Tituba, who was well versed in the magic of the Spanish countries. A number of the girls of the colony, ranging in age from nine to twenty years, met at the house of her owner, Rev. Samuel Parris, to watch Tituba display her arts. "The time was spent in telling fortunes and ghost stories, reading palms, tipping tables, listening to spirit rappings, and inducing hypnotic spells" (Gemmill). We are told that under the influence of these performances the girls became hysterical, had violent fits, and screamed loudly, as well as doing many other out-of-the-way things. Two of the girls were epileptic; eight of them could not write their own names. Three were domestic servants and were responsible for the accusation and hanging of their employers.

In February 1692, the girls were examined by a physician, Dr.

Gregg, who, for want of any better explanation of their strange actions, declared that they were bewitched. The girls refused to tell who bewitched them. Tituba offered the following charm: "Take four ounces of rye meal, mix it with children's water, roll it in a biscuit, bake it in ashes, and feed it to a dog. If the dog gets sick, the girls will tell who bewitched them."

This was done and, whatever the reason may have been, the girls began to talk. By the time they stopped talking, twenty persons had been hanged and upwards of two hundred had been imprisoned. Almost all of the accusations of witchcraft in Salem were made by one or more of these girls. One of them, Ann Putnam, testified in all of the cases but one which resulted in hanging. Another, Mary Walcott, is recorded as having testified in all but two such cases. The whole group of girls would usually attend the sessions of the court, where they rolled upon the floor, threw fits, and accused the prisoners of sticking them with needles or pins and of pinching them. We are told that upon some occasions the judges were so aroused by the presence of spirits in the courtroom that Chief Justice Stoughton, "with a large switch in hand, rose and struck wildly about the room in order to drive the evil spirits away..."

The court established by Governor Phipps met for one hundred twenty days. During that time, it put to death twenty people. At the time of its dissolution, there were about one hundred persons in jail, some of them under sentence of death. A court of Common Pleas was created, and on January 5, 1698, it tried twenty-one persons for witchcraft. Of these, all but three were acquitted, and those found guilty were returned to jail and afterwards pardoned. In May 1693, Governor Phipps issued a pardon to all remaining in jail. By this time the people had begun to think and were recovering from the delusion. Seven prominent persons, among them the wife of Governor Phipps and the wife of the minister, Reverend Hall, were accused of witchcraft. Probably this had something to do in causing the sudden ending of the period of persecution.

The awakening of Salem was the beginning of a similar experience in all the countries in which witchcraft trials had been prosecuted. England was the last to fall under the delusion and also the first to recover from it. England executed her last witch in 1716, Scotland in 1722, Germany in 1793, Switzerland in 1780, and Spain in 1781.

On October 17, 1711, the sum of five hundred seventy-eight pounds and twelve shillings was appropriated to be paid to the heirs of those executed in Salem. Damages were also awarded to the heirs of those who died in prison after conviction.

With the passing of the Salem witchcraft delusion came to an end one of the most disgraceful chapters in the history of the American continent. Gradually, the various countries came to realize their errors, and at the present day accusations of witchcraft are very rare.

The belief in witchcraft, or the exercise of supernatural power by witches, was directly and indirectly the result of the ignorance of natural law of the people of all countries. No one who understands the causes of storms, why winds blow, the causes of lightning flashes, could possibly believe that these phenomena of nature can be caused, for instance, by a woman pulling off her stocking or muttering the Lord's prayer backwards. When the natural explanation of a phenomenon is understood, there is no necessity for a supernatural explanation. The belief in devils, like the belief in gods, ceases with the understanding of the causes which produce the results previously supposed to be the result of supernatural power. Understanding of the laws of nature, of the relation of cause and effect, leaves nothing for a god or a devil to do, and no place for him in the scheme of things.

Ignorance, whether it is exhibited in the burning to death of helpless persons for witchcraft, or in the imprisonment of thinkers for daring to think out loud, or in the prohibition of the teaching of scientific facts, is the chief foe of progress. To do away with the results of ignorance, we must first do away with the causes.

Heroines of Freethought

*T*HIS WAS one of Queen's most popular lectures, both with her personally and with her audiences. As an unabashed feminist, Queen believed that the contributions of women to freethought had been not only immense, but unique. They wedded the cause of women's rights to that of freedom of conscience to create a broader context for rationalism.

Earlier in her lecturing career, however, Queen did not give a great deal of attention to the contributions of women. The only other existing lecture she delivered on the general history of freethought mentioned one woman. The lecture was "Pioneers of Freethought," reprinted in *Queen Silver's Magazine* 1, number 4 (Third Quarter 1924): the woman was Hypatia. The passage read:

> There is another woman of ancient times, whose name ought never to be forgotten by anyone who loves freedom, or who values knowledge. Her name was Hypatia, and for forty years she taught such truths as were then known. I want to tell you about her, but before I do so, I must tell you about the great college wherein she taught.
>
> Several hundred years before the Christian era, an Egyptian king, Ptolemy Soter, founded a college and library in the city of Alexandria. Almost all of the dynasty of kings known as [the] Ptolemies were interested in promoting scientific knowledge. They added to this library from time to time, until, shortly before it was destroyed by a mob of Christians in the year 391, it possessed seven hundred thousand volumes of manuscripts. Every student or learned man who came to Egypt was asked to set down in writing his knowledge, that they might preserve it for all time. Every foreigner who brought into Egypt a manuscript from any other country was obliged to lend it to the library, while they made a copy of it for preservation. At Alexandria were collected all the known works of all the writers and philosophers of the ancient world. Part of this library was accidentally destroyed by Julius Caesar. His successor, Antony, presented to Cleopatra the great collection of Pergamos, to take the place of the works destroyed.
>
> In connection with this library, which was kept in two great buildings, a great university was maintained. Ten thousand students were accommodated. Anyone who felt he had a message to deliver, or who wished to teach, went to one of the great courtyards, and sat, or stood, with his students around him, as long as they cared to listen. Learning was free. Anyone might teach, and anyone might come to study. Poor students were fed at public expense. Anyone might, if he chose, sleep on the floor at night. Any subject might be taught by anyone. In other words, the Alexandrian college was a great, free, open forum. If you can imagine Los Angeles Street multiplied twenty-five times, and if you can imagine it without any Christian or other religionists, and if you can picture a library of three-quarters of a million books accessible to the public free of charge, and if you can picture what all this would be like if we possessed absolute freedom of speech—then you will have a fair idea of what the university and library of ancient Alexandria was like. The modern world has no such place of learning as that.
>
> In the year 391 a mob of fanatics, recently washed in the blood of

Jesus, led by sanctified bandits and monks, destroyed the larger wing of the library, with more than half of the priceless manuscripts possessed by the institution. This act of vandalism was instituted by the great Christian emperor, Theodosius, and carried out under the direct supervision of Theophilus, Christian bishop of Alexandria. Theophilus said: "If these books disagree with the Bible, they are heretical, and ought to be burned. If they agree with the Bible, they are useless, and ought to be burned." So he burned them anyway. He was a true Christian, carrying out god's command to Adam, "Of the tree of knowledge thou shalt not eat." But the college still remained, and possibly a third of the books which were in the other building were preserved.

In this college, at this very time, lived and taught Hypatia, the greatest woman philosopher of which history has told us. She was the daughter of the great Cleon, an astronomer and mathematician. It is said that in her infancy she showed proof of rare genius, and that accordingly her father educated her with great care. While no more than a child, she mastered the different languages of antiquity, and while still a young girl, took her place as a teacher of the school.

In those days women were kept in seclusion, and it is said that the beauty and youth of Hypatia made so great an impression upon the men who were unaccustomed to see women in public places, that Hypatia usually wore a heavy veil, that her students might not have their attention distracted by her face. Her lectures drew all the educated people of the city to the school, as well as regular students. People came from all over the Roman world to listen to her wisdom and eloquence. She was held in such high regard that the judges of the city took their difficult cases to her for judgment. Theophilus, holy father, saint, and bishop, hated her intensely, but he felt she was too powerful for him to attack. The Christians were not yet sufficiently powerful to force their dogmas on the government of Alexandria, for that city was the last stronghold of Science and Reason. But when his nephew Cyril became bishop, the end of freedom came. Dirty—he never bathed—filled with fanaticism and holy fervor, he set out to make Alexandria saintly, Christian, and ignorant. It is said by some historians that he became jealous of Hypatia, because the people flocked to her lectures instead of coming to his church. He preached to monks and empty seats while thousands attended the lectures of Hypatia. However that may be, Cyril and his crazy monks seized Hypatia as she was riding through the streets, tore the clothing from her body, dragged her at the end of a rope through the city, and brought her to Cyril's own church. They took her inside, to the foot of their Christian altar, and with hands and teeth and knives, those Christian savages tore her body to pieces. Pieces of her flesh were dis-

tributed among the mob as souvenirs. Cyril thus became supreme.
Science was intimidated and destroyed. Cyril was a saint, and superstition held sway without opposition for more than a thousand years,
as far as the Christian world was concerned. Christianity teaches that
Hypatia, the woman who taught Truth for forty years, went to hell,
and that Cyril, the saintly bishop who murdered her, went to heaven.

In later years, Queen acknowledged many, many more contributions of women to freethought.

Heroines of Freethought

I am always a little reluctant to discuss women as opposed to men
because I don't like segregating people in this way. However sometimes
it is necessary, and in this case I think it is especially so because finding
the names and activities of women in the freethought movement took a
bit of digging. And, when I did find references, it was often to a "Mrs.
So-and-So," who was the wife of some prominent freethinker. The reference will say "Mrs. So-and-so is also very active." You are lucky if you
find out the woman's first name, let alone her place or date of birth.
These women lived in what someone has called "the seven-story blanket
of insignificance." I'm not sure whether it is because most of the histories have been written by men or because the women back then were
retiring and did not like to get into the public eye. Thus, the women
often wrote under pen names or anonymously.

Nevertheless, many women have made important contributions to
the freethought movement. When I got deeply enough into the research
I found that not only did I have enough for an evening, but I had enough
for five or six evenings. After I had cut the talk down to the nineteenth
century in the United States, I still had about sixteen women whom I
couldn't overlook. That talk is too lengthy for me to give tonight.

What I propose to do instead is to first talk about what freethought
is and, then, try to examine how women in the nineteenth century
became freethinkers or became involved in freethought organizations.
We have a stereotype in this country that women are the pillars of the
church. They are the mainstay of religion through their potluck suppers
and all the unpaid labor they donate. And, it is true, churches would be
in a bad way if they did not have women volunteering their labor for

generations. Women are said to have a special relationship with their churches. So I want to discuss what encourages or discourages women from becoming freethinkers. Then, I will talk about a very few individual women.

First of all, let me define what I mean when I say "freethinker." The term "freethinker" has been used in different contexts over the years. For a long time, the word "freethinker" referred to anybody who rejected authority and insisted on thinking for themselves in any field. Later on, it referred to people who used reason to decide about religious matters rather than appealing to divine revelation. In other words, rational religion as opposed to revealed, supernatural religion. "Freethinker" came to be a term for atheists, agnostics, and—generally speaking—heretics.

Both senses of the word "freethinker" are still in use. For example, in the *Viking Desk Encyclopedia*, it says "those who reached conclusions by reasoning, rejecting supernatural authority and ecclesiastical tradition." In another definition, "freethought is that thought which is free from dogmatic assumptions, usually religious dogmas, and seeks the answers to all questions through rational inquiry."

I like the statement attributed to the father of Hypatia, "Reserve your right to think, for even to think wrongly is better than not to think at all." He also said "all formal dogmatic religions are fallacious, and must never be accepted by self-respecting persons as final." I also like the definition Gordon Stein used in his book *Freethought in America*: freethought is thought that is free of dogmatic assumption and seeks the answer through rational inquiry.

So, in the spirit of this definition, I think the words "freethinker" and "freethought" can be applied to a great many areas other than religion because it is really an attitude, or a way of thinking.

During the nineteenth century, there was a great deal of freethought activity in the United States under the aegis of various organizations. They called themselves secularists, rationalists, liberals, and by many other names. They rarely called themselves "atheists" because of the climate of extreme intolerance. But there were such organizations as the Free Inquirers Association, the American Rationalist Association, the National Liberal League, the United Secularists of America, and local groups such as the Los Angeles Liberal Club. Then, later in the early years of this century, came more specialized groups. In 1925, after much struggle, we had the organization incorporated in the state of New York as the American Association for the Advancement of Atheism. Since then there has been American Atheists, the Freedom from Religion Foundation, and Atheists United. There are also humanist organizations, which could be in the category of freethought.

What discourages freethinking in women? In the nineteenth century, thinking was not popular when it was done by women. Freethinking was not popular when it was done by anyone. Those of you who know the history of the women's rights movement know that the climate then was not conducive to freedom of any kind for women. Rebellion was unacceptable. A woman was supposed to be a lady, which meant keeping quiet and doing what she was told and not rocking the boat. Also, women were economically very dependent and they did not have financial independence. The person who has the purse strings in the family is the person who usually dictates what others in the family are going to do and say.

Also, women in the nineteenth century had a very confined life. Their role in society was rigidly defined for them. For example, if a woman spoke in public at all on any subject, she was considered to be very unladylike and extremely unacceptable, even if she spoke in a religious meeting or in the Ladies Aid Society, or something of this sort. It was unacceptable for women publicly to speak or write or agitate. In those days, a respectable woman never got her name into the paper. Or if she did, it was only on three occasions: when she was born, when she was married, and when she died. Anything else was completely out of the question. This was a period in which women were advised, when arranging their bookshelves, to put titles by male authors on a different shelf than ones by women for the sake of propriety.

So the early women speakers—most of whom started out in the antislavery movement—began by going to women's living rooms and just talking to women. Men would stray in occasionally and this would create a great scandal because women were not supposed to speak at a meeting where both men and women were present. When the women finally went out to lecture in public, the Congregational church issued a pastoral letter condemning the practice and calling attention to the "danger to the female character" by virtue of such activities.

Moreover, the women who became pioneers usually had families and home responsibilities. In the 1800s, raising a family required a great amount of sheer activity. It was not as easy as it is now, and many women feel it is not so easy now. But cooking on a wood stove, heating water with wood you had to chop, doing laundry by hand in the wash basin on the stove—this sort of labor takes a physical toll on a person. Also, there were no childcare facilities. So not only did these women lack opportunities to develop their minds, they also had no time or physical strength to pursue anything beyond the day-to-day necessities. Often the women were not able to get out and become active until after the children could take care of themselves, or the older children could care for the younger ones.

There was also a patriarchal family structure, in which daughters were discouraged from pursuing intellectual matters at all. One of the first things a woman would hear as a small child would be, "Oh, I am so sorry you are not a boy, otherwise I would send you to college."

Church was often the only socially acceptable and available way for women to get out of the house and participate in society. It provided an emotional support system and a social life that, especially in farm communities, women did not have otherwise. When they did go to church, however, women found they were supposed to do a great deal of the work and have no say in how things were run. So, there was oppression within the religious community but, at the same time, there was little alternative to it. For a women to be a freethinker required either extreme personal stubbornness or a very supportive family who were willing to provide her with economic support. Or, she had to be able to earn her own living.

Often, men came to the freethought movement by directly questioning religious dogmas or through their education. But most of the women came into the freethought movement through different avenues. How did women enter the movement? Well, sometimes they were fortunate enough to be born into a family of freethinkers or liberals, and they got their education in rationalism naturally. But more frequently they came either by way of the women's rights movement or the antislavery movement, or sometimes in reaction to a very rigorous and orthodox home environment.

Often, they became involved in some other movement which, in turn, led them into freethought. This is not always true but it is very often true. For example, in the early days of the antislavery movement, many women wanted to take part in the agitation. But they found it was unacceptable for a woman to take part actively because she *was* a woman. As you will recall, the women's rights movement in this country grew out of the fact that women had been barred from the World Anti-Slavery Conference. They were not allowed to be delegates to that convention and, so, they started the Woman's Rights Convention. Everything broke loose from then on.

Women in the antislavery movement found that the chief spokesmen against their public agitation were ministers. The church was also a main support for slavery. The chief material quoted against women and against the slaves were biblical quotations. So it was natural for women to question some religious matters and, when you question one religious dogma, you are apt to doubt all the other dogmas. So from questioning the divine right of slavery, you are likely to question the divine right of men over women. This is what antislavery women did, and they drew some unpleasant comparisons between the status of women and the status of slaves.

But, as I said, few of the women who went into the freethought movement were single-tracked people. Most of them were radicals in a number of other areas. I have seen many men in freethought who get one idea, and having one idea, stopped. As I used to say, "They are half-baked and need to be turned over to cook on the other side." But perhaps because it was such an effort for the women to become assertive about anything, when they did speak out they started raising questions about all sorts of things.

I am going to start trying to cover just a few of the women—not all of them by any means—but a few who were prominent in their period and who made a definite contribution.

The first is a woman named Mrs. Dorothy Johns. I know nothing about her except that she was the wife of a very close friend of Jack London, probably Cloudsley Johns. In 1908, the preachers in Los Angeles were taking advantage of the streets to shout about religion. They occupied a great deal of public space and made noise. Johns and three other women decided that preachers should not be allowed to have the streets to themselves. The freethinkers and radicals should also be able to speak on the streets. So, the four women asserted their rights. They were all promptly jailed and held for some time. Thirty-five men were also arrested. Among them was Edward Adams Cantrell, a minister who went on to become one of the two leaders of the Los Angeles Liberal Club—a freethought club in Los Angeles at the time I arrived in 1916. Although they had not yet been tried, the men were either put out on the chain gang or put in jail. Eventually, the prisoners were all acquitted.

As a result, Los Angeles opened up part of its streets for speaking. [The author] Channing Severance wrote:

> The Socialists and Freethinkers of Los Angeles have won a notable victory for free speech—that is, the right to speak unmolested on the street—and religious ranters no longer enjoy a monopoly given them by pinheaded officials afflicted with the idea that only believers in the Christian superstition have any rights under a secular government.

I will add a personal note on this: in 1916 when my mother and I came to Los Angeles the free speech zone was at that time on Los Angeles Street from 1st Street to 2nd Street. The religious people more or less hung toward 1st Street and the left-wingers hung toward 2nd Street but sometimes they got too close to each other. Then there was some friction. There was one incident where a truck was purposefully driven into one of the street meetings and two people were killed, with several others injured. Nothing was ever done to the people who drove the truck. On other occasions, rocks were thrown. By and large, however, it was peaceful.

My mother carried on open-air meetings there over a period of some years and I spoke a great deal when I was young. I grew up in that situation. After some years, the free speech zone was moved because the respectable merchants in the area were getting perturbed. It moved to the Los Angeles Plaza—what is now Olivera Street—and it was clear into the '30s and I believe into the '40s (I remember speaking there myself, but not in the '40s). Then, when Olivera Street was remodeled, then, of course, it was no longer respectable to have street speakers. The Department of Parks built a small park that was never used by speakers because it was so difficult to get to.

The postscript to the Johns story is that, in 1917, my mother was holding a meeting on Los Angeles Street. She was making a freethought speech. She read a newspaper clipping that said the city of Riverside had just passed an ordinance prohibiting people from kissing on the streets of that city. The law was meant to protect the morals of the American soldiers who were stationed in an army base close to Riverside. Mother remarked that if these young men had not had good Christian upbringings, but had been given rational moral training, they wouldn't need to have their morals protected by the police department. That cost her a week in jail, and a $50 fine for disturbing the peace. But I think she got enough fun out of it to feel well paid.

The second woman freethinker I want to discuss was one of the inspirations for America's greatest poet. When Walt Whitman was about ten years old, his father took him to hear Frances Wright lecture. His father was an ardent fan of Frances Wright. He attended all of her lectures, and took his son along with him. Years later Walt was to say that she was one of the very few who inspired in him tremendous respect and love. She was described as being extraordinarily eloquent, with an almost unequaled command of words.

She was born in Scotland in 1795. Of her father, all we know is that he was an admirer of Thomas Paine and a graduate of Trinity College. However, both her parents were killed when she was two years old. So Frances and a younger sister were raised by various relatives. Then, they went to live with a great uncle who taught moral philosophy at Glasgow College. Of course, he had books and Frances read widely.

She published a freethought booklet entitled *A Few Days in Athens* when she was nineteen. Then, in 1818 she came to America for the first time and later published a book on her travels entitled *View of Society and Manners in America.* She became active in the movement to do away with slavery, however, she was a moderate who felt it would be best to buy the slaves and send them to colonies. Beginning in 1828, she became a freethought lecturer and edited the *Free Enquirer* with the social utopian Robert Dale Owen. In 1829 she settled in New York where she purchased a small church and converted it into a Hall of Science, which was used for freethought lectures for the next several years. In addition to freethought, she advocated equal rights for women, freedom for the slaves, liberal divorce laws, and birth control. These were unpopular views at this time and certainly things women were not supposed to talk about. She was branded by the newspapers as the "great red harlot of infidelity."

She died in 1852 as the result of a freakish accident in which she sustained a broken hip that did not recover. She had separated from her husband and both of them were on the same icy street, each going in different directions. They bumped into each other and she fell down. The aftereffects eventually killed her.

The next woman acquired the nickname of "Ingersoll in soprano" and, at that time, no higher compliment could be paid to a freethought lecturer. Col. Robert Ingersoll was *the* outstanding freethought lecturer in the country. She was born Alice Chenowethl in 1853 in Virginia, but she is known to history as Helen Hamilton Gardener. Her father was an Episcopalian who later became a Methodist circuit rider, and quite orthodox. However, he did have the courage of conscience because when he decided slavery was wrong, he freed all the slaves he had inherited and moved his family to Indiana. During the Civil War, he served as a guide for the Northern troops. Gardener's mother remained a very orthodox Calvinist all her life.

It is not clear why she left home as early as she did, probably the orthodox environment in the family had a great deal to do with it. By 1873 she had gone to Cincinnati, where she graduated from high school and normal school. She then taught for a number of years until her first marriage. She began writing and, perhaps because she didn't want family arguments, she published under various male pseudonyms. Remember that it was not ladylike for a woman to write books, and it was only just becoming acceptable for women to write novels. As far as women writing on more abstruse subjects, a woman's brain wasn't considered equal to the job and shouldn't be strained. Nevertheless, she attended Columbia University and studied biology. After several years, she adopted the name Helen Hamilton Gardener, which is the name she kept both personally and professionally for the rest of her life.

As well as writing, she became an outstanding public speaker and one of the very few people who was equally brilliant with written and spoken words. She became a friend of Robert and Eva Ingersoll, who greatly influenced her. It was through Robert Ingersoll's prodding that she gave her first series of lectures in 1884, which were published the next year under the title of *Men, Women, and Gods and Other Lectures* by the Truth Seeker Co. She also became a contributor to the *Free Thought Magazine*.

During the period of her first lectures, Gardener had dealt extensively with the degradation of women as taught through the Bible. Following up on this line of thought, she became very active in the feminist movement. In 1887, the *Popular Science Monthly* published an article written by a neurologist who said it was inherently impossible and impractical for women to have equality as their brains were measurably inferior to those of men. This annoyed Helen Gardener, so she decided to answer the article. So, with the assistance of another neurologist, she prepared a research paper on sex and the brain. This was read before the International Congress of Women in 1888. Also she pointed out that the brains of men studied by the research scientists have been usually those of prominent men who had accomplished a great deal. But when they studied women's brains, the ones they used were from the prisons or the insane asylums or other places of that sort. To provide another source, she arranged for her own brain to go to Cornell University after her death. A research paper on the brain of Helen Gardener was published shortly after her death in 1925 in the *Journal of Physical Anthropology* (October–December 1927).

She was a prolific writer, with two novels, numerous short stories, including some based on scientific matters of heredity. She wrote many, many articles in *Popular Science Monthly* and other magazines and she contributed to the *Free Thought Magazine* for a period of about ten years. Because her writings were translated into many languages all over the world, she came into contact and corresponded with leading biologists and anthropologists worldwide.

After her first husband died, she remarried to a retired army officer. For the next six years, they traveled and she was not active in any reform. However, upon her return to Washington, the feminist leaders urged her to get into the campaign for the passage of the suffrage amendment, and she became an unofficial lobbyist in that field. Because of her husband's position, she was able to have contact with a great many officials, including President Wilson on at least twenty occasions. She earned a new nickname, "Our Diplomatic Corps." Maud Wood Park, chairman of the Congressional Committee of the North American Woman's Suffrage Association which worked for the suffrage amendment, wrote,

> Her work can rarely be reported because of its confidential nature, but this may truly be said, that whenever a miracle has appeared to happen in our behalf, if the facts could be told they would nearly always prove that Mrs. Gardener was the worker of wonders.

The next woman I want to discuss is Matilda Joselyn Gage, primarily because one book she wrote became a classic in freethought. It was *Woman, Church and State.* Gage originally came through the women's rights movement. Although she was born in 1826, she didn't become active in freethought until many years later. She came out of a free-thinking home, which served as a gathering place for reformers. It was also, reportedly, on the underground railroad that hid runaway slaves. She was tutored by her father at home, including biology that women generally did not study in those days. In fact, when my mother was going to school around the turn of the century, the physiology textbook had no section of reproduction. Sections such as digestion were over in the appendix. Although mother was told to read this, it would not be discussed in class. Women were expected to grow up without realizing they had any of this equipment.

Gage was never an outstanding public speaker. She was primarily a writer and an organizer. As one of the radicals within the women's rights movement, she felt it was not enough to work for suffrage. It was also necessary to work for equal property, for birth control, and especially for economic rights for women—the right to keep their own earnings and the right to own property. By about 1880, she had become convinced that the primary obstacle to woman's equality were the organized churches. She tried very hard to get the women's organizations to take steps along this line, without success. It was this belief that led her to publish *Woman, Church and State* in 1883.

In 1890, she formed the Women's National Liberal Union with two goals in mind. First, Gage wanted to show the relationship between the teachings of the church and the struggle for equality. Second, she wanted to counter the growing trend of churches trying to interfere with government. Anthony Comstock by this time was in his heyday and Matilda Gage's book was threatened with prosecution under the Comstock Act because of things that she quoted from the Bible. She was never actually prosecuted.

Gage was closely allied with Elizabeth Cady Stanton who was also very prominent in the women's rights movement. She and Stanton collaborated, with a committee of other women, to produce *The Woman's Bible* which was a commentary on the Bible and its relation to women's rights. She died at seventy-one at the home of her daughter Maud, wife of L. Frank Baum, author of *Wizard of Oz*.

The next woman has the distinction of getting arrested under the Comstock laws in 1885: Elmina Drake Slenker. She was affectionately known as Aunt Elmina. She was the eldest daughter of Thomas Drake, a Quaker preacher who was expelled by the Quakers for heresy. He then became a liberal. Growing up in an atmosphere of debate and argument, Elmina became an atheist. Unfortunately she couldn't be a public speaker because of a speech impediment—a hare lip—but she became a prolific writer. For a number of years she edited a publication known as *The Little Freethinker*, which was published for children. She wrote a number of freethought books for children, which is something we are sadly lacking today. Slenker wrote *Little Lessons for Liberal Sunday School*, *The Darwins*, and *Little Lessons for Little Folks*. She corresponded with almost all the liberal journals of that period and was very devoted to the freethought cause, a substantial contributor.

Her arrest came on the charge of contaminating the public mails with obscene material. We speak of entrapment at the present time. One of the agents of the Comstock Anti-Vice Society went to her office, engaged in conversation, and expressed an interest in her views, which were somewhat explicit but rather conservative in their content. He succeeded in having her mail some material to him and she was arrested for contaminating the United States mail. She was indicted by the federal grand jury, brought to trial, and found guilty by the jury. However, the judge delayed sentencing and her attorney made a motion to quash the indictment because it was technically defective. The judge, probably being happy to get rid of the case so easily—it had become quite controversial—granted the motion to dismiss.

The *Truth Seeker*, which was the leading freethought paper for many, many years, had raised the money for her defense fund. Over two thousand freethinkers, liberals, and scientists from all over the world had contributed to the defense fund for her, even though the charge against her was not technically a freethought issue. In the book *Fifty Years of Freethought*, the editor of the *Truth Seeker*, George MacDonald, wrote:

> Mrs. Slenker was an Alphite, or one who admitted the legitimacy of marriage for no other purpose than to perpetuate the species. She circulated literature bearing on this question and probably treated of the propagative act with considerable freedom. The agent of the Vice Society got her into the trap by pretending to be interested in her work.... The National Defense Association conducted the defense of Mrs. Slenker and *Truth Seeker* readers paid the expenses. Her most ardent advocates were women. She was indicted on July 12 (1887) and held for trial by the U.S. District Court for the Western District of

Virginia at Abingdon. She was arraigned before Judge Paul and a jury, which found her guilty. When the judge postponed sentence, the court discharged Mrs. Slenker from custody.

Elmina died in 1908.

The next woman is a westerner—the others were in the eastern part of the country. She spent much of her life in Portland, Oregon, which I'm happy about because I was born in Portland myself. Katie Kehm Smith was born about 1868 in Illinois but moved westward after graduating from high school in Iowa. She taught school there for about six years. She had become a freethinker at sixteen and at seventeen gave her first freethought lecture.

In 1891 she married D. W. Smith of Washington and they later moved to Oregon where she became the secretary of the Oregon State Secular Union. She and her husband established the First Secular Church of Portland in January 1893, and later the Portland Secular Sunday School. She lectured every Sunday at the church to an audience that usually ranged from 300 to 400 people, which was as much as any of the orthodox churches in the city. She died in 1895, at the age of only twenty-seven.

The next woman I want to discuss came out of a rather hostile religious environment. Her father was a rabbi in Russian Poland. The name she later adopted was Ernestine Louise Rose. There is next to no information on her early background, which was presumably a traditionally orthodox Jewish one. Her father regretted having her as a daughter because he said she had a boy's head in a woman's body. When he told her that little girls should not ask questions, she said "why?" She was a rebel at five and a heretic at fourteen. Upon the death of her mother shortly before she was sixteen, an inheritance came to her and her father decided it would be a good idea to marry her off, using the inheritance as a dowry. The selected husband was almost her father's age, so she took her case before the court of a town many miles away. Ernestine argued so eloquently that she won her case. Returning home, she encountered a new stepmother who was about her own age. They didn't get along very well.

Abandoning most of her inheritance, she left and never went home again. Her travels took her to Berlin where she earned a living through inventing a household deodorant. Later she traveled to Holland, Belgium, and France, and became involved in the revolution in France in 1830. Afterward, in England, she became a disciple of Robert Owen, the reformer. She married another of his disciples and they moved to America in 1836. From then on she was active in all types of reform, becoming an eloquent speaker for both women's rights and freethought. She acquired the title of "Queen of the Platform." She published a popular pamphlet entitled *In Defense of Atheism* and for fifty years was a contributor to the *Boston Investigator*, a freethought weekly.

She became increasingly active in the women's rights movement, lecturing in more than twenty states. Her outspoken freethought ideas made her very unpopular with the more conservative women's organizations and groups, causing her to be overlooked by some histories of the suffrage movement. However, she sustained the support of both Susan Anthony and Elizabeth Cady Stanton. Anthony, when asked about women's rights pioneers, said, "Begin with Mary Wollstonecraft, then Frances Wright, then Ernestine L. Rose." She died in England in 1892.

There are others I would like to mention but there is no time. So I will end with Elizabeth Cady Stanton and discuss an aspect of Stanton which is often swept under the rug. Most people know of Stanton as a women's rights advocate, but few people know how strongly she spoke for freethought. The biographical sketch in the *Encyclopaedia Britannica* mentions her as an advocate of woman's suffrage and lists organizations to which she belonged, but very conveniently forgets her anticlerical and antireligious activities. It doesn't even mention *The Woman's Bible.*

All during the period that Stanton had been active for women's rights, at every turn she found churches and religious organizations in her way. When she went to rural areas and talked to women in their homes, she found they were not so shocked at what she said about birth control as they were by her unorthodox religious opinions. Whenever she argued a point on behalf of women, someone in the audience always quoted a Bible passage to show that you couldn't or shouldn't do it. She came to believe that organized religion was the greatest obstacle in the way of women's rights and, unless the obstacle was overcome, the movement was not going to succeed.

She tried to convince others in the organizations to which she belonged of this, but was largely unsuccessful. So she organized a separate group, the Women's National Liberal Union, for the expressed purpose of combating organized religion. When she was eighty years old, in 1895, she published one of the fundamental contributions of women to freethought—*The Woman's Bible.* It was put together by Stanton, and a group of nineteen other women who wrote commentaries on the scriptures in the Old and New Testament pertaining to women. The book was a best-seller, but it created a storm of protest and Stanton was accused of killing the women's rights movement. As she said later on,

> When I introduced the resolution at the first convention that we should demand the vote, they accused me of killing the women's rights movement. When I introduced resolutions calling for easier divorce laws and for the woman's property law, they accused me of killing the women's rights movement. And now I have published *The Woman's Bible* and they accuse me of killing the women's rights movement. The women's rights movement still lives.

The book *Notable American Women* summarized her contribution as follows,

> Perhaps Mrs. Stanton's greatest contribution was her effort to emancipate women's minds. She was essentially a torchbearer whose liberal thinking and courageous outlook were potent factors in freeing women from the psychological barriers which hedged them in, and in pointing the way to wider interests and activities.... [S]he urged women to reject encumbering traditions and to dare to question any edict or church or state which limited women's sphere.

So here we have a very brief outline of a few of the women involved in nineteenth-century American freethought. Some became very famous and known all over the world. Others remained obscure. Some were orators. Some were writers. Some were great organizers. Others did the ordinary day-to-day work that must be done by someone. All of them probably made mistakes, as they all made contributions. But because of such people we have the freedoms we have now.

Several themes run through the lives of these women. One of them is that very few were single-track liberals. Unlike many male freethinkers, who might have their heads screwed on very well in one direction but not in other directions, the women have been pretty well-rounded. They were not afraid to apply their freethinking to all areas of life, not just religion. Another theme is that the women who became freethought lecturers and advocates were able to find a way of earning their own living and of being independent financially so they did not need to ask someone's permission to do these things. They could openly speak their minds. But, then, there were other women like Ella Gibson who wrote the book *Godly Women of the Bible*. When it was published Gibson didn't put her name on it for various family reasons: the author's identity went on as "An Ungodly Woman of the Nineteenth Century." Later on, the book was republished under her own name.

We also find that women had to overcome much greater handicaps in terms of social pressure against them and criticism of their activities. And this, of course, is true even now. If a man makes a vigorous speech and is very assertive, it will be reported as "Mr. So-and-So gave a very dynamic exposition of his case." But if a woman does the same thing, this is not dynamic, this is just plain aggressive. And for a woman who is aggressive there is a nasty, nasty word. For a woman to be a freethinker involved a great deal more than for a man to be a freethinker.

Notwithstanding all these things, these women overcame all these obstacles, and left a contribution to the freethought upon which the rest of us can build.

The Many Sides of Mark Twain

*I*N OCTOBER 1995, the Humanist Association of Los Angeles circulated the following announcement:

> Queen Silver, Freethought Activist/Pioneer, recipient of the HALA-Negri Award as well as many other awards. Topic: The Many Sides of Mark Twain. Queen is a third-generation feminist and a second-generation Freethinker. She was educated entirely by her mother, who was an activist/speaker who traveled a great deal. She is Vice-President Emeritus of HALA and is active in many organizations.

A precocious child, Queen received her first library card at the age of 5 and was able to sign (not print) her own name on the card.

She speaks with much humor and wit—don't miss her![1]

Mark Twain was one of Queen's two favorite authors, and a source she drew upon throughout her life. In 1930, she had written in *Queen Silver's Magazine*:

Mark Twain was known in his lifetime as a humorist; since his death, he has become even more famous for his philosophy and his radical free-thinking. *What is Man?*, a small book which he first published in a very limited edition, for private circulation only, and most of which was bought up and suppressed by his relatives, is now to be had from his regular publishers, as are also five other attacks upon religion, *The Mysterious Stranger, Christian Science, Captain Stormfield's Visit to Heaven, Adam's Diary*, and *Joan of Arc*. In the first of these, the devil is portrayed as much superior to god, and man's inferiority to the other animals is said to be due to his possession of "moral sense." One of the most striking denunciations of god ever written may be found in *The Mysterious Stranger*. It is, in part, as follows:

A God who could make good children as easily as bad, yet preferred to make bad ones; who could have made every one of them happy, yet never made a single happy one; who made them prize their bitter life, yet stingily cut it short; who gave his angels eternal happiness un-earned, yet required his other children to earn it; who gave his angels painless lives, and yet cursed his other children with biting miseries and maladies of mind and body; who mouths justice and invented Hell; mouths Golden Rules, and forgiveness multiplied seventy time seven, and invented Hell; who mouths morals to other people and has none himself; who frowns upon crimes, yet commits them all; who created man without invitation, then tries to shuffle the responsibility for man's acts upon man, instead of honorably placing it where it belongs, upon himself; and finally, with altogether divine obtuseness, invites this poor abused slave to worship him.[2]

Queen Silver's Magazine quoted Twain elsewhere, as well, as follows:

At a dinner party, the subject of eternal life and future punishment came up for a long discussion, in which Mark Twain, who was present, took no part. A lady suddenly turned to him and exclaimed: "Why do you not say anything? I want your opinion." Twain replied gravely: "Madam, you must excuse me. I am silent of necessity. I have friends in both places."[3]

During the last days of her life, one of the last requests Queen made was for me to look up a quote in the set of Mark Twain she had given to me as a gift years before. She was sketching out another talk on Twain in her mind.

The following transcript has been edited together from various cassette-recorded versions of this lecture, using as a guide the same set of file cards Queen used herself when delivering "The Many Sides of Mark Twain."

Notes

1. The speech was given on November 5, 1995. In contradiction to the introduction, Grace claimed that Queen received her first library card at the age of six.

2. *QSM* 5, no. 4 (July–August 1930): 15.

3. *QSM* 6, no. 2 (March–April 1931): 14.

The Many Sides of Mark Twain

I am not an authority on Mark Twain. He is one of my two favorite authors,* and I have probably read the published works of Mark Twain multiple times. But tonight I would like to get into things that are not usually discussed about Mark Twain because people, when they hear his name, say, "Oh, yes, he wrote *Tom Sawyer.*" And if they are erudite, they remember he also wrote *Huckleberry Finn.* And that is about as far as it goes.

But Mark Twain was a many-sided individual. He was, in his lifetime, a printer, a laborer, a miner, a newspaper writer, a newspaper owner, at times an inventor—he had three patents to his credit. Often he was also a social critic, although he refrained from saying many things he would have liked to have said. We will never see all of Mark Twain's work. When he died, he left behind hundreds of thousands of words of unpublished material. Some of it he had marked "not to be printed for fifty years." Some "not to be printed for one hundred years." Some "not

---

*The other was Jack London, on whom Grace wrote articles and seemed to know personally.

to be printed for two hundred years." It was his feeling that his heirs would probably be burned alive should they publish these writings.

As you know, there is a new attempt to censor *Huckleberry Finn* and take it out of the libraries. I would like to read a letter Mark Twain wrote in 1902 to a librarian who had contacted him because another librarian was attempting to get rid of *Huckleberry Finn.* He said, "Dear Sir. I am deeply troubled by what you say. I wrote *Tom Sawyer* and *Huck Finn* for adults exclusively. And it always distresses me when I find boys and girls have been allowed access to them." This is, of course, tongue-in-cheek: they were boy's books.

> The mind that becomes soiled in youth can never again be washed clean. I know this by my own experience and to this day I cherish an unappeasable bitterness against the unfaithful guardians of my young life who not only permitted but compelled me to read an unexpurgated Bible through before I was fifteen years old. Most honestly do I wish I could say a softening word or two in defense of Huck's character since you wish it. But, really, in my opinion, it is no better than those of Solomon, David, and the rest of the sacred brotherhood. If there is an unexpurgated in the children's department, won't you please help that young woman remove Tom and Huck from that questionable companionship.

After some biographical information on Twain, I will spend the greater part of the time talking about some works people are not familiar with. But some details seem necessary. In 1835, Florida, Missouri, was not even what we would call today "a wide spot in the road." It held a hundred people and I am not sure that excluded slaves, but it probably did. When Mark Twain was born on November 30, 1835—the year of Halley's comet—he increased the population by 1 percent, which is more than most people do for their birthplaces.

The house into which he came as a premature, unhealthy baby already was occupied by a father, mother, four other children, a slave girl, and possibly a man slave. So probably another child wasn't terribly welcome, but in those days they took what the Lord sent and tried to be happy about it. His father, John Marshall Clemens, was an agnostic and an anticlerical. Not in sequence but often simultaneously, he was a farmer, a merchant, a lawyer, and sometimes a justice of the peace because, in that day and in that town, you had to be at least several things in order to make any kind of living. Just before he died, he was selected as town clerk but was unable to take that position. He had moved several times before Mark Twain's birth. We should say Samuel's birth, I suppose, because his name was Samuel Langhorne Clemens. But I am going to use Mark Twain. They had moved several times before Twain's birth trying to better themselves economically and, in the course of his lifetime, they moved several more times.

His mother, Jane Lampton Clemens, had been a vivacious character, a great dancer, and fond of good times when she was young. By the time Samuel was born, however, she had become a very pious person, a Presbyterian. She was a strict disciplinarian and had lost that earlier joy of living by having received too much religion. But she was a compassionate and courageous person in defending animals who were mistreated and in defending women who were beaten—if the women happened to be white. She did not extend that feeling to the slave girl who was repeatedly punished rather severely.

Mark Twain was a sickly child. At one time, they did not expect he would live. The death rate for children in those days was much steeper than it is now and it was a novelty to raise a sizable family and not lose at least one or two children along the way. Twain was constantly dosed with patent medicines of the period, ranging all the way from the painkiller which he describes in an episode in *Tom Sawyer* to a number of other cures. He was also subjected to curative treatments, such as the water treatment, and in spite of all this he managed to survive.

He was not exempted from being disciplined because of ill health and, in those days, much of what we now punish as child abuse was a routine part of daily living. It was standard discipline. The maxim was "spare the rod and spoil the child." And never did they spare the rod. The attitude was that if the child didn't do one thing, he or she deserved it for something else. The father was the king in the household and the children were the underclass, to put it mildly.

In addition, Twain had to go to church and Sunday school, and when he had done anything wrong he got extra church service as punishment. He was indoctrinated into the Presbyterian faith and afterwards wrote that his "nights were filled with terror." Whenever there was a thunderstorm or lightning or a flood or something happened, he was sure that it was a warning if he did not improve his ways the Lord would be coming after him next. Whenever one of his schoolmates became ill or had a mishap, this again was a warning that he had better straighten up and fly right, or else he would be the next one in line. All these things were special providences for him. He got the superstitions of church, plus those of the slaves with their stories about witches and other occult things. And years later, he wrote of the chronic anxiety this brought up in him and how, "I look back with shuddering horror upon the days when I believed that I believed."

When he was four and a half years old, the family moved to Hannibal, Missouri, which was somewhat bigger. The Mark Twain memorial house there is much bigger and better than the one in Florida. When he was five years old, he was sent to what was called a "dame's school." It was a school taught by one of the women of the village for twenty-five cents a week for each pupil. And that is where the children of that period got their beginning education. Then, when they were a little older, they went to similar schools taught by men. But all the way through the discipline was severe. On the first day Twain was in school, he committed some infraction and was sent out to get a switch with which he would be beaten. He brought back a long shaving that a carpenter had discarded and that looked to him very suitable. The teacher was neither amused nor satisfied and she sent one of the other children out to get a switch. He brought back a much more satisfactory switch, at least to the teacher. Twain got punished severely at school and then at home. In those days, if you got punished in school and the family found out about it, you got punished at home for being punished at school.

When Twain was twelve years old his father died. He was taken out of school and put to work in a print shop, becoming what they called a "printer's devil"—a child who did all the dirty work and had all the jokes played on him. Later he was apprenticed, becoming a journeyman printer. At one time, his brother had a print shop and a newspaper called the *Hannibal Journal.* Twain worked there as a printer, and when his brother was out of town on certain occasions, he would take over editing, though not in a way that pleased his brother. He said later on, however, that he should have let Mark have his way because the circulation increased about 100 percent when he was editing it.

Working for his brother became unbearable and Mark left, wandering about as a journeyman printer could in those days, going from town to town and getting work in the local print shop or the local newspaper without a great deal of difficulty. He wandered for about a year and a half including a trip to the St. Louis World's Fair and to New York City. When he came home he was still unsettled. I suppose about a generation ago, he would have fitted in with the young people who said they were trying to find themselves. In my generation, we were trying to find a job and we didn't have time to look for ourselves.

Twain read about the Amazon and he thought it would be good to explore. Perhaps he could make his fortune in the mining which was going on there. One day when he was going down the street, a wind blew a $50 bill up against his feet. He picked it up and, as he said later, after advertising the find, he left town promptly. However, when he got to where boats to the Amazon departed, he found there would be no ships for at least a year. He was still without a profession but every boy growing up in Hannibal had one of two ambitions: one was to become a minister, and the other was to become a river pilot. Mark had the customary ambition to become a minister but he lacked one essential ingredient: he didn't have the religion. So he decided to become a river pilot and he got his certificate in 1859. He thought his fortune was made. He was getting good wages—$250 a month, which, in those days, was a tremendous amount of money. It was more money than most of the families saw in cash in the course of a year.

But something went wrong—the Civil War broke out. The boats on the Mississippi soon found themselves targets for whatever gunfire was going on. So Twain quit piloting and joined a little band of freelance soldiers on the Southern side called Marion's Rangers. At the end of the two weeks of constantly running away from people that he didn't know but who wanted to kill him, he decided he didn't like the idea of people who hadn't done each other any harm wanting to kill each other.

One of the reasons for his next move was probably to get as far away from the Civil War as possible. In later years, he might have gone to Canada. In his time, Twain went to Nevada which was not yet a state, but still a territory. His brother had been appointed secretary to the governor of Nevada and Twain agreed to go along, at no salary, as secretary to the secretary. Unfortunately there was not enough money to spread over two people. In fact, Twain later said that his brother's salary wouldn't support even the unabridged dictionary he had in his office, much less a relative. So he became at times a miner, at times a laborer, at other times a freelance writer or newspaper reporter. After some problems with the editor of a newspaper caused a challenge to a duel, Twain left for San Francisco.

In those days, newspaper offices had what they called a "local-item"—all one word—who was the person who went around gathering the odds and ends of local news to be printed in the paper. Even in those days Twain was something of a social critic. It was the habit of the San Francisco police to deal with the Chinese population much in the same way that some other police departments today are known to deal with blacks or Latinos. He wrote a satirical piece one day about the persecution of a boy who had been arrested for throwing something at a Chinese. He wondered how the boy could know that this was wrong when every day he saw the San Francisco police department mistreating the Chinese population. Well, his editor had a little discussion with him and said the newspaper, the *San Francisco Call*, was operated for the Irish washerwoman trade, and they did not like the Chinese. So Mark found himself censored for the first time, and without a job.

Along about this time, he published the story that everyone associates with Mark Twain. It was called "The Celebrated Jumping Frog of Calaveras County" and I won't go into it because for one thing it has been told a lot of times. The story hit people in the right spot and it made him famous on the West Coast and, then, on the East Coast when it was included in a book there. Twain was disgusted because he had written so many other things he considered to be more worthy of note, but it did make a name for him.

In 1866, he had an opportunity to take a trip to the Sandwich Islands—what is now Hawaii—as a correspondent and to write letters back to a newspaper in San Francisco. After he returned, having no job and wanting to eat, he decided that the best thing he could do would be to lecture on the subject, and he was very successful at it. Later he said he had not done a day's work since. I do not agree. I think lecturing is very hard work.

In the next year he traveled about lecturing, eventually ending in New York City. There the *Quaker City* steamer was gathering passengers for an excursion to the Holy Land and, possibly, around the world. He managed to persuade a Sacramento newspaper to pay the $1,250 it would take for the trip on the understanding that he would write letters back to be published by them. The trip itself was actually sponsored by a church, with a famous minister of the time aboard along with other notables. Twain and a number of other young men on the ship thoroughly scandalized the rest of the passengers whom they referred to as "the Pilgrims." In an early part of a book he wrote afterward, Twain said, "Look at them. Here are all these people in the parlor praying for a favorable wind to go one way across the Ocean, and they are one ship. There are a hundred ships going the other way and they do not even think of the other ships."

Two things came out of the *Quaker City* excursion. One was that his letters, along with other material, became a book entitled *Innocents Abroad, or the New Pilgrim's Progress*. In case you don't recall, a book called *Pilgrim's Progress* was very popular in those days and contained a gruesome account of what you go through trying to attain salvation. Undoubtedly, the Pilgrims did not appreciate the title of the book. The other thing that came out of the trip was a friendship with Charlie Langdon, one of the other young men who scandalized the Pilgrims so much. Charlie showed Twain a miniature—a very small oil portrait—of his sister, Olivia. Twain fell in love with the portrait on sight. Some years later he married the original.

After Twain's return he visited Langdon's family in Elmira, New York, and met Olivia in person. His courtship encountered stern opposition from the family. They asked him for references and the names he provided wrote back to the effect that Twain had been born to be hung, if he didn't die of intemperance first. Remember that Twain was coming from the West: he was a very rough type compared to what the family were accustomed to. He was a miner, his language was a little bit flamboyant at times, he had an expert use of profanity and very rarely refrained from using it. He said that a well-placed curse offers a solace not equaled by prayer. After some years of courtship, however, the couple married and the family presented them with a very nice home, furnished, as a wedding present. Although he had quite a job getting the consent, once the family gave it they accepted him wholeheartedly. Twain was a devoted husband until Olivia died some years before he did.

Innocents Abroad was an almost instant success for two reasons. First was the subject matter itself. Second was the humor. The book gave people a new way of looking at the world outside America. Americans were still in the middle of what could be called an inferiority complex. Everything European was better than everything American. Our books were not as good. The food was not as good. The art was not as good. Then Twain looked at all these things without much reverence and turned the light of humor on them.

After a brief time of newspaper editing, Twain devoted himself to writing books and touring as a lecturer. Those were the days of the lecture circuit. The lecture platform was a major source of entertainment and education for people. They did not have the distractions we have now, like television or the radio. Ridpath Lecture Bureau, and other agencies, had what could be called a stable of lecturers who could be hired for from $25 to $1,000 per appearance. Some were what Mark called "house-emptiers." Twain, from his very first lecture about the Sandwich Islands, was a house-filler, playing to capacity crowds willing to pay a dollar or more—a lot of money in those days—in order to hear him. In what was probably the original block-booking system, groups who wanted a house-filler had to take a certain number of house-emptiers as well. Just as movie distributing companies require cinemas to buy or take several unpopular movies in order to get a blockbuster, the lecture halls had to take bad speakers in order to get a good one.

Twain formed an arrangement with the American Publishing Company to issue his books over a period of many years. Then Mark and his brother-in-law formed their own publishing company called Webster and Company. From then on they printed the Mark Twain books, as well as a great many others. One was an instantaneous success—it was the personal memoirs of Ulysses S. Grant. Twain discovered that another publisher was going to pay Grant virtually nothing for his material. He stepped in and insisted Grant let his company publish it. The large royalties he sent back to Grant's family took care of them.

When Twain was sixty years old, Webster and Company failed due to a general financial crisis and he was forced into bankruptcy. Normally, bankruptcy means you do not pay your debts and you are discharged with what assets you have. Some of Twain's assets were safe because they belonged to his wife, like the copyrights on his books. But he believed he was morally obligated, though not legally obligated, to pay every dollar he owed.

He was never broke in the sense in which you and I use the word. When I say "I'm broke," I mean I don't have a place to live, I don't have anything to eat—or, at least, in a day or so, I won't have anything to eat. I have been there so I know what this means. In his case, it meant he had to reduce his standard of living drastically. He had built a house called Stormfield at Redding, Connecticut, now a historical showplace. They closed up the house and went to live in Europe where they could live much more cheaply. Also, other people wouldn't be around to see how cheaply they actually were living.

As old as he was, Twain took off on what he called a "raiding tour"—a lecture tour—around the world. As a result of this trip, another travel book, *Following the Equator*, was published. It includes a chapter on the religions of India [chapter 15] entitled "How to Make Salvation Sure." Here he writes, "There are several ways. To get drowned in the Ganges is one, but that is not pleasant. To die within the limits of Benares [a religious city] is another; but that is a risky one, because you might be out of town when your time comes. The best... is the Pilgrimage Around the City. The tramp is 44 miles.... But you will have plenty of company." Then, of course, the salvation must be recorded in order to be sure. "You can get this done at Skhi Binayak Temple.... Within is a god whose office it is to record your pilgrimage. ... You will not see him, but you *will* see a Brahman who will attend to the matter and collect the money."

The book and the lecture tour earned Mark enough money to pay his debts, penny for penny. I think of how many religious people who think nothing of going into court and walking away from their debts. Yet Twain, who was by this point a thoroughly ungodly man, insisted on paying off his debts. In fact, Twain made enough money that some was left over. It was invested with good advice from friends so that by the time he died a few years later, he left about $600,000 for his family.

In the last part of his life, Twain was severely ill. Many people have seen the picture of Twain writing in bed, where he had to be propped up on a series of pillows. When I was young I thought rather highly of that picture, because my favorite way of reading books was and is in bed, with a few pillows and anything else I happen to want for refreshment near by.

Twain is probably one of the most prolific of American writers. And if you add in the material that isn't going to be published, I don't think there is anybody who has ever done that much. He wrote one manuscript on a typewriter, then he gave the typewriter away and went back to writing by hand. When he couldn't do as much as he would like by this method, he would dictate to a stenographer who then brought the work into manuscript copy.

The edition of Twain that I had was twenty-four volumes and some of them dual volumes—two volumes bound in one. A lot of new material was printed after that volume or separately. The unpublished work

Twain left behind is probably equivalent to what had already appeared. All of his papers now are in the hands of the Mark Twain Foundation in the University of California at Berkeley, and grants have enabled them to work with the papers. So, often a new volume or a revision of an old one comes out to show what was censored from the first edition. But I have no idea of how much material exists. His notebooks alone— he always carried a notebook with him—have been made into a few thick volumes by themselves. And his "autobiography," which he dictated to a stenographer, had a lot of comments about politics and religion. About nine or ten years before he died, Twain started his autobiography which was really a stream of consciousness. It was published in a two-volume edition and later rearranged into a one-volume edition. But a tremendous amount of it has not been published.

Twain had a mystical feeling during most of his life because of having come into the world with Halley's comet. To superstitious people, the sight of this comet in the sky in 1835 was a tremendous thing. My mother once told me of being on the observation platform of a train in 1910, and going out to see Halley's comet. Twain had a personal attachment to it. He claimed, "The Almighty has said, here are these two sublime freaks. They came in together and they must go out together." And, lo and behold, on April 21, 1910, when Halley's comet was again visible, Mark Twain died. He had a long and successful life, but he had also had great sorrow. Twain had lost all but one of his four children before his own death.

I want to take a few minutes to cover some other aspects of Twain, such as religion. I mentioned that, as a boy, he was thoroughly indoctrinated with Presbyterianism. His nights were filled with terror and frequent nightmares.

As to his later religious beliefs, I do not think you can call him an atheist in the modern sense of that word. He was certainly an atheist in terms of any orthodox religion of his period. But in most of his writing he seems to come somewhere between being a deist and a pantheist. When he was courting Olivia Langdon, her family wanted a Christian son-in-law and she wanted a Christian husband. Twain did his very best, attending church regularly and even saying prayers over each meal. But after the couple had been married for some time, Mark told Olivia she could do whatever she wanted but he simply couldn't go on pretending to believe in religion. In the long run, Olivia lost virtually all of her religious faith.

You hear a great deal about Twain having been censored, and it is definitely true. His manuscripts were read by his wife and others to judge what things should be taken out. Sometimes Twain would put things in just for the fun of seeing them argue with him. One place where I think you find sentiments that really represent his point of view is in the little aphorisms on what he called *Puddn'head Wilson's Calendar*. There is one about freedom of speech that says, "It is by the goodness of God that in our country we have these unspeakably precious things, freedom of speech, freedom of conscience, and the prudence to practice neither of them." I wonder what he would have done if he had the material of Joseph McCarthy to work his humor on. We could have used Mark Twain during the McCarthy era.

But there were many occasions on which Twain spoke out, not only on religion but also on politics. One of them was in his *King Leopold's Soliloquy*. King Leopold of Belgium—the Beast of Belgium—was at the head of an effort of a number of countries to control the Congo. In the course of taking over this area of Africa, his policies caused the death of millions of people. Twain was very active in the Anti-Imperialist League, an organization that tried to block Leopold's efforts. When Andrew Carnegie donated $1,000 to print the pamphlet, the Anti-Imperialist League issued it.

Another soliloquy—*The Czar's Soliloquy*—was written after Bloody Sunday, 1905, when peaceful workers and peasants were shot down in front of the Winter Palace. Twain was an advocate of revolution and he looked forward to the time when the last king would lose his throne. Twain was a strong supporter of the Russian revolutionists who were, in large part, rather violent. He considered it possible that the only remedy to having a czar was to keep the position vacant by dynamite until no one would dare accept the job. This view did not make him popular. On the other hand he refused to support Maxim Gorky because Gorky came to the United States with a woman to whom he was not legally married. Twain was quite conventional in some respects.

Politically speaking, Twain rejected the idea of binding himself to one political party and became what was referred to as a "mugwump"— one who deserted his party and voted for the candidate who best expressed his principles. He said, "Loyalty to petrified opinion never yet broke a chain or freed a human soul in this world and never will." This statement came in a time when some Republicans refused to support the presidential nominee of their party and voted for the Democratic candidate, Cleveland, instead. A minister of Twain's acquaintance almost lost his pulpit for doing so. They didn't have secret ballots in those days so everyone knew how you voted.

Twain was also strongly critical of American conduct in the Spanish-American War. At the beginning, he believed it was a war to free Cuba, but when he discovered America was not planning to free anybody, only to annex them, he became a critic. In his book *Mysterious Stranger*, Twain had Satan say,

> There has never been a just one, never an honorable one—on the part of the instigator of the war. I can see a million years ahead, and this will never change in so many as half a dozen instances. The loud little handful—as usual—will shout for the war. The pulpit will—warily and cautiously—object at first; the great big dull bulk of the nation will rub its sleepy eyes and try to make out why there should be a war, and will say, earnestly and indignantly, "It is unjust and dishonorable, and there is no necessity for it." Then the handful will shout louder. A few fair men on the other side will argue and reason against the war with speech and pen and at first will have a hearing and be applauded, but it will not last long; those others will out-shout them, and presently the anti-war audience will thin out and lose popularity. Before long you will see this curious thing: the speakers stoned from the platform and free speech strangled, by hordes of furious men who in their secret hearts are still at one with those stoned speakers,—as earlier, but do not dare to say so! And now the whole nation—pulpit and all—will take up the war-cry, and shout itself hoarse, and mob any honest man who ventures to open his mouth, and presently such mouths will cease to open.

I want to run through a few of Mark Twain's books, as well as his beliefs. We are all familiar with *Tom Sawyer* and *Huckleberry Finn*. I mentioned the attempts to censor Huck Finn. In the early days, censors attacked Huck because he was just not the kind of boy they wanted their sons to grow up to be. And, in all fairness, had there been a juvenile court in Hannibal at the time when Twain was growing up, the chances are they would have tried to reform him. In later days, the censors attacked the book because it dealt bluntly with slavery. Twain used the word "nigger" in *Huckleberry Finn*. After all, he was writing about a specific time on the Mississippi River, in a southern state, in a slaveholding town, and that was how people talked. Earlier, Twain had written an article about Fenimore Cooper, ridiculing Cooper because all the Indians in *The Last of the Mohicans* talked as though they had graduated from college recently. So Twain decided to write in the vernacular of his time.

The actor Hal Holbrook used a long passage from *Huckleberry Finn* in his one-man stage performance, "Mark Twain Tonight." It is the one where Huck is wrestling with his conscience about knowing that the slave, Jim, is running away. Huck's conscience was a well-educated Presbyterian one and it told him to turn the slave in. After a few pages, Huck asks himself, "Will I feel better this way or will I feel better that way?" Figuring he will feel bad no matter what happens, Huck decides he might as well go to hell and does not turn in his friend. So it is short-sighted to censor such a book for being racist just because it was written in the vernacular of its time.

In the two-volumed novel *The Gilded Age*, written with Charles Dudley Warner, Twain exposed the corruption of the political system in the United States. In the book, he says, "I think we have a Congress which brings higher prices than any other legislative body in the world." In one sequence, he told about the cost of getting a particular bill passed—$3,000 for this lobbyist, and $5,000 for another. It was well-received as a novel, but somewhat frowned upon because people thought he shouldn't criticize the government in that way.

Puddn'head Wilson is one of his lesser-known books. Its title comes from a stranger in town who makes a witty remark that is not understood by the townsfolk. They believed anyone who would say something like that was a "Puddn'head." At the start of each chapter, Twain had an aphorism from "Puddn'head Wilson's Calendar." I think these were the things he wanted to say in his books but felt he couldn't get away with.

And now for some works that most people don't know about.... One is *Captain Stormfield's Visit to Heaven*. A woman of that period had published a book called *Gates Ajar about the Christian Heaven*, about somebody who went there, and it described the battlements, the angels, and so forth. And Twain thought this was a pretty picayune type of heaven. If people wanted a description, well, he would describe heaven for them. Captain Stormfield dies and starts to heaven, but he gets off course because he races with a comet for awhile. This makes him turn up in a part of heaven that never heard of the earth, never heard of the human race, and couldn't care less. Finally, after much persuasion, the heavenly agents go up in some kind of an aural balloon and they find earth way up on a heavenly map. They come back and say, "Oh, yes, we found it. We call it the wart."

In conclusion, because time has run out, I would like to mention a rather remarkable thing about Mark Twain. There are lots of people who are censored by the right wing. There are a lots of people now who are censored by the left wing. Mark Twain has the distinction of being if not the only author, then one of the very few, who has been censored at one time by the right wing, during another period by the left wing, and by the middle wing frequently in between. If you get censored by the right, the left, and the center, you must be pretty good.

Our Secular Constitution

*Delivered October 21, 1988,
for the Humanist Association of Los Angeles*[*]

*T*he Humanist Society of Friends flyer that announced this lecture read "Atheists United Secretary, Queen Silver, whose appearance on the platform is always a treat, will address the Humanist Society of Friends (of which she is the 2nd VP) on Thursday, October 21.... Her topic: Our Secular Constitution: Why We Have It and Why We Must Keep It."

The Constitution of the United States and the Bill of Rights were both lifelong passions

---

[*]The text as it appears in this book is actually a mixture of several versions of the same speech which I have edited together.

for Queen, even when she was still a child. For example, the November–December 1929 issue of *Queen Silver's Magazine* carried an article by Henry Roser entitled "Fundamentalist Treason":

The United States Constitution distinctly provides that:

"All executive and judicial officers, both of the United States and of the several states, shall be bound by oath OR AFFIRMATION...but no religious test of any kind shall ever be required as a qualification to any office of public trust under the United States."

If it is particularly specified that the president may take oath OR AFFIRMATION, it seems rather strange that Herbert Hoover, descendant of five generations of Quakers, all of whom have during their entire history steadfastly refused to take any oath, did not claim the constitutional right of affirmation. He took the regulation oath and kissed the Bible, all of which is contrary to Quaker teaching.

Nowhere in the Constitution does the word "god" occur; nor is there in that document any expression of belief or confidence in a supreme being. This Federal Constitution is recognized as the supreme law of the land, and the laws of Congress and the laws and the Constitutions of the several states are supposed to conform in letter and spirit to its provisions.

Queen was an absolutist about the First Amendment, regarding both its guarantee of free speech and of the separation of church and state. Indeed, she saw an unbreakable connection between the two guarantees. Freedom of speech is essential to any society that values truth and progress: the suppression of speech leads to ignorance and stagnation. And the most common manner by which censorship becomes embedded into society is through the state granting privilege to some voices while silencing others. Throughout history, religion has often been granted such privilege, while religious dissenters have been silenced. To prevent religion from stifling free inquiry, Queen believed it was necessary to keep the church and the state entirely separate from each other.

The separation of church and state was vital to the health of feminism, as well. Generally speaking, religion has not promoted the psychological independence or sexual liberation of women. Thus, when the church uses the state to promote its own interests, the interests of women often suffer. For example, abortion rights and the access to birth control come under attack. Thus, for the sake of feminism as well as freedom of speech, the church had to be denied any special status under the law.

Our Secular Constitution: Why We Have It and Why We Must Keep It

I am considered by some people to be a fanatical defender of civil liberties, but this means I believe civil liberties are indivisible and nonnegotiable. And that means freedom of speech even for the people whose opinions I detest. I believe that the Constitution means exactly what it says and it should be followed. Unfortunately, there are a great many people, including people in high places, who do not agree with that idea. President Bush is on record as saying he does not believe in the separation of church and state, he does not believe atheists can be good citizens or should be considered citizens of the United States, because this is a nation under God.

What is the Constitution? Why do we have it? And why is it important to us, even though we may find imperfections, to keep that Constitution from being further eroded?

The American Constitution is a unique achievement in modern times and perhaps in all times in terms of government. There was a time many, many years ago, in prehistory and into early history, when the priesthood and the government were one and the same. If you didn't get along with the priest, you also didn't get along with the government. Gradually, over the years, those powers have been separated. We have gone through many revolutions and conflicts about changes in that structure. But, to my knowledge, even though the idea of a republic has come down to us from many hundreds of years ago—and it was not given to us by the Christians, it was given to us by the Greeks—it was not a republic in the sense of the one in this country.

The Constitution is also a new concept about where the authority for a government comes from. A book of Mark Twain's called *A Connecticut Yankee in King Arthur's Court* has some very cute cartoons in the original edition. Some of them tell how authority manifested itself. In one, the bishop is kicking the king, the king is kicking one of the lords of the manor, the lord is kicking one of the lower orders who in turn is kicking one of the serfs. The serf had no one to kick except, perhaps, to go home and beat up his wife which he probably did. This cartoon is typical of the way authority has been conceived.

People say that the United States was founded upon the Christian religion and upon the Bible. Democracy is not part of the Bible. In there are only monarchs and kings and lords. The American concept was based on the idea that the people give the power to the authorities who in turn exercise that authority as long as it meets the satisfaction of the people. The Declaration of Independence spells this out very clearly. "We hold these truths to be self-evident. That all men are endowed by their Creator with inalienable rights, that among these are life, liberty, and the pursuit of happiness." And then it goes on to say that whenever any government becomes destructive of those rights, it is the right of the people to alter it or to abolish it.

Many years ago, during the hysteria over World War I, people were brought into court on charges that they had distributed some seditious literature, including certain quotations of this kind from Thomas Jefferson and others of that period. The judge who tried them had probably just arrived from another country and had been placed in his position by the procedure they used back then—politicians met the boat, they took the person down to the voting place and had them registered to vote, next they took them to the police department, then shortly after that they became judges. And this particular judge looked at the document [the seditious literature] and he said, "This is the most seditious document I have ever read in my life and I want you to go out and arrest that guy Jefferson."

So we are unique. We did something that has never been done in the history of the world. We said that the people are the repository of all power. Power must come from them and only by their consent, and from nowhere else. This principle has been violated many, many times in the history of the country, but it is what we started with. There is no king. There is no divine right. And this was an interruption of something that had been in existence for many years: the idea that God gave power to the king who exercised it, in turn, over his people. It was only when the pope, back in English history, decided that King John had done bad things and sanctioned an insurrection against King John did one occur. It resulted in the signing of the Magna Carta. In this document we get the idea that the people had certain rights that the king could not take away. But until that time, the king had absolute right, because his authority came from God through the pope.

In the nineteenth century, the National Liberal League and secular organizations in the United States were extremely active. They were probably responsible for the fact that none of the Christian amendments to the Constitution ever got passed. Every so often, the religious people got up and introduced an amendment to specify that the United States was founded upon the Bible, that we acknowledge God as our savior and Jesus Christ as his son, etc., etc. And only by the activities of organizations such as the Liberal League was it possible for us to avoid these amendments. Within this century, we have had at least three attempts of the same kind.

What the freethinkers and secularists couldn't do, the businessmen did. They forced the repeal of the observance of Sunday as a sabbath. They didn't want to give up the profits on the seventh day of the week by observing the sabbath. Sunday laws have pretty much gone all over the country.

Before we get into some of the arguments of the people on the other side, we should also define a few terms. A secularist, by definition, is a person who says that religion in any form whatsoever must be separate from government of any sort whatsoever. The two must be kept completely separate. Religion has no place in government and government has no place in religion. This is the concept behind the separation of church and state. A secularist may be an atheist or an agnostic, but not necessarily, because many people who have supported separation of church and state have been religious people. In experiencing persecution, as Baptists did in the early days, many people found that the only way they could serve their own religion as they wished to was to grant that right to other people as well.

Other definitions to keep in mind when we are talking about the Founding Fathers are the words "theist" and "deist." For a long time the two words were used interchangeably. But actually a deist is a person who believes in the existence of a God who created the universe and set it in motion, but who does not interfere with the operation of the universe. He does not violate the laws that he put in place. Or, as we used to say jokingly, "God is not dead, he just doesn't want to get involved." Deism is sometimes called "natural religion" or "religion of nature."

A theist, on the other hand, is a person who believes in a personal God who created the universe—presumably in six days, or a reasonable facsimile thereof—and who continues to interfere with the operation of the universe. He continues to govern it and to perform miracles, such as having the sun stand still when a general wanted to carry the battle on for a few more hours. This is the position of the theist. He does believe in a God who has a place in Heaven, who is very jealous of his power, and who insists that man adore him. This is rather inconceivable to me. If God is an all-powerful being, why he should care what one man or one woman down here thinks about him surpasses my comprehension. But, then, I am not a theologian.

A pantheist is a person who considers all of nature and the universe as being God. He may or may not believe in an essence, a being who is separate from reality, and is God. But generally speaking, the universe and God are one and it operates under the laws of nature. He does not believe in a God who interferes and stops the operation of the laws of nature.

Bearing these definitions in mind, let's consider some of the arguments that we get. When we talk about a secular constitution, we get a lot of flak from the other side.

And one of the first things they say is, "This is a Christian country; it was founded by Christians."

When they talk about the Founding Fathers they speak as though there were some sort of a generic brand of Founding Father, one Founding Father who was a prototype and they all had the same ideas and the same beliefs. Nothing could be farther from the truth. The thirteen colonies, the colonies that became the United States, were very diverse. There were people who were Anglicans and adhered completely to the Church of England. There were Nonconformists who didn't like some things about the Church of England but still wanted to remain within it. And there were separatists who didn't want anything to do with the Church of England. Then, there were Quakers, a few Jews, and many Catholics.

We hear about the Mayflower Compact signed on November 11, 1610, by the Pilgrims who came to Plymouth. They were independent religionists who had repudiated the Church of England. According to many antisecularists, the Mayflower Compact was the prototype for the American colonies. But the Mayflower Compact was only in one colony.

And of the 101 people who made the trip on the *Mayflower* only forty-one signed the Mayflower Compact. The others were women, children, indentured servants, or military men who had been hired to protect the colony.

The Puritans who settled Massachusetts in 1630 were Nonconformists who did not openly break with the Church of England. The Massachusetts colony had three covenants: a covenant between God and man, a covenant between Church and members, and one between the state and its citizens. They set up what they called a Bible Commonwealth. This is the purpose for which my family came over here, the part of the family that did not make the boat [the *Mayflower*].

In each colony, the religion of the people who had founded it became the dominant religion. There is a lot of talk about how people came over here to practice religious freedom and follow the dictates of their consciences. There is not much talk about how they acted once they were over here and had that freedom. They often started forcing everyone else to worship the same God they did, and do it according to their conscience, not according to the other person's conscience. There was a religious reign of terror in one colony after another.

And, so, we entered into a reign of religious persecution in this country in which the Jews were persecuted by everybody whenever there was a Jew around, and there weren't many. They got it from all sides. The Catholics persecuted the Protestants until people finally got so fed up with it that, in Maryland, there was a revolt against the Catholic establishment. By 1689, the most stringent anti-Catholic laws that have ever been passed in America were passed in Maryland. A poll tax was put on Irish immigrants. They said that all children of "mixed" marriages must be brought up as Protestants, anyone who had a child baptized in the Catholic church was subject to imprisonment, anyone who sent a child overseas to be educated in a Catholic school would be severely punished. It was a complete reaction to former persecution by the Catholics who, in previous times, had been persecuting the Protestants. By 1775, no public expression of Catholicism was allowed except in Pennsylvania, which had a declaration of liberty of conscience, though it was not always adhered to.

The Quakers were persecuted in almost every colony, though not so badly in Rhode Island where the Charter of 1663 provided for religious freedom regardless of differences of opinion. Only in Pennsylvania did they have a refuge where they were not persecuted, or at least not treated so badly. And, of course, the Jews were persecuted by everyone.

Anyone in the colony who did not conform to what the colony said—and bear in mind that in the early colonies the government and the church were virtually the same thing—was a nonperson. You couldn't be married, you couldn't be buried. This is the period when America had blue laws. They severely punished anyone who would walk on Sunday except to and from church, anyone who kissed his wife on Sunday... people had to observe the Sabbath and, of course, they had to pay to the church and they must obey all the church's regulations.

But by the time we started the ferment of the American Revolution, people were fed up with this sort of thing. They were very well aware of what happens when one religious group gets control and gets established. And remember, you had what amounted to an established church in most colonies, although not all of them. In New York and in Pennsylvania, for example, they did not have an established church. An established church meant that, if you wanted to be in good standing with the community, you had to be in good standing with the church. But it also meant that everyone was taxed to support that particular church, whether he believed in it or belonged to some other sect. To belong to something else, you still had to pay for the support of the dominant sect. In one place, it would be the Catholics, in another the Anglicans, in another the Dissenters. But all of them had the same idea. Pennsylvania became the refuge of the Quakers and also a great many freethinking people. It is no accident that Benjamin Franklin settled there and he was one of the early publishers of both books under his own name and books which he published anonymously, because it was not popular to state certain types of opinions.

In the progress toward revolution and the Constitution, we can see a definite pattern. There were so many diverse groups that all of them were afraid of any one group getting control. So, progressively, as we go down through the documents we find fewer references to the deity and more references to rights.

When the Mayflower Compact was signed, it started out, "In the name of God, Amen," and it was a religious compact. When the Declaration of Rights was published by the Stamp Act Congress in 1765, we had gotten to the point that there was nothing in its declaration that had anything to do with God or religion. The Stamp Act Congress recited the rights, obligations, and grievances of the colonists, but it did not speak of freedom of religion. By 1774 the Continental Congress issued a Declaration of Rights that did not have any references to God, but it did express some concern over the establishment of the Roman Catholic religion in Quebec, Canada, which had been done under the Quebec Act.

Then, when we come to the Declaration of Independence, it gets more nebulous. There is one reference to nature's God and to the Creator endowing all men with inalienable rights. But note that the person who authored the Declaration of Independence, Thomas Jefferson, was a deist. In one of his campaigns for president, he was attacked bitterly by the opposing party as an atheist. This, however, did not keep him from getting elected, which speaks well for the people of that period.

Thomas Jefferson was a deist and, as far as that time and period was concerned, that was almost as bad as being an atheist. Most people did not adopt the term "atheist" and there was a good reason for that. Until Darwin and the theory of evolution, until the development of modern science, there was not a satisfactory way of explaining the origin of the universe and of man. So, although intellectually a man might find the idea of "God" inconceivable, he couldn't back his objections up with evidence that the universe could have come about any other way.

The Declaration of Independence was also heavily influenced by the writings of Thomas Paine, whose *Age of Reason* is one of the best critiques of the Bible ever published and it is still in print, selling many copies every year. He did not publish that until after the Revolution. And he felt, because of publishing it, he had lost the good repute he'd had by being a father of the American Revolution.

When we come to the Articles of Confederation, which were finally ratified in 1781, the only references to religion are the date—"the year of our Lord"—and mention of a "great Governor" of the world. This is a deistic concept, far from the Christian concept of a personal God the father, the son, and the holy ghost. And, remember, in that period, if you did not believe in the Trinity, you were not a Christian within the definition employed in the colonies.

By the time we came to the Constitution of the United States, there is no reference to God. And the preamble is: "We the people of the United States, in order to form a more perfect Union...." And then it goes on to proscribe certain things. The only references to religion are restrictive. Article VI, paragraph 3, provided for oath or affirmation by members of Congress, executive and judicial officers, which binds them to support the Constitution but provided that "...no religious test shall ever be required as a Qualification to any Office or public trust under the United States." The reason for this was that colonists came out of countries where in order to serve in government you had to belong to the church that was in power at that particular time. You had to have allegiance not only to government but to whatever God the government wanted you to believe in. So this was a prohibition of that.

Article II, section 1, paragraph 8 provides for the swearing in of the oath of office to be taken by the president, the Congress, and so forth. And that is by oath or by affirmation and it has no reference to God or the Bible in it. Those are the only two places you see religion in any shape or form in the Constitution and it is restrictive.

Several of the states would not ratify the Constitution until they were presented with a Bill of Rights. Two states in particular—Rhode Island and North Carolina—held out. The first thing that started the Bill of Rights was that Congress should make no laws concerning religion and the free exercise thereof. By the time these people had gone from 1620 to 1789, they knew what religious persecution could do to a country and they were determined that they would not have this kind of persecution. The fact that some of their descendants have tried to introduce it doesn't alter the fact that the country started out with that idea.

I submit to you there was no reason to mention something in the Bill of Rights unless the people felt there was a real need for it. If you look at the items enumerated in the Bill of Rights you will get a clear picture of what conditions were like in that period. For state/church matters, we are primarily interested in the First Amendment, which states, "Congress shall make no law respecting an establishment of religion, or prohibiting the free exercise thereof...."

Amendment VIII is a prohibition against cruel and unusual punishment, because they were trying to avoid the types of things done to prisoners in England and Europe. In the Fifth Amendment, there is a prohibition against self-incrimination. This comes from the fact that not only were people required to testify against themselves, but often they were tortured to make them testify as the prosecuting attorney wanted them to. The prohibition against what is called "a bill of attainder" comes from the fact that, in the old country, when they found a person guilty, they would take away not only his property but they would also extend this to the next generation or even the third generation in the biblical theory that the sins of the father are visited upon the sons. So a man convicted of certain kinds of crimes, like treason, could see his children and grandchildren stripped of everything. There was another prohibition against excessive bail, which was intended to stop the practice of making bail so high that people could not get out of jail.

The reason these prohibitions are in the Bill of Rights is because the colonists were coming out of a society in which they had been subjected to abuses, including religious abuses. And this is why religion is mentioned in terms of prohibitions, not of establishing religion.

Was America, then, established as a Christian country? All the evidence points to the contrary. It was set up deliberately as a secular government. Common to all of the documents on which the United States is based is the idea of natural rights that do not come from a king and do not come from a Christian type of God. The rights come to them because they are human beings who are entitled to such rights. One of the first expressions of this is in the Treaty of Tripoli which was signed in 1797 between the United States and the Bey and subjects of Tripoli. Article XI stated:

> As the government of the United States of America is not, in any sense, founded on the Christian religion, as it has in itself no character of enmity against the laws, religion, or tranquility, of musselmans; and as the said states never entered into any war, or act of hostility against any Mahometan nation, it is declared by the parties that no pretext, arising from religious opinions, shall ever produce an interruption of the harmony existing between the two countries.

You must remember that a treaty, once ratified, becomes part of the law of the land just the same as any other law. The treaty was negotiated during the term of office of George Washington, and ratified during the office of John Adams.

The next argument religious people will bring up to show America is Christian is that we have "in God we trust" on our money and we pledge allegiance to "one nation under God." As a matter of fact, "in God we trust" did not appear on any coins in the United States until April 1864 when they were in the middle of the Civil War and were probably in the same hysteria that accompanies every war. In 1865 Congress authorized "in God we trust" to be put on gold and silver coins if the coin's design allowed it.

In 1907, under President Theodore Roosevelt, a new issue of coins omitted the phrase "in God we trust." In answer to criticism, Roosevelt wrote a letter to a clergyman in which he said:

> My own feeling in the matter is due to my very firm conviction that to put such a motto on coins, or to use it in any kindred manner, not only does no good but does positive harm, and is in effect irreverence which comes dangerously close to blasphemy...

Nevertheless, there was so much opposition that the motto was put back on the coins. We did not have it on the paper money until 1956, in the Eisenhower years when "atheist" and "Communist" became one word. In an effort to show how nonatheistic and non-Communistic America was, the administration had "in God we trust" put on the paper money. Parenthetically, I would add that it doesn't seem to have done the paper money one bit of good. It seems to be worth less and less ever since they put it on.

The argument is, of course, that because this has happened, another thing should be allowed to happen. That is, because we have "in God we trust" on the money, then we should have prayer in the schools. Well, if a thief enters my house and takes my stereo, it is not a good argument for him to come the next week and say his former theft allows him to take the TV. Yet the religious argument is the same logic. There has been one violation of separation of church and state and, so, there should be another. We should always remember the fable of the camel who pleaded with his master in a tent, saying, "Oh, master, it is so cold outside, please let me put my nose in the tent to keep warm." And the master allowed it. Then the camel said, "Oh, master, it is still so cold outside, please let me put my head in the tent to keep warm." And the master allowed it. Soon the whole camel was in the tent and the master was outside. By the same reasoning, the religious people say because they have gotten away with doing an injury, then they should be allowed to do another injury. That does not make good logic, except to the religious mind.

So, to repeat the question, Was America established as a Christian nation? I want to end with the words of James Madison in *Memorial and*

Remonstrance concerning a law proposed by Virginia to provide for teachers of the Christian religion.

> Who does not see that the same authority which can establish Christianity, in exclusion of all other religions, may establish, with the same ease, any particular sect of Christians, in exclusion of all other sects? That the same authority that can call for each citizen to contribute three pence only of his property for the support of only one establishment, may force him to conform to any one establishment, in all cases whatsoever? ...
>
> During almost fifteen centuries has the legal establishment of Christianity been on trial. What have been its fruits? More or less, in all places, pride and indolence in the clergy; ignorance and servility in the laity; in both, superstition and bigotry, and persecution.... What influences, in fact, have ecclesiastical establishments had on civil society? In some instances they have been seen to erect a spiritual tyranny on the ruins of civil authority; in many instances, they have been seen upholding the thrones of political tyranny; in no instance have they been the guardians of the liberties of the people.

Index

287